The Evolution of a State

The Evolution of a State *or*

BY NOAH SMITHWICK

Compiled by His Daughter
Nanna Smithwick Donaldson

Foreword by L. Tuffly Ellis
Illustrations by Charles Shaw

Barker Texas History Center Series, No. 5

UNIVERSITY OF TEXAS PRESS, AUSTIN

Recollections of Old Texas Days

International Standard Book Number 0-292-72043-2;
0-292-72045-9 (pbk.)
Library of Congress Catalog Card Number 82-51249
Copyright 1900 by H. P. N. Gammel
Copyright © 1983 by the University of Texas Press
Printed in the United States of America
Second University of Texas Press Edition, 1984

CONTENTS

[v]

FOREWORD

"It is extremely improbable that I shall ever see Texas again, as the first of January, 1899, ushered in my ninety-second year, but I will cherish the memory of the long ago spent on her soil, and wish her a prosperous future. I am proud to note the progress she has made, though I can scarcely realize the transformation that progress has wrought," spoke Noah Smithwick, as he concluded *The Evolution of a State or Recollections of Old Texas Days*, a classic in the field of Texana. The author died less than ten months after dictating the above to his daughter. He never saw Texas again, but his wish for a prosperous Texas certainly came to pass.

When North Carolina–born Noah Smithwick came to Texas as a recruit for Sterling C. Robertson's colony in 1827 at the age of nineteen, the population of the Mexican frontier province numbered only a few thousand. Indians still controlled much of the area. Wildlife was abundant: deer, bear, panthers, buffalo, wild horses, and even alligators. After more than one hundred years of occupation, Spain had left its imprint on Texas, but the latter still remained only sparsely settled when it became Mexican territory in 1821. Mexico opened Texas up to colonization by foreigners, and Americans quickly took advantage of the government's generous land offer. For Smithwick, however, a life of adventure, not land, served as the attraction. By the time he left Texas in 1861—he opposed secession—the population totaled more than 600,000. By the time of his death, railroads crisscrossed the state and more than 3,000,000 people called themselves Texans. The frontier era had ended. No wonder that he could "scarcely realize the transformation that progress had wrought."

Smithwick was not an *empresario*; he held no major military command or important civil office; he amassed no great landholdings—he "had a strong aversion to tearing up God's earth." His trade was that of a gun- and blacksmith; his schooling was from nature. His *Recollections* are those of a man who loved nature and enjoyed life. There is no bitterness, no regrets. His observations on social, military, and personal events are laced together by a kind of harmony with his environment and friendship for his fellow frontiersmen. He blacksmithed in San Felipe, smuggled tobacco across the Rio Grande, fought in the Revolution, farmed on Webber's prairie, and operated a mill near Marble Falls; but whatever the occasion or wherever the place, he was observant. His descriptions of Mexican life in San Fernando, where he stayed for awhile after his smuggling venture, are as vivid, although much briefer, as are his remarks about life in San Felipe de Austin.

Smithwick's social commentary offers a perspective on a wide range of life of the period. The hospitality of the frontier is reflected in the sharing of bed and board, however humble, with friend or stranger. Dress ranged from buckskin to "store clothes," even at weddings. And weddings were special occasions—filled with conviviality—and included, in addition to the ceremony, supper and dance. "When young folks danced those days, they danced; they didn't glide around; they 'shuffled' and 'double shuffled,' 'wired' and 'cut the pigeon's wing,' making the splinters fly."

Historians and anthropologists have frequently borrowed from his observations about Indian life. His comments about the Karankawas have been woven into the literature about those coastal people. But it is the Comanche life and culture that Smithwick most enlightens us about. He spent three months among them negotiating a treaty; he succeeded, but both sides ignored it. During his stay with those people, he came to respect them and to appreciate their effort to protect their ranging grounds.

His observations on Comanche life include remarks about the place of women, the deferential treatment accorded older tribe members, and his inability to grasp their religious practices or to learn much about their language. Boys—future warriors—were the center of parental affection and pride; girls were generally neglected. During Smithwick's stay with the Comanches, meat constituted the only element of their diet and buffalo ranked as the major staple. The white hunters' wanton slaughter of those animals constituted one of the Indians' principal grievances. Their sense of sport leaned to lassoing turkeys, deer, mustang, and buffalo calves rather than the destruction of their staff of life.

In 1835 Smithwick stood with his comrades at Gonzales and Concepción; and his accounts of the battles are exciting and exacting. His description of the citizens' army that comprised the revolutionary forces during those critical days reveals initially a rowdy band of patriots—men undisciplined, ill-prepared for war, and overconfident, yet unawed by Mexican military strength. But it is his commentary on the Runaway Scrape that is most gripping: "The desolation of the country through which we passed beggars description. Houses were standing open, the beds unmade, the breakfast things still on the tables, pans of milk moulding in the dairies. There were cribs full of corn, smoke houses full of bacon, yards full of chickens that ran after us for food, nests of eggs in every fence corner, young corn and garden truck rejoicing in the rain, cattle cropping the luxuriant grass, hogs, fat and lazy, wallowing in the mud, all abandoned. . . . Wagons were so scarce that it was impossible to remove household goods, many of the women and children, even, had to walk. . . .

"And, as if the arch fiend had broken loose, there were men—or devils, rather—bent on plunder, galloping up behind the fugitives, telling them the Mexicans were just behind, thus causing the hapless victims to abandon what few valuables they had tried to save. There were broken-down wagons and household goods scattered all along the road."

But one must read for oneself the entire passage for the full effect of the plight and trauma that settlers felt in the wake of Santa Anna's victory at the Alamo.

In a few years Texans will commemorate the sesquicentennial of their independence from Mexico. It is particularly fitting that in anticipation of that event the University of Texas Press issue this new edition of Noah Smithwick's *Evolution of a State*, for this volume is unmatched among recollections and reminiscences of early Texas settlers.

Smithwick had been gone from Texas for close to forty years when he died in 1899, but he never lost interest in the land he called home for almost thirty years. Through the *Dallas Morning News* and other sources he kept informed of developments in the state. He contributed articles in 1896, 1897, and 1898 to the *News*. These pieces were incorporated into *Evolution of a State* when H. N. P. Gammel, an Austin publisher, printed the volume in 1900. The work has enjoyed a continuous popularity ever since. In 1935 and 1963 the Steck Company and the Steck-Vaughn Company, respectively, published facsimile editions of the original.

Any reader, whatever the age, who begins this book will almost certainly finish it, for Smithwick has provided an account of frontier life that will interest and fascinate everyone who wants to know how the evolution of Texas occurred as seen through the eyes of a man who was there for the most exciting period of its history.

L. Tuffly Ellis

PREFACE

In presenting this volume to the public, I desire, in justice to the deceased author, to explain that, though the facts it embodies were furnished by the person whose name appears on the title page, owing to impairment of vision the work of preparation was of necessity committed to an amanuensis. That the material was good, probably few will deny; therefore, whatsoever of merit the work may possess, belongs of right to the author, while the amanuensis accepts whatever of blame that may attach to the defects the reader may discover.

The work primarily begun to beguile the tedium incident to the author's loss of sight was partly published in the Galveston-Dallas News, where it seemed to attract favorable notice; in so much that we were repeatedly urged to put it in book form for preservation. The extreme age of the author, he being then 89, rendered it expedient to hasten the work. Sixty years was a wide gulf for a single memory to span, and being away in California where he had neither the benefit of old associations to refresh his memory, nor the advantages of extended historical research to assist him on doubtful points, and his death occurring before the final revision was completed, it is quite possible there may be slight errors. For these, if they exist, we beg the readers' indulgence.

Nanna Smithwick Donaldson

Austin, Texas

BIOGRAPHICAL SKETCH
OF THE AUTHOR

Noah Smithwick was born in Martin Co., N. C., on the 1st day of January 1808. He came of good old revolutionary stock, his ancestors on both sides having fought in the patriot army. The Smithwicks came from England to America early in the 18th century, procuring land in North Carolina, the original title deeds to which, bearing date of 1661, are still in the family. The family was of Scotch descent. Edward, the father of Noah Smithwick, moved to Tennessee in 1814, settling near Springfield, from which place the son drifted with the tide of emigration to Texas in 1827; remaining with the state till 1861, when he moved on to California, settling first in Tulare Co., and later at Santa Anna, Orange Co., at which latter place he died Oct. 21, 1899, aged 91 years, 9 months and 21 days. His wife, Thurza N. (Blakey) Smithwick (prior to her marriage to him the widow Duty), also a pioneer Texan, died in 1871. Of their five children but two survive; Edward, in Santa Anna, Cal., and the writer of this sketch, now in Texas.

Nanna Smithwick Donaldson

The Evolution of a State

CHAPTER I

What the discovery of gold was to California the colonization act of 1825 was to Texas. In the following year Sterling C. Robertson, who had obtained a grant for a colony, for each 100 families of which he was to receive a bonus of 23,025 acres of land, went up into Kentucky recruiting. The glowing terms in which he descanted on the advantages to be gained by emigration, were well calculated to further his scheme. To every head of a family, if a farmer, was promised 177 acres of farming land—bottom land or land susceptible of irrigation, for the Mexicans considered no land arable unless irrigable—and 4,428 acres of pasture land for stock; colonists to be exempt from taxation six years from date of settlement, with the privilege of importing, duty free, everything they might desire for themselves and families; an abundance of game, wild horses, cattle, turkeys, buffalo, deer and antelope by the drove. The woods abounded in bee trees, wild grapes, plums, cherries, persimmons, haws and dewberries, while walnuts, hickorynuts and pecans were abundant along the water courses. The climate was so mild that houses were not essential; neither was a superabundance of clothing or bedding, buffalo robes and bear skins supplying all that was needed for the latter and buckskin the former. Corn in any quantity was to be had for the planting, and, in short, there the primitive curse was set at defiance. Mexican soldiers were stationed on the frontier to keep the Indians in check. Of the hardships and privations, the ever increasing danger from the growing dissatisfaction of the Indians, upon whose hunting grounds the whites were steadily encroaching, and the almost certainty of an ultimate war with Mexico, he was discreetly silent. Viewed from that distance, the prospect was certainly flattering, and it should not occasion surprise that men with large families—for families increased in geometrical ratio those days—were induced to migrate thither with the hope of securing homes for themselves and children.

I was but a boy in my nineteenth year, and in for adventure. My older brothers talked of going. They, however, abandoned the project; but, it had taken complete possession of me, so early in the following year, 1827, I started out from Hopkinsville, Kentucky, with all my worldly possessions, consisting of a few dollars in money, a change of clothes, and a gun, of course, to seek my fortune in this lazy man's paradise. Incredible as it may seem to the present generation, seeing the country traversed from ocean to ocean and lakes to gulf with innumerable lines of railroad, there was not then a mile of railroad in operation in the United States; and though twenty years had elapsed since the Clermont made her triumphal trip from New York to Albany, few steamboats plied the western waters and none had ventured out to sea. I saw the first one that went up the Cumberland river—the Rifleman, a sternwheeler. Its progress was so slow that one had to take sight by stationary objects to determine if it moved. The stage coach, being the only public overland conveyance, took me down to the mouth of the river, where I intended to take steamer for New Orleans; but the steamboat had not arrived and no one knew when it would. My impatience could brook no delay, so I took passage on a flatboat, or as they were known in river parlance, a "Mississippi broadhorn," the poor man's transfer. Out on the broad bosom of the Father of Waters these boats floated from the Ohio, the Cumberland, the Tennessee and numerous smaller tributaries, laden with the products of the vast region contiguous, to be floated down to New Orleans and thence distributed around the seaboard by sailing vessels. The flatboat having served its purpose, it was broken up and sold for lumber and fuel, while the owner pocketed his cash and wended his way home, generally on foot up through Mississippi, where he was liable to be interviewed by footpads and relieved of his money if not his life. Many were the gruesome stories of robbery and murder thus committed by old John A. Murrill and his band of freebooters. My transport was loaded with ice, artificial ice being a thing unheard of. The crew consisted of three men, whose principal duty was to look out for "sawyers," sunken trees, and to keep clear of eddies, for a boat once drawn into the swirl would go floating around indefinitely, in danger of colliding with the ever-accumulating drift and being sunk. As flatboats never returned and seldom passed each other, the slow, leisurely drifting, day after day, became intolerably monotonous. So I stopped off at Natchez and waited for a steamboat. Very poetical it was, no doubt, this dropping down with the rippling stream, but I had not started out in search of the poetical. By the time I reached New Orleans my exchequer was running low and mechanics were getting big wages, so I went to work as finisher in the old Leeds foundry. It was but a small affair, then employing only about twenty-five men. When I revisited it in 1835 it had spread over a whole block and employed over a hundred hands. It was a rough place for a boy to drift into. The men all got good wages and most of them spent their money either at the gambling table or in other disreputable resorts. When I went to work they eyed me with ill-concealed displeasure. I was so young to stand up beside old mechanics and do equal work; but they soon found more serious cause for dissatisfaction; I did too much work. Finally old Father Blair, the pattern maker, who took a friendly interest in me, cautioned me to go slow or I would have all the men down on me. I was "green from the states" then and felt indignant at being told that I must shirk. "Our employer pays me for my time; do I not owe him all I am capable of doing in that time?" "No," said they, "he pays for so much work. You get no more for your big day's work than we do for ours, and if you go on like this you will make trouble for the rest of us," and the words were accompanied by a look that said plainly, "No sprig of a boy must presume to set the pace for us," and so I was forced to slow down and drift with the tide. This was Labor Unionism in its incipiency.

When the sickly season came on and the men began to leave, I again took up the line of march for Texas, this time on board a coasting schooner owned by parties in New Orleans, chartered by Carlysle & Smith and laden with supplies for the Mexican army. A steam tug towed us out to the mouth of the Mississippi as far as steamers ventured. The weather was lovely as a dream of Venice, and we rounded the Balize and sped away on the wings of the trade winds over the placid waters. We passed Galveston island in plain view. There was no sign of human habitation on it; nothing to give promise of the thriving city which now covers it. It was only noted then as having been the rendezvous of Lafitte and his pirates, and as such was pointed out to me. The trip was a delightful one and I was in fine spirits, when on the third day we threaded the Paso Caballo and ran into Matagorda bay, having made the run in a little over forty-eight hours, a remarkable record in those days. We cast anchor in the mouth of the Lavaca river, where we had calculated to find the Mexican troops, but the movements of the troops, as well as the government, were very uncertain, and there were no troops, no agent, no one authorized to receive the goods. There was not an American there. The colonization law exempted from settlement all land within twenty-five miles of the coast, so the territory was given over to the Karankawa Indians, a fierce tribe, whose hand was against every man. They lived mostly on fish and alligators, with a man for fete days when they could catch one. They were the most savage looking human beings I ever saw. Many of the bucks were six feet in height, with bows and arrows in proportion. Their ugly faces were rendered hideous by the alligator grease and dirt with which they were besmeared from head to foot as a defense against mosquitoes. They rowed outside to our vessel in their canoes, but Carlysle warned them to leave their arms on shore, enforcing the argument by the presence of a wicked looking little cannon, which was conspicuously pointed in their direction. The mate and I had made special preparations for their reception, having molded several pints of bullets with which to load the cannon, and we were eager for a chance to turn it loose among them, but they gave us no provocation. It was a dreary place for a lone stranger to land. A few Mexicans came around, but they spoke no English and I understood no Spanish. At length two men, Fulcher and McHenry, who had squatted on land six or eight miles up the river, sighted the schooner and came down in a dugout. They took me in with them and I spent my first night in Texas in their cabin. My first meal on Texas soil was dried venison sopped in honey. After having spent some months in New Orleans, where everything of the known world was obtainable, it looked like rank starvation to me, but I was adaptive. The sea voyage had sharpened my appetite and I was possessed of a strong set of grinders, so I set to and made a meal, but I was not anxious to trespass on their hospitality, so next morning I set out on foot for Dewitt's colony, ten miles further up the Lavaca. Even at that early date there was a controversy between the government and colonists with regard to the meaning of the line of reserve, the government contending that it was ten leagues from the indentation of the gulf and bays and the colonists that it was ten leagues from the outer line of the chain of islands that extend around the coast, precisely the claim that England is now setting up in Alaska. The Texans made their own claim stick; it remains to be seen how John Bull will come out. Fulcher accompanied me up to the station. The beautiful rose color that tinged my visions of Texas while viewing it through Robertson's long-distance lens paled with each succeeding step. There were herds of fine, fat deer, and antelope enough to set one wild who had never killed anything bigger than a raccoon, but, to my astonishment and disgust, I could not kill one, though I was accounted a crack marksman; but I found it was one thing to shoot at a mark, the exact distance of which I knew, and another to hit game at an uncertain distance.

The colonists, consisting of a dozen families, were living—if such existence could be called living—huddled together for security against the Karanka-was, who, though not openly hostile, were not friendly. The rude log cabins, windowless and floorless, have been so often described as the abode of the pioneer as to require no repetition here; suffice it to say that save as a partial protection against rain and sun they were absolutely devoid of comfort. De-witt had at first established his headquarters at Gonzales, and the colonists had located their land in that vicinity, but the Indians stole their horses and otherwise annoyed them so much, notwithstanding the soldiers, that they abandoned the colony and moved down on the Lavaca, where they were just simply staying. The station being in the limits of the reserve, they made no pretense of improving it, not even to the extent of planting corn, one of the first things usually attended to, for the Texan Indians, unlike their eastern brethren, scorned to till the soil, and the few Mexicans scattered through the country did so only to the extent of supplying their own wants; so when the colonists used up the breadstuff they brought with them they had to do without until they raised it. This, however, was no very difficult matter near the coast, where there were vast canebrakes all along the rivers. The soil was rich and loose from the successive crops of cane that had decayed on it. In the fall, when the cane died down, it was burned off clean. The ground was then ready for planting, which was done in a very primitive manner, a sharpened stick being all the implement necessary. With this they made holes in the moist loam and dropped in grains of corn. When the young cane began to grow they went over it with a stick, simply knocking it down; the crop was then laid by. Game was plenty the year round, so there was no need of starving. Men talked hopefully of the future; children reveled in the novelty of the present; but the women—ah, there was where the situation bore heaviest. As one old lady remarked, Texas was "a heaven for men and dogs, but a hell for women and oxen." They—the women—talked sadly of the old homes and friends left behind, so very far behind it seemed then, of the hardships and bitter privations they were undergoing and the dangers that surrounded them. They had not even the solace of constant employment. The spinning wheel and loom had been left behind. There was, as yet, no use for them—there was nothing to spin. There was no house to keep in order; the meager fare was so simple as to require little time for its preparation. There was no poultry, no dairy, no garden, no books, or papers as nowadays—and, if there had been, many of them could not read—no schools, no churches—nothing to break the dull monotony of their lives, save an occasional wrangle among the children and dogs. The men at least had the excitement of killing game and cutting bee trees. It was July, and the heat was intense. The only water obtainable was that of the sluggish river, which crept along between low banks thickly set with tall trees, from the branches of which depended long streamers of Spanish moss swarming with mosquitoes and pregnant of malaria. Alligators, gaunt and grim—certainly the most hideous creatures God ever made—lay in wait among the moss and drift for any unwary creature that might come down to drink. Dogs, of which every well regulated family had several, were their special weakness, and many a thirsty canine drank and never thirsted more. This was not perhaps from any partiality for dog meat; on the contrary, when the alligator went foraging under cover of night he evinced a decided preference for human flesh, particularly negroes, and many blood-curdling stories were told of alligators stealing into sleeping camps and seizing an inmate. One story, in particular, I remember as being told by an eye-witness. A company of emigrants were camped at the mouth of the Brazos waiting for teams to take them up to Austin's colony. One night they were aroused by piercing screams, and rushing to the place from whence they proceeded found a huge alligator making for the river, dragging a 14-year-old negro girl by the arm. He had crawled into a tent, where a number of persons were sleeping, and, whether from accident or choice I cannot say, seized the darky and struck a bee-line for the river, which he would have reached on time with his prey but for his inveterate foes, the aforesaid dogs, who rushed upon him and, though finding no vulnerable point of attack, swarmed around, harassing and delaying his retreat till the men pulled themselves together and came to the rescue, when, seeing the odds decidedly against him, his alligatorship relinquished his prize and sought his own safety in the river. Their bellow was just such a hideous sound as might be expected to issue from the throat of such a hideous creature, and was of itself enough to chase away sleep, unassisted by the tuneful mosquito, whose song, like the opera singer's,

[5]

has a business ring in it. I had heard the bellowing nightly while in New Orleans, but heard amid the noise and lights of the city there lurked in it no suspicion of the horror it could produce when heard amid the gloom and solitude of the wilderness. Wolves and owls added their voices to the dismal serenade. I had heard them all my life, but I had yet to learn the terrible significance that might attach to the familiar howl and hoot. The whippoorwill's silvery notes filled in the interludes, but they seemed strangely out of tune amid such surroundings.

Newcomers were warmly welcomed and entertained with all the hospitality at the command of the colonists. Sleeping accommodations were limited to mosquito bars, a provision not to be despised, since they were absolutely indispensable to sleep. The bill of fare, though far from epicurean, was an improvement on dried venison and honey, in that the venison was fresh and cooked, and Colonel Dewitt, my host, had bread, though some families were without. Flour was $10 a barrel. Trading vessels came in sometimes, but few people had money to buy anything more than coffee and tobacco, which were considered absolutely indispensable. Money was as scarce as bread. There was no controversy about "sound" money then. Pelts of any kind passed current and constituted the principal medium of exchange.

Children forgot, many of them had never known, what wheaten bread was like. Old Martin Varner used to tell a good story of his little son's first experience with a biscuit. The old man had managed to get together money or pelts enough to buy a barrel of flour. Mrs. Varner made a batch of biscuits, which, considering the resources of the country, were doubtless heavy as lead and hard as wood. When they were done Mrs. Varner set them on the table. The boy looked at them curiously, helped himself to one and made for the door with it. In a few minutes he came back for another. Doubting the child's ability to eat it so quickly, the old man followed him to see what disposition he made of the second. The ingenious youngster had conceived a novel and altogether illogical idea of their utility. He had punched holes through the center, inserted an axle and triumphantly displayed a miniature Mexican cart. And I assure you, from my recollection of those pioneer biscuits, they were capable of sustaining a pretty heavy load; shouldn't wonder if that was the first inception of the paper car wheel. Game was the sole dependence of many families and I fixed up many an old gun that I wouldn't have picked up in the road, knowing that it was all that stood between a family and the gaunt wolf at the door, as well as the Indians. Domestic animals were so scarce that the possession of any considerable number gave notoriety and name to the possessor; thus there were "Cow" Cooper and "Hog" Mitchell. Failing to secure more choice game, there were always mustangs to fall back on. Over on the Brazos lived Jared E. Groce, a planter from South Carolina, who had over 100 slaves, with which force he set to work clearing ground and planting cotton and corn. He hired two men to kill game to feed them on, and the mustangs being the largest and easiest to kill the negroes lived on horse meat till corn came in.

CHAPTER 2

The outlook was a gloomy one to me. Colonel Dewitt having a colony to settle, was as enthusiastic in praise of the country as the most energetic real estate dealer of boom towns nowadays, but land had no attractions for me, as I had a strong aversion to tearing up God's earth, to which fact I owe what little schooling I got. Disliking the restraint of school, I was given the alternative of going to school or working on the farm. That seeming to be the least of the two evils I chose the school, which I abandoned for the gun and blacksmith trades, becoming sufficiently skilled therein to do journey-work before I was eighteen. There were plenty of old guns to work on, but no tools, and no money to pay for work. By this time the last vestige of color had faded from my landscape, and if there had been an opportunity, I think I should have turned my back on it before it assumed a more than leaden hue. About that time Elhanan Gibbs came round from the salt works at the mouth of the Brazos, where Asa Mitchell, the first settler there, had opened a salt factory, bringing a load of salt. He wanted to take a trip inland and wanted a traveling companion. Glad to avail myself of any opportunity to get away from the stagnation of the station, I promptly offered my services. Gibbs was a hardy, muscular man, and looking doubtfully at my boyish face, he said: "My son, I'm afraid your face is 'most too smooth to keep me company." My pride was up in arms at once; was I not almost twenty, and had I not stood up beside men in shops day after day and done more work than any of them? I drew myself up to my fullest height and answered with dignity: "When I give out, Mr. Gibbs, you needn't wait for me. You can go ahead and leave me." With that understanding we started out. There were no horses to be had, but we were directed to a wealthy old Mexican ranchero over on the Guadaloupe who had horses galore. We struck out on foot and reached Victoria, or De Leon's town, as it was then called, without accident or incident worthy of relation.

There was but one white man in the place and with him we stopped. After supper we heard a regular series of hand-claps going on which naturally reminded us of the "Juba" dance among the negroes. "Let's go round there and see those fellows pat Juba," said Gibbs. We approached a hut from which the sound seemed to emanate; but, instead of the merry dancers we expected to find, there was a woman down on her knees before a little bed of glowing coals on which lay a piece of sheet iron on which a couple of tortillas were baking, while by a series of pats she was preparing a third one for the griddle. There the patient creature knelt with her bowl of hulled corn beside her on one side and her metate on the other. The metate is simply two flat stones between which the softened corn is mashed into dough; after which it is rolled and patted and tossed in the oven, i.e., on the heated iron; the manipulator keeping up the milling and baking with the regularity of clock work, taking off one, turning another and putting on a third, then preparing another until there is enough for the family meal.

Martin De Leon had settled his grant with Mexicans, most of them being his peons and vaqueros. He had a large stock of both horses and cattle, and between the Comanches, who stole his horses, and the Cronks, as the Karankawas were called, who killed his cattle, he had a troublous time of it. Becoming exasperated at the constant depredations of the Cronks, he determined to take matters into his own hands. He organized his retainers into an army, and mounting a four-pounder swivel gun on a jackass, set out to annihilate the tribe. He ran them to cover, brought his artillery to bear and touched it off, but he did not take the precaution to brace up the jackass, and the recoil turned him a flying somersault, landing him on top of the gun with his feet in the air, a position from which he was unable to extricate himself. The Mexicans got around him and tried to boost him, but the jackass had had enough of that kind of fun and philosophically declined to rise until released from his burden, so they had to dismount the jackass. By that time the Indians had disappeared and if any were killed they were taken off the field.

Captain Buckner, one of the first white men in the colonies, concocted a scheme to rid the country of both Karankawas and Tonkawas. Buckner kept a trading post down on Bay prairie. The two tribes of Indians were always bickering with each other and finally agreed to meet at a certain time and place and fight it out. The Karankawas came and reported the arrangement to Buckner and said if they only had arms and ammunition they would make short work of their foes. Buckner readily furnished the munitions of war, and directly the Tonks came with the same plea for assistance. The obliging Buckner also fitted them out, and when the time for the battle arrived, repaired to the designated field of conflict, field glass in hand, hoping to see both parties annihilated. The meeting place was a prairie half a mile across. The Cronks came yelling out of a belt of timber on one side, and the Tonks came from a similar shelter on the other, and both opened fire before they were within striking distance, shooting away all Buckner's ammunition without drawing a drop of blood; each party retiring in good order and claiming a glorious victory.

The Karankawas seem to have disappeared with the dominion of Mexico; just how I don't know; but there was a story to the effect that Captain Dimmit was incidentally the prime factor in the problem. Dimmit had a ranch near the mouth of Lavaca at a place called Dimmit's landing. Finding a pacific policy best in dealing with the Cronks, he was in the habit of giving them beef whenever they came around. During the Texas revolution Dimmit left to aid in the struggle. The Indians, knowing nothing of the nature of the trouble, went to Dimmit's ranch and finding it deserted went out and drove in the cattle and helped themselves to a beef. While thus engaged a party of Mexican soldiers came up and demanded to know what they were doing. "Oh," said the Indians, "it's all right; we are Captain Dimmit's friends." Upon hearing that, the Mexicans charged them, killing some and putting the rest to flight. The unlucky Cronks next met a party of Americans, and fearing another attack, shouted "Viva Mexico!" whereupon the Americans fell upon them and the remnant that escaped, either hid themselves in the canebrakes or took to their canoes and paddled out to sea. At any rate, I don't remember of ever hearing of them after the revolution.

Senor De Leon was the very essence of hospitality, as, indeed, I found the Mexicans everywhere to be. He had his caballada driven in for us to choose from. The vaqueros rode in among them, carajoing and swinging their lariats, the horses reared and snorted, and we concluded walking would be pleasant pastime compared to riding such steeds, so we continued our journey on foot. The weather was so hot that we were obliged to lay up a good part of the day, and so were nine days going from Victoria to Gonzales, and it rained every day. The streams were all swollen, and as Gibbs could not swim, I had to raft him across when the water was too deep to wade. We trudged through black mud, wading and swimming streams, sleeping on wet grass, killing and broiling our meat, our only care being to keep our powder dry. Gonzales consisted of two block houses and the inhabitants of two men, John W. Smith and ———— Porter, the families having all gone down to DeWitt's station. Finding nothing to tempt us to further explorations, and still unable to procure horses, we struck out for the Colorado. There were droves of handsome, sleek mustangs all around, and Gibbs concluded to catch one. It was said that a shot through a certain place in the top of the neck, called "creasing," would stun a horse and cause it to fall, when if one would be quick about it he could get a rope on it before it could recover. Gibbs killed a wild cow, braided a lariat of the hide and watched for a favorable opportunity to "crease" a mustang. By and by a drove came down to drink, and selecting a fine specimen, he fired. The horse fell and lay quivering. Gibbs dropped his gun, grabbed his lariat, ran up to the prostrate courser, slipped a noose over his head, and taking a turn around a tree, braced himself and waited for his prize to recover; but the horse never even kicked. He had broken its neck.

We reached the Colorado at Burnham's station, a few miles below where LaGrange now stands, then the highest settlement on the river. There Gibbs procured a horse and returned to the mouth of the Brazos, where he soon after died. Things looked more promising there than any place I had seen.

The settlers were doing some farming and all had milk cows, poultry, etc. Corn was in "roasting ear" and the people feasting. They boiled it and fried it and roasted it, either by standing the husked ears on end before the fire and turning them till browned all around or buried them husk and all in hot ashes, the sweetest way green corn was ever cooked. When the corn began to harden they made graters of old tinware, coffee pots being most in vogue. They were ripped open and spread flat on a board and punched full of ragged holes. They were then bent into an oval and the straight edges nailed to a board. The corn was of the large, soft, white Mexican variety and grated easily, and the bread was very rich and sweet, if a bit heavy. Next came the mortar and sweep. A good, sound tree was cut off some three or four feet above the ground, and the stump was hollowed out by alternate burning and scraping till it would hold sometimes a peck of shelled corn. Then a long pole, to the butt end of which a pestle was attached, was swung into the fork of an adjacent tree and the corn was pounded into meal, which, often without sifting or salt, was mixed with water and baked, not a very tempting dish from an epicurean standpoint, but to people who had not tasted bread for months it was a delicious change. When cold weather came on there were huge kettles of "lye hominy." Captain Jesse Burnham had a nice family, one only of whom is at present living.* He was anxious to have a school and when he found that I had mastered the rudiments of the three "R's" he offered me a situation as teacher. But I had no predilection for pedagogy. Upon inquiry I learned that there was a shop down at Judge Cummin's station, some miles below on the Colorado, so I went down there. The judge had two daughters and there were the two Miss Beasons, all nice, agreeable girls, and altogether it was not a bad place to stop, so I went to work. Here too I first met Captain Jim Ross and Colonel John H. Moore, who later married the Misses Cummins. But the unaccustomed exposure incidental to my jaunt brought on fever and I was bedridden for weeks. There was no doctor, but the judge was equal to the occasion. He nursed me as tenderly as if I had been his son. By the time I was able to get around my last cent was gone and I had even sold part of my clothes and I was the most homesick boy that ever left a comfortable home and loving, indulgent parents in search of adventure. In that condition Colonel Little, a man who had known my father in the old north state, found me. He had been over into Mexico for a drove of mules, which he was taking back. Shocked to find me so far from home amid such surroundings, he offered to take me home, an offer which I was all too glad to accept. I was very weak, but the thought of getting home buoyed me up to make the attempt. Colonel Little fitted me out with a nice easy-gaited horse and I started, but I had miscalculated my strength and by the time we reached San Felipe I was exhausted. Colonel Little, loth to leave me, waited for me to rest

*Robert. He died November 11, 1899, after the above was written.

[14]

up and I made another start, but only got across the Brazos, where I was again prostrated and my friend was obliged to leave me. I found asylum in the family of Churchill Fulshear, who took me in and with the rude hospitality which ever characterizes frontier people, did all in their power to alleviate my suffering, but, living, as they did, without any of the conveniences even of those times, it was impossible to do more than supply actual necessities. As I lay there day after day, burning with fever, tormented with gnats and mosquitoes, and loathing the coarse and unpalatable food which was all those good Samaritans had to offer, I would have given the whole territory of Texas had it been mine, to feel myself once more at home in a comfortable bed, with mother's loving face beside me. So thoroughly homesick was I that I was determined to resume my journey as soon as I got able, even if I had to walk. I thought if I could only get down to the mouth of the Brazos, where vessels came in, I could get back to New Orleans, where I had friends who would help me home. As soon as I felt able to undertake the jaunt I thanked my kind entertainers—I had nothing else to give—and started out to walk by easy stages. I skirted the river timber for several miles till I struck a trail leading through the bottom to Fort Bend (Richmond), where White & Knight had a trading post and ferry. My weakness prevented me from making good time and night overtook me while I was still some miles short of my destination. It was not an enviable situation. Weak, unarmed, not even a pocket knife—I had parted with everything except the clothes I had on—alone in a dense forest inhabited by Mexican lions, panthers, leopards and numerous smaller members of the feline race, all more or less inimical to man. There was no moon, and the tall timber made a darkness so intense that I had to feel rather than see my way along the narrow trail. I confess I felt rather uncomfortable, and every time a twig snapped I looked and listened for some nocturnal beast of prey. Now and then there was a rustle of leaves as some small animal scurried away in the darkness. With every sense alert and strained, I at length descried a moving object in the trail a short distance ahead of me. Concentrating all my powers of vision upon it, I made out that it was traveling leisurely in the same direction as myself, apparently unconscious of my presence. I walked on, unintentionally gaining on it, when, to my horror, it suddenly stopped and seemed to swell to double its former size. I could see that it was mottled light and dark, and at once jumped to the conclusion that it was a leopard. Knowing that it was a characteristic of all the cat family to turn their hair the wrong way when displeased, I felt my hair raise, for I thought he was about to spring upon me. Presently he started on and, it being out of the question to turn back, and not caring to remain in the woods, I had no alternative but to follow. Not daring to lose sight of him, lest he lie in wait for me, I kept along at a respectful distance behind. His pace was exasperatingly slow, and again and again when I got a little too near to suit him he stopped, and every time he seemed to take on greater dimensions. This

[15]

process of doubling had by this time brought him up to the size of an ordinary dog, and feeling that it would be extremely hazardous to permit any further increase in his proportions, I desperately resolved to bring matters to a crisis. I stooped, still keeping my eye on the enemy, and felt around for a good sized club. Trying it on the ground to test its soundness, I took it in my left hand and felt for another, resolved to make the best fight possible. Thus armed, I started on. Again the animal halted and I felt that the time for decisive action had arrived. I raised my chunk and with a strength born of desperation, hurled it at him and grabbed the missile from my left hand to be ready in case he should resent my familiarity. But there was no need. My shot struck him square and landed him some distance ahead, and then—well, then he didn't look any bigger than a polecat. With the release from excitement came the reaction; my overtaxed strength gave way and I wouldn't swear that I didn't cry. Anyway I had to sit down and rest before I could proceed. Waiting till the smoke—or rather scent—of battle cleared a little, I went on and soon saw the welcome gleam of light that betokened a human habitation, and never was the sight more welcome. Hungry and worn out, I reached the cabin, where Captain White received me and ministered to my needs. In return I recounted my adventure, the denouement of which elicited roars of laughter, in which I could then afford to join. The next morning I crossed the river and went my way. Before I was out of the timber I met a panther face to face. We both stopped, one as much surprised as the other. I yelled at him, but he didn't budge. I suppose he wanted to see what manner of beast or bird I was, probably never having seen a white man before. He made no hostile demonstration, so I yelled again, when, apparently satisfied with his observations, he turned and went his way. He was a big fellow, but he didn't look half so formidable as the polecat. I have faced death many times since, when bullets and arrows flew thick around me, but I never afterwards felt the sickening horror that seized me every time that wretched little skunk stopped and threw up his brush.

The next settlement I struck was Josiah Bell's, where Columbia now stands. There I learned that Johnny McNeal, out on the gulf prairie, was in need of a blacksmith. There were quite a family of the McNeals. They had raised a crop of cotton and were building a gin. They had a shop and tools, and so I went out and in the intervals between relapses of the fever I made the gin irons. Iron was a scarce article, but we found an ample supply in the wreck of an old vessel that lay high and dry in a belt of timber at least five miles back from the gulf. The timbers were all rotted away; the knotted hearts of two pine trees that had once been the masts alone remaining. The irons though deeply encrusted with rust, were in a fair state of preservation. There was nothing to give a clue to its age or nationality. It had evidently been there many a long year, probably driven ashore by a tidal wave, or one of

those fierce tornadoes which sometimes drive the water far out over the prairie. It may have been one of La Salle's vessels.

Sterling McNeal was something of a doctor and he treated me so successfully that I soon began to mend. The members of the family were the embodiment of kindness. By this time the weather was growing cool and I went bear hunting with the boys, and my homesickness melted away. I shot away many pounds of lead in vain attempts to kill a deer, but the balls invariably struck the ground many yards short of the intended victim. At last old Johnny McNeal told me not to fire till I could see the eyes. Acting on the suggestion, I went out one day alone and brought in a deer on my back, as proud and happy as a boy with his first pantaloons. The boys saw me coming and raised a shout: "Run here everybody; Smithwick's killed a deer." They lifted me and the deer on their shoulders and bore us in triumph to the house. After that it was no trouble for me to kill deer. The Mexican garrison at San Antonio was in need of an armorer and Stephen F. Austin procured me the appointment. I was quite elated with the prospect, but when I got to San Antonio I found everything so different to anything I had ever before encountered that I was thoroughly disgusted. There were but few Americans there, and but one American family. Captain Dimmit, with whom I stopped, had a Mexican wife and was, for all practical purposes, a Mexican. I had to do all business through an interpreter. The upper crust of society took no notice of me and the under crust was, to my mind, much lower than the negro slaves, and I couldn't think of coming down to their level. Old Gasper Flores was land commissioner and had almost unlimited power in the way of land grants. He offered me any quantity of land, accompanied by the hand of his daughter, a little squatty girl, dark, almost, as an Indian. I was young then and disposed to be rather fastidious in such matters, and so declined the honor of the alliance, thus throwing away the chance of a lifetime.

The tools they offered me to work with were at least a century old in design. The anvil was simply a square block of iron; the bellows, two cylinders into which were fitted valvular pistons, worked by hand; the operator standing behind and working them alternately. And such hammers! They baffle description. The Comandante offered to send to New Orleans and get an outfit if I would make out a list, but I was not to be tempted by even such a flattering deference to my judgment, so after a ten days' sojourn, I foolishly threw up my commission and, in company with ———— Duncan and "Mustang" Brown, set out on my return to San Felipe. At the Salado we met a couple of men, with one of whom (Parker) I was slightly acquainted. Upon learning my destination he handed me $6 in silver and an old brass pistol with the request that I deliver them to Cooper & Cheaves, who had a store in San Felipe. At Gonzales we stopped with Joe McCoy; Joe was a famous mustang catcher and had just made a catch. Among the lot was a nice looking black mare which proved to be perfectly gentle; she took my fancy and I traded my horse for her. Arriving at San Felipe I went straight to the store of Cooper & Cheaves to deliver the goods committed to my care by Parker. Cooper—commonly called "Sawmill Cooper," from having been engaged in the business of manufacturing lumber—was at once attracted by the mare. He walked around her, looked at the brand and asked me where I got her. I told him. "H'm," said he, "it's a little curious." "Why?" I asked, somewhat nettled by his air of incredulity. "Why, that's the very mare we sold to Early, who left here about two weeks ago with Parker to go over to Mexico to buy mules." "I met Parker," I replied, "but the only man I saw with him was Tomlinson." Several persons had gathered around, and there appearing to be something peculiar about it, I called on my two traveling companions to verify my statement and relieve me from an awkward position. Early was a comparative stranger, having lately come in from Kentucky with quite a sum of money, which he proposed investing in Spanish mules, they being in demand for farming purposes in the cotton states. Being unacquainted with the country and language, he wanted some one to go with him, for which service Parker was engaged. Being flat broke, Parker borrowed from Cooper $6 and a pistol, which some strange motive prompted him to return by me. There was certainly something suspicious about it, but San Antonio was 300 miles away and the only means of communication was by chance travelers, but as time passed on and Early did not return, Ned Cullen, an old acquaintance of his, became uneasy and began to make inquiries, which revealed the fact that Parker was in San Antonio spending money freely, but nothing had been seen of Early. At this juncture Parker, ignorant of the turn affairs had taken, returned to San Felipe. On being questioned he said that Early had gone on to Mexico, but upon being confronted with the facts in possession of Cullen and others, he betrayed such evident confusion that he was at once placed under arrest pending investigation. There was no jail, so I was called on to put him in irons, the first time I had ever performed such an office, but I put them on to stay until the affair was cleared up, for, as you may readily suppose, I felt resentful for the suspicion he had laid me under. A searching party was made up, and at Plum creek, where the mare was found, they discovered the remains of Early, together with his saddle, bridle, blankets and saddle-bags, all sunk in a hole in the creek. They had been deposited there when the creek was flush and were well hidden till the fall of the water exposed them. The mare had been turned loose with the mustangs, which an avenging Nemesis delivered into the hands of Joe McCoy.

Texas and Coahuila then constituted one state, with the seat of government at Saltillo, and in all Texas there was no tribunal for the trial of murder cases. The custom was to take down the evidence and send it to Saltillo. While this was being done it transpired that Parker was not his true name, which, for the sake of an honest family, I withhold. Under circumstances similar to the present he had murdered a man in his native state, of which his father was at

[19]

the time governor. The evidence was so conclusive that all efforts to save him were futile, though the trial was obstructed in every way possible and his father well nigh impoverished himself trying to defeat the ends of justice. Parker lay in jail nearly two years and at length in a fit of despair attempted to cut his throat, but either his strength failed him or his courage, and he only succeeded in severing the windpipe, which would have answered every purpose but for the interposition of the physician, who inserted a silver tube to secure his breathing. Failing to secure his release, after exhausting every other means, the heart-broken father—a father still, even to the extent of sacrificing his honor—exercised his executive prerogative to save his guilty son from the gallows and immediately resigned his office. The murderer fled from the fury of an indignant people and sought safety in the land of refuge—Texas—only to continue his career of crime. The facts in the Early murder case were taken before the alcalde and dispatched to Saltillo, but, before there was any return made, Parker was taken sick; there was no physician near, and he was left to the care of old Jimmy Whiteside, who finally announced that he was dead, and, assisted by his negro man, forthwith proceeded to prepare the body for burial, accounting for the haste on the ground that, having died of fever and the weather being very warm, decomposition at once ensued. There was no coroner, and, when the few whom curiosity led thither arrived at Whiteside's cabin, the body was already nailed up in a rough box, from which a sickening odor emanated. Everybody was satisfied, and the incident was almost forgotten when a citizen of San Felipe, having business in Mobile, Ala., met and talked with Parker in the flesh. On returning to San Felipe he reported the meeting; the coffin was exhumed and found to contain only a cottonwood chunk, which, when green, was about the weight of a man. The artful scoundrel had worked on Whiteside's sympathies with a pitiful story of persecution, from which he was trying to escape to Mexico, of a quarrel with Early whom he was forced to kill in self defense, and thus prevailed on his kind-hearted jailor to assist him to escape. Well, he was gone and not at all likely to trouble that community again, so Uncle Jimmy Whiteside was not brought to time for his breach of the law.

An article published in the Louisville Courier Journal since the above was written, furnishes the clue to an interesting sequel thereto. The statement was to the effect that the late Minister Willis, who represented the United States in Hawaii during Cleveland's last administration, discovered in the person of a native Hawaiian missionary a son of the quondam Parker by a native woman; Parker having resumed his family name, which, being a peculiar one, led to his identification by Minister Willis, who, being a native of the same state with Parker, was familiar with all the circumstances of his first crime.

When and by what means the double-dyed murderer who had twice almost miraculously escaped the gallows effected his retreat to those then savage, far away islands, and how many more victims paved his way thereto, will never be known; but could the story be revealed it would doubtless make an interesting chapter.

CHAPTER 3

"Young man, you have thrown away an independent fortune," was Col. Austin's impatient comment when informed of my hasty rejection of the position tendered me by the government. And he was no doubt correct, but I still had a good trade to fall back on and this I forthwith prepared to do, purchasing the outfit of San Felipe's pioneer blacksmith, David Carpenter, and establishing myself in business at Bell's Landing where the proprietor of the premises, Col. Josiah Bell, was laboring to bring into being the town of Columbia.

A fine specimen of the old Kentucky gentleman was Col. Bell, who was among the first of Austin's colonists, both chronologically and socially. As a proof of the high esteem in which he held Col. Bell, Austin, when compelled to go on to Mexico in 1822, in order to get his father's grant confirmed, committed the affairs of the colony into the former's hands during his absence.

Of Col. Bell's children who were then quite small, I remember distinctly only James H., who later distinguished himself in the legal profession, attaining therein the honorable prefix by which he was long designated. It was not in that character, however, that Judge Bell first introduced himself to my special notice.

During a visit to the home of Col. Bell, my head covering a fur cap which I had deposited on the floor beside my chair having attracted the attention of the embryo jurist, he crept softly up in my rear and laid his hand cautiously upon it. This mode of examination, though apparently establishing the general character of the material of the cap, failed to reveal the specific character. But the incipient lawyer showed forth his determination to get at the bottom facts. Looking earnestly up into my face, he gravely inquired, "Is this a wool-'kin or a bear-'kin?"

Bell's Landing was the depot for all the supplies for the settlements above. Here Davis and John R. Harris, the founders of Harrisburg, had opened a store; they also owned a small trading schooner which plied between Columbia and New Orleans. I think they had a store at Harrisburg, but it may have been at a later date.

Among others that I recall as residents of the incipient town were my host and hostess, Mr. and Mrs. Farr, the latter a daughter of Capt. Brit Bailey (Mrs. Farr subsequently married David Milburn, at one time alcalde of San Felipe); Joseph H. Polley, also a son-in-law of Capt. Bailey's; (Capt. Bailey lived on a farm in the vicinity); Oliver Jones, who later represented Texas in

the congress of Coahuila and Texas; Thomas Westall, whose daughter married Brown Austin and after his death Zeno Philips—both gentlemen residents of Brazoria municipality; Alexander—or, as he was generally known, Sandy—Calvit; Mrs. Jane Long, widow of General James Long and sister to Mrs. Calvit; Mrs. Pamelia Pickett, also a widow, with her son John and a daughter; Dr. Samuel Angier, who subsequently married Mrs. Pickett; Martin Varner, Jesse Thompson, the Alsburys, Alleys, Dr. Wells, John H. Moore, the McNeals—the last four on San Bernard—and many more whose names have slipped my memory, lived in the vicinity.

I had also many patrons in Ft. Bend municipality, among them William Morton, Jesse Cartwright, Horatio Chriesman, Mills M. Battles, alcalde, Thomas Barnet, later "Big Alcalde," i.e., president of the ayuntamiento, Joseph San Pierre—French; Churchill Fulshear, the widow McNutt, Moses Shipman, Martin Allen, Elijah Alcorn and a host of others; for in these two districts, Ft. Bend and Brazoria, were located the majority of Austin's colonists; and here, too, was concentrated the greater portion of the wealth in the colony.

Most of the men I have mentioned were men of means, many of them having slaves with which they had already opened up quite respectable plantations.

Of these old pioneers, Churchill Fulshear occupies the largest space in my memory, because of the generosity extended to me when I was left to his care, sick and a stranger, as previously related. He was a small man, somewhat lame, with very homely features, but a warm, true heart. The old man had been for years a follower of the sea, at which trade he had accumulated some money. This fact becoming known, there were frequent calls for loans. If the applicant were a man that he wished to oblige, Fulshear would remark that he had "little or none," but would see what he could do, and drawing a purse from his pocket, manage to scrape up the required amount. In other cases he would solemnly declare that he "hadn't a dollar in the world," and draw out an empty purse to prove it. Having been present in both cases, I probably betrayed some surprise when, after having heard him assert that he "hadn't a dollar in the world," he turned right about and loaned 50 or 100 dollars to another party.

"You doubtless think me lying when I say 'I haven't a dollar in the world,'" said he, in explanation, "but I'll show you that I am not. This," said he, drawing the empty purse from his pocket, "I call 'the world' and you can see for yourself that there isn't a dollar in it. And this," exhibiting one containing money, "I call 'little or none.'"

Capt. Horatio Chriesman, head surveyor for Austin's colony, was the soul of generosity. It was told of him that he loaned a friend a league of land to assist him in the consummation of a trade and it was further told that the loan was never repaid, but a league of land those days was of less consequence than a horse.

Jesse Thompson, living on the San Bernard, though possessed of a number of slaves, devoted his attention mostly to stock. There was much dissatisfaction over the uncertainty of legislation on the slavery question and Thompson, among others, was at one time on the point of returning to the United States with his slaves, and it was probably due to this uncertainty that he had neglected farming interests. One of his slaves, Mose, impatient for the promised freedom, ran away to Mexico to obtain it, but he soon wearied of "husks," and, returning voluntarily, surrendered himself to his old master, preferring slavery under Thompson's lenient rule to freedom in Mexico.

The negroes soon became aware of the legal status of slavery in Mexican territory, and it was probably owing to their ignorance of the language and country that more of them did not leave. Jim, one of McNeal's slaves, openly announced his determination to leave, and, acting on the impulse, threw down his hoe and started away. Pleasant McNeal, to whom he communicated his intention, ordered him to return to work, but Jim went on, whereupon Pleasant raised his rifle.

"Jim," said he, "if you don't come back I'll shoot you!" Jim, however, kept on and true to his threat McNeal shot him dead.

Another type of the old colonists, but one that played a no less important part in the development of the country, was Thomas B. Bell, who lived up on the San Bernard above McNeal's. He came several times to my shop during my stay at McNeal's, and he being an intelligent, well-bred man, I took quite a fancy to him and gladly accepted an invitation to visit him. I found him domiciled in a little pole-cabin in the midst of a small clearing upon which was a crop of corn. His wife, every inch a lady, welcomed me with as much cordiality as if she were mistress of a mansion. There were two young children and they, too, showed in their every manner the effects of gentle training. The whole family were dressed in buckskin, and when supper was announced, we sat on stools around a clapboard table, upon which were arranged wooden platters. Beside each platter lay a fork made of a joint of cane. The knives were of various patterns, ranging from butcher knives to pocket-knives. And for cups, we had little wild cymlings, scraped and scoured until they looked as white and clean as earthenware, and the milk with which the cups were filled was as pure and sweet as mortal ever tasted. The repast was of the simplest, but served with as much grace as if it had been a feast, which, indeed, it became, seasoned with the kindly manners and pleasant conversation of those two entertainers. Not a word of apology was uttered during my stay of a day and night, and when I left them I did so with a hearty invitation to repeat my visit. It so happened that I never was at their place again, but was told that in the course of time the pole cabin gave place to a handsome brick house and that the rude furnishings were replaced by the best the country boasted, but I'll venture to say that the host and hostess still retained their old hospitality unchanged by change of fortune.

They were a social people these old Three Hundred, though no one seems to have nöted the evidence of it. There were a number of weddings and other social gatherings during my sojourn in that section, the most notable one perhaps being the marriage of Nicholas McNutt to Miss Cartwright. There was a large number of invited guests, both the families occupying prominent social positions. Jesse Cartwright, father of the bride, was a man in comfortable circumstances and himself and family people of good breeding. They were among the very first of Austin's colonists, Cartwright being a member of the first ayuntamiento organized in Texas. The bridegroom was a son of the widow McNutt, also among the early arrivals. The family, consisting of mother, two sons and three young daughters, came from Louisiana, where they had been very wealthy, but having suffered reverses they came to Texas to recoup their fortunes. Bred up in luxury, as they evidently had been, it was a rough road to fortune they chose, but they adapted themselves to the situation and made the best of it. Mrs. McNutt had three brothers, the Welches, living on Bayou Rapids, La., whom I afterwards knew; she also had a sister, Mrs. Dr. Peebles living with her husband in San Felipe. Dr. Wells later married a Miss McNutt, and Porter another. But to get back to the wedding. Miss Mary Allen, daughter of Martin Allen, a very pretty girl and a great belle by the way, was bridesmaid, and John McNutt, brother of the bridegroom, was groomsman. There being no priest in the vicinity, Thomas Dukes, the "big" alcalde, was summoned from San Felipe. The alcalde tied the nuptial knot in good American style, but the contracting parties had in addition to sign a bond to avail themselves of the priest's services to legalize the marriage at the earliest opportunity.

Among the guests present I remember Mrs. Long and her daughter Ann, Miss Alcorn, daughter of Elijah Alcorn, Miss Mary, daughter of Moses Shipman, Mrs. McNutt and daughters, none of the latter then grown, Capt. Martin, Elliot and John Alcorn.

The first and most important number on the program being duly carried out, the next thing in order was the wedding supper, which was the best the market afforded. That being disposed of, the floor was cleared for dancing. It mattered not that the floor was made of puncheons. When young folks danced those days, they danced; they didn't glide around; they "shuffled" and "double shuffled," "wired" and "cut the pigeon's wing," making the splinters fly. There were some of the boys, however, who were not provided with shoes, and moccasins were not adapted to that kind of dancing floor, and moreover they couldn't make noise enough, but their more fortunate brethren were not at all selfish or disposed to put on airs, so, when they had danced a turn, they generously exchanged footgear with the moccasined contingent and gave them the ring, and we just literally kicked every splinter off that floor before morning. The fiddle, manipulated by Jesse Thompson's man Mose, being rather too weak to make itself heard above the din of clattering feet, we had in

another fellow with a clevis and pin to strengthen the orchestra, and we had a most enjoyable time.

One other wedding to which I was bidden was that of Dr. Angier and Mrs. Pickett, Mills M. Battles, I think, officiating. The wedding, which took place at Captain Bailey's, was a very quiet affair, no dancing or other amusements being indulged in.

Another dancing party in which I participated was at Martin Varner's, near Columbia. When we were all assembled and ready to begin business it was found that Mose, the only fiddler around, had failed to come to time, so we called in an old darky belonging to Colonel Zeno Philips, who performed on a clevis as an accompaniment to his singing, while another negro scraped on a cotton hoe with a case knife. The favorite chorus was:

"O git up gals in de mawnin',
O git up gals in de mawnin',
O git up gals in de mawnin',
Jes at the de break ob day,"

at the conclusion of which the performer gave an extra blow to the clevis while the dancers responded with a series of dexterous rat-tat-tats with heel and toe.

Ah, those old memories, how they throng around me, bringing up forms and faces long since hidden 'neath the sod. So long ago the events herein narrated occurred that I question if there is now another person living who participated in or even has heard of them.

Other weddings among the Old Three Hundred in that vicinity to which I was not fortunate enough to get an invitation were the daughters of Wm. Moreton of Fort Bend, one of whom married Stephen Richardson, at one time partner with Thomas Davis in a store at San Felipe, and the other, William, son of George Huff, on San Bernard; Samuel Chance and Miss San Pierre, daughter of Joseph San Pierre. They have probably all passed away, but to their descendants, for such I take there are, I extend the greeting of their father's friend; may they prove worthy of such parentage.

My associations with those worthy people were pleasant, and, had I been content to remain with them, much of the remainder of this book might never have been written. But the spirit of adventure was still the dominating influence and, falling in with a lot of congenial spirits, I forsook the ways of civilization for a time, returning no more to those peaceful shades.

CHAPTER 4

Under the colonization act the Texas colonists were permitted to import, duty free, everything they desired for their own use; but, in order to carry merchandise into Mexico, they were required then, as now, to pay a heavy import duty. Coffee and tobacco were contraband—the government reserving to itself the sole right to deal in those commodities. Citizens were even restricted in the cultivation of tobacco, the government, it is said, having passed an act prohibiting any one person from planting more than an almnd (one-sixth of a bushel) of tobacco seed. Traders, even in illegitimate lines, had to pay a heavy duty to get their goods into market, and a still heavier duty to get their money out; so smuggling was largely resorted to, notwithstanding the strict patrol maintained along the border. The official optic, however, was not proof against the dazzle of coin. Therefore there was little to fear from that source; the principal risk lay in the cupidity of the Mexican soldiery.

Life in the colonies becoming stale and not so profitable as I could wish, I sold out my shop down at Bell's Landing (Columbia), invested the proceeds in tobacco, and, in company with Joe McCoy, Jack Cryor, and John F. Webber, set out for Mexico on a smuggling trip.

Altogether we had about 1,000 pounds of leaf tobacco, done up in bales of 100 pounds each, which we packed on mules. The first town we struck on the Rio Grande was Laredo. Finding that some other trader had got in ahead of us and stocked the market, we proceeded on up the river to find fresh territory. On the way up one of those interminable Texas rains set in, and we were compelled to strike camp and cover up our tobacco. We ran out of food, and, there being no settlements near and no game but wild horses, the very thought of eating which sickened me, there was a prospective famine, at least for me. The other boys had been in Texas long enough to get rid of any fastidious notions about clean and unclean beasts, so when provisions ran out they killed a mustang and were provisioned for a siege. I turned from the horse-meat diet with disgust, vowing I would starve before I would eat it. I fasted two days, and still the rain god, as if enjoying the situation, continued to pour out his moist blessing with no sign of cessation. On the third day of my fast I sat hungry and disconsolate by the camp fire, while Webber was frying out some horse fat with which to grease our packs and lariats. At length, when the fat was all fried out, Webber lifted out the "cracklings," brown, light and crisp, laying them on a rock to the windward of me. I sniffed the air hungrily, and finally, when I thought the action unperceived, reached over and possessed myself of a crackling. I bit off a piece and found that it had no bad taste; on the contrary, it seemed to me no meat ever tasted better. My prejudice took wings, and I went for a horse steak which I could scarcely wait to cook, so famished was I. The boys said I was "broke in," and I ate horse meat with the rest of them; still I can't say I should do so of choice.

[29]

The weather finally cleared, and we went on up to Presidio del Norte, but the rains had raised the river and there were no boats except rawhide ones, which were not very safe, with the river a quarter of a mile wide and running with a swift current. We hid our tobacco out in the chaparral and laid around watching for some chance to cross the river.

Over opposite our camp was a goat ranch. Under pretense of getting milk, Cryor and myself swam our horses over and reconnoitered the situation, seeing which the Mexican soldiers concluded to emulate our example and investigate us. Their ponies were not strong enough to breast the current and were carried down to a point where the bank was so steep they could not effect a landing. One soldier was drowned, and the others, after drifting down lower, scrambled out. They found our tobacco and helped themselves to as much as they could conceal, making no attempt to arrest us, as their duty required. To have done so would have necessitated the surrender of the goods, which they had no intention of doing. Surmising that they proposed returning for the bulk of our cargo at their convenience, we removed it. We then paid another visit to the goat ranch and by a little tangible persuasion succeeded in getting possession of a rawhide boat, which we took across the river after dark, swimming and towing it. In the same manner we ferried the tobacco over and had it safely hidden before morning. There was more tobacco than could be disposed of advantageously in one little town, so we divided it, Webber and I taking our part up to San Fernando, Cryor and McCoy got in with the alcalde, but the custom house officers got wind of the affair and arrested the alcalde. He succeeded in giving the boys warning and they skipped out, leaving their tobacco buried in the sand.

Webber and I had better luck. Arriving at San Fernando in safety, we hunted up the only white man in the place, John Villars, and made him our confederate. Villars had been in the place several years, having gone out there during the Mexican war of independence with one Boone, who was a gunsmith, and was appointed armorer for the Mexican army. Boone dying, Villars succeeded to the position, marrying the widow, who in turn died, and was succeeded by a Mexican woman. Through the assistance of Villars we found safe hiding for our wares with an old Mexican woman, Doña Petra, who enjoyed the distinction of being the widow of a white man (one John Smith), and consequently the steadfast friend of all Americans, considering it an honor to have them make her house their home. Therefore our being domiciled there was quite a matter of course, occasioning no suspicion. We had to dispose of the tobacco in small parcels, which took time. In order to avert any suspicion that an apparently aimless sojourn might arouse, Villars suggested that one of us should be "doctor," American doctors being in demand among the Mexicans, who had no regular physicians. I caught at the idea at once but I was so boyish looking that we feared the natives might distrust my skill, so we decided Webber must shoulder the responsibility.

Villars had a store which was the principal advertising medium in the vicinity. Its facilities were ample, and "Dr." Webber's services were soon in requisition. It was summer time, and bilious disorders prevalent. We had taken out a lot of simple medicines for our own needs, consisting for the most part of calomel, quinine, and tartar emetic. As I spoke better Spanish than the "doctor," I accompanied him on his professional visits, ostensibly as interpreter, really to see the fun and help him out if he got into deep water. With an air of importance that would have done credit to a professional, Webber noted the symptoms, shaking his head, knitting his brows, and otherwise impressing the patient with the seriousness of his condition.

Tartar emetic was the doctor's favorite prescription, and his doses were liberal. I looked on the Mexicans as scarce more than apes and could with difficulty restrain my enjoyment at the situation when the medicine got in its work, seemingly turning the poor devils inside out, they meanwhile swearing and praying alternately. And I felt no twinge of remorse for the monstrous imposition we were practicing upon them when they finally emerged from the doctor's heroic treatment looking as dry and shrunken as so many pods of chili colorado (their favorite article of diet), and loaded him with thanks for his ministrations. I managed to keep down my risibles while in attendance on the patients, but I gave full vent to them when I got back to Villars' store and rehearsed the performance for his benefit. The doctor's fame went abroad and he soon had a large practice, just the same as impostors of the present day. Occasionally he varied his treatment by bleeding, though between the red pepper with which the natives plied the inner man, and the hot summer sun beating on the thinly clad outer surface, blood-letting seemed something of a paradox. The only case we ever had which baffled Dr. Webber's skill was that of an old Mexican woman, fat as only a Mexican woman can get. The doctor decided she needed depletion, so he corded her arm, but here he encountered a difficulty for which his practice furnished no precedent: the vein was too deeply imbedded in the fat to be discernible to the eye, and his knowledge of anatomy did not enable him to otherwise locate it with any degree of accuracy; therefore the only resource was to prospect for it. He jabbed the lancet in several times, but either from failure to get his bearings right, a miscalculation of the capacity of his lancet, or the thickness of the stratum of fat, it had no more effect than if he had stuck it into a fat porker, and he had to fall back on tartar emetic.

When not "professionally" engaged I divided my time between my study of the Spanish language and tinkering at my trade. Villars gave me the freedom of his smithy, but his outfit was so meager and ancient that it was almost like learning the trade anew.

Every kind of work was done in the most primitive manner. Their plows were counterparts of the one Romulus used in laying out the city of Rome, being simply forked sticks, one prong of which served for share, another for

handle, and the third for a tongue, which was tied on to a straight stick, the latter in turn lashed to the horns of a pair of oxen. Carts with great, clumsy, solid wooden wheels were the only vehicles they had there; there were not even dugouts, their only boats being made of cow hides sewed together and stretched over a framework of poles, the whole thing put together with raw-hide thongs.

Rawhide entered into the construction of pretty much everything they used. When they slept, it was on a rawhide bedstead; when they sat, it was on a rawhide; and when they ate, a rawhide laid on the ground did duty for a table—around this the family squatted, eating with their fingers, like Indians, their only table service consisting of rude pottery and gourds.

The women ground their corn on the metate, after first hulling it like hominy, and baked their tortillas on flat stones, or at best on a sheet of iron. Their spinning and weaving would have made even a lazy man tired. Such things as cards, wheels and looms were unknown. Wool was colored and then picked open by hand. For spinning, they used a kind of top, attaching a bit of wool to the peg or spindle, then giving it a dexterous twirl between the thumb and finger and dropping it into a bowl, drawing out the thread while it spun round. It took weeks and weeks of this kind of patient work to spin thread enough for the warp of a blanket, and then came the weaving, which took months. The warp was stretched upon a frame and the filling of unspun wool worked in and out with the fingers and driven up with a board which was passed over and under the threads and stood on edge while the filling was being placed, then turned flat and the filling driven up close, after which the board was taken out and changed for the next layer. I presume they are still working the same way in some portions of Mexico. Their blankets were beautiful, and much more durable than might be supposed.

Old Doña Petra had a wheel that her deceased husband had made. It was a grotesque looking affair, but an improvement on the top. The old lady was also the proud possessor of several chairs, the handiwork of the lamented John Smith. The houses had no chimneys, the little fire necessary being kindled in the center of the room, like an Indian wigwam. The one only lux-ury they enjoyed was an abundance of pure, clear spring water, brought through a cement aqueduct from a large spring some miles distant.

There was an old grist mill in the outskirts of the town which had fallen into disuse for want of patronage, presumably. We went out and took a look at it with a view to its rehabilitation, but it would have required more capital than we were possessed of to put it into running order.

To illustrate how ignorant even the best of the inhabitants were, I will re-late a couple of incidents that came under my observation during my sojourn in San Fernando. A rumor had reached them that Bradburn and Staples had applied for a charter to run a steamboat up the Rio Grande. As not one of them, not even Villars, had ever seen a steamboat, they sent out for Webber

and myself to attend a meeting of the council and explain its workings to them. I, being spokesman, spread myself, expatiating on the speed, carrying capacity, etc., but I overshot the mark. The very point that I had depended on to recommend it proved its condemnation. After listening to my glowing eulogies, they consulted together, gravely shook their heads, and announced their decision: that "it would never do; it would throw all the cartmen and packmen out of employment." The same argument used by the Mississippi flatboatmen.

At another time there was an excitement about the landing of the French army at Vera Cruz. Having no idea where Vera Cruz was, they again sent for me to help them. There was an old atlas among Villars' possessions, and with its aid I succeeded in allaying all fears of an immediate attack on San Fernando.

And, speaking of the French invasion, reminds me of another story. There was a band of Empirico Indians in town, one of whom had a horse that I very much coveted. It was a mountain mustang, in color a strawberry roan, as beautiful a piece of horseflesh as I ever laid eyes on. I was determined to have the roan, and on making overtures for him was struck dumb with astonishment and delight when told that if I would make twenty silver buckles with which to bedeck the Indian's long braid of hair, I could take the horse. I accepted the offer with alacrity, and at once set about fulfilling my part of the contract. I took twenty old Spanish hammered dollars, worth 75 cents on the dollar, and worked industriously to convert them into buckles, in a fever of anxiety lest the Indian go back on his agreement. I had almost completed the job when news came that the French had been repulsed, whereupon the Mexicans got up a grand parade to celebrate the event. The Indians mounted their horses and took part in the demonstration. The horse that I had bargained for, being frightened by the blare of trumpets, became unmanageable and ran over another horseman, throwing its rider and falling on him. The Indian never regained consciousness and lived but a short time. Then, notwithstanding the whole band of Indians knew of the bargain I had made, they would not give the horse up. They held that inasmuch as he had not been delivered to me, he was still the property of the dead brave, and as such must be killed so as to accompany his master to the happy hunting ground. In vain I offered them twice and even thrice the sum agreed upon. It was an Indian law, and they were determined their unlucky comrade should make a good appearance when he rode into the happy hunting grounds. I experienced no regret for the untimely taking of the Indian, but it did sore grieve me to see that noble animal sacrificed to a blind superstition. Decked out in all the glory of warpaint, the doomed steed was led away beside the remains of his dead master, followed by the chief mourners with shorn heads and blackened faces, giving vent to their sorrow in loud, blood-curdling shrieks and howls. Wrapped in his buffalo robes, with his bow and arrows beside him, the departed brave was laid to rest in a shallow grave. His saddle and bridle were placed at his feet, and the grave filled in and tramped down hard. The horse was then led up beside the grave and shot, the remains being cremated. There were twenty silver buckles for sale and no buyers, as not one of the tribe would take them. Villars gave me back my $20 and took the buckles off my hands.

About that time I got a letter from Dr. Long, who had invested in some old silver mines in the Le Juana Mountains, which he thought very rich, offering me a liberal share in the investment. I started at once, going out on the Saltillo road to La Punte, a considerable town at the foot of the mountains, where we left the road. The arrival of an American being an unusual event, the news spread quickly, and at once brought forth the only white man the place contained. He was very friendly, and, having to present my passport to the alcalde, I asked him to go with me. As he informed me he had been some time in Mexico, I supposed he had learned to speak the language fluently, and asked him to interpret for me. When we came into the alcalde's presence, Blerton commenced to explain the object of our visit in a mixture of English and Spanish unintelligible to any one. The alcalde listened politely, and when Blerton had finished turned to me with a puzzled expression. "Alba uste Spanola, senor?" said he. "Poquito," I replied. "Then," said he, "I wish you would try and do your own talking; I can't understand this man." Poor Blerton was terribly crestfallen, but he did not in the least abate his friendliness. He accompanied me up to the mines.

Dr. Long's mines lay some thirty miles back in the mountains. When I reached the place I was disgusted to find only a few of the lowest class of Mexicans there, pecking out a few grains of silver, enough to purchase the bare necessities of life, instead of the lively camp I expected to find. The hills were honeycombed with old tunnels and there were huge piles of cinders, showing that much ore had been taken out, but there were no smelting works and no way of getting supplies except by pack trains, so I took no stock in it. Long was dead broke, and having his family up there with him, I divided what money I had with him, which would enable him to get back to Montevideo, where he had left a good practice, and myself returned to San Fernando. Americans were held in high esteem in Mexico at that time, and I could have traveled through the length and breadth of the land without spending a dollar.

In spite of the abject poverty of the Mexican peons, they extracted a good deal of enjoyment from life. The men worked out in the hot sun all the week, with only thin cotton trousers on, and on Saturday night donned a shirt and went to the fandango perfectly happy if they had a few cents with which to buy a cup of mescal and a cigarette. On Sunday morning they all attended mass and got their sins wiped out, the afternoon being devoted to horse racing, chicken fighting, and kindred amusements, the padre making a full hand.

When I reached San Fernando I found Webber had disposed of all our tobacco, also his stock of medicine, so we at once set out on our return to Texas. At Presidio we learned that the old alcalde was still in jail for his intrigue with Cryor and McCoy, and we asked permission to visit him. He was taking his incarceration quite philosophically; said his "time would soon be out."

We had sold our tobacco for a good price, getting as high as $2 a pound for some of it, but with what the soldiers stole and the money we necessarily spent, we hadn't more than the law allowed us to take out duty free, so we had no difficulty leaving the state. Traders who did a large business, though, found the export duty rather onerous, and resorted to many devices to evade it.

Some time later the McNeal boys went out with a load of general merchandise, which they disposed of to advantage, the proceeds amounting to several hundred dollars, which being all in silver, was quite bulky. However, they managed to conceal the greater portion of it, only paying export on a small part. After they had gone the officials became suspicious and sent a detachment of soldiers after them. Finding they were pursued, the boys dropped their money, which was put up in stout bags, into one of those dry-weather crevices which are so frequently met with on the mesquite prairies. Marking the spot, they rode on, allowing the soldiers to overtake and search them. Then, waiting till the coast was clear, they returned for their money, but the cleft was so deep and the ground so hard they could not dig it out without picks and spades, which they could not obtain without returning to the colonies, several hundred miles away, and before they got in the rain came on, obliterating their landmarks, and if anybody wants to search for buried treasure there is his chance, if it hasn't gone through to the other side of the world.

Billy Eaton used to tell a good story on himself that clearly illustrates the ruses the soldiers resorted to to cheat the government. Billy and a confederate were endeavoring to land a load of tobacco in Laredo during the night when they were surprised by a squad of soldiers. The other fellow got away, but they captured Billy and the tobacco. Disarming Billy, they placed him between two soldiers, while a third led his horse with a slender rope. Billy said when they got within sight of the town he began to think about the calaboose, and he didn't relish the prospect of a sojourn therein. It was quite dark, and he got out his pocketknife, opened it, and cut the rope around his horse's neck; then, snatching his water gourd, which hung by a strap to his saddle, and was a large one almost full of water, he struck the soldier on his right over the head with it, smashing the gourd to flinders and knocking the Mexican from his horse. He then dashed the spurs to his horse, and before the soldiers could unsling their carbines he was out of range. They gave chase, "carajoing" and firing their carbines; but it was all for effect. They soon relinquished the pursuit and Billy said he heard them laughing hilariously over the escapade. Had they taken him in they would have been obliged to produce the contraband.

We reached the Rio Frio without incident worthy of mention. Camping for the night, we hoppled some of our horses and turned the others loose. There were no resident Indians in that section, and we had seen no sign of any roving band, nor of mustangs either, and so felt quite secure. In the night, however, we heard a commotion among our horses, and then heard them running away. Our first thought was Indians, so we kept still till day broke. Then, eating a hasty breakfast, we took our guns and a little grub and started on their trail, which was easily followed, my saddle horse being shod. About 10 a. m., we came in hearing of them across a little rise. Stealing cautiously to the top of the ridge we saw a mustang stallion trying to whip my horse out of the band, which he was driving away. My horse was fighting him, and so much absorbed were they in combat that they didn't perceive us. We knew that the only chance of recovering our horses lay in killing the stallion, so we crept up in range, and, both taking aim at him, fired, both shots taking fatal effect. After waiting till our horses recovered from their fright consequent on the killing of their captor, I went out toward them. My horse immediately recognized me and came to me. You may imagine our relief. It wasn't a pleasant predicament to be left afoot several hundred miles from anywhere. Those old mustang stallions, after lording it over their bands for years, would finally get whipped out by some younger aspirant. They were termed then "old mokes" by the Spaniards, and would leave the band, roving round in search of another, trying to take possession of any drove they came across. So desperate and vicious they often became that it was not safe to interfere with them.

Without further trouble we in due course of time reached San Felipe de Austin, no richer than when we left, but we were a little wiser, and had had "heaps of fun."

CHAPTER 5

San Felipe de Austin! The shibboleth that flings the door of memory wide; the spell that bids the tide of years roll back, and from the ashes, where it has lain these sixty years and more, conjures up the old town which formed the nucleus of the movement that eventuated in the extension of the great American Union in an unbroken plane from the Atlantic to the Pacific.

Here, in pursuance of the scheme which cost Moses Austin his life, his indomitable son, Stephen Fuller, established his headquarters, from thence distributing the colonists who followed him into the wilderness seventy-six years ago.

San Felipe de Austin! Itself but a phantom, what a host of phantoms the name summons back to repeople it.

Though not one of the Three Hundred, the writer was but a few years behind them, and knew them all by repute, many of them personally. The town was still in its swaddling clothes when the writer made his advent therein in 1827. Twenty-five or perhaps thirty log cabins strung along the west bank of the Brazos River was all there was of it, while the whole human population of all ages and colors could not have exceeded 200. Men were largely in the majority, coming from every state in the Union, and every walk in life.

There seeming to be a good opening for my trade in San Felipe, I bought a set of tools from George Huff on the San Bernard and set up business in the parent colony in the year 1828. In the absence of a more comprehensive view, a pen picture of the old town may not be uninteresting. The buildings all being of unhewn logs with clapboard roofs, presented few distinguishing features. Stephen F. Austin had established his headquarters something like half a mile back from the river on the west bank of a little creek—Palmito—that ran into the Brazos just above the main village. Just above Austin's house was the farm of Joshua Parker. Austin's house was a double log cabin with a wide "passage" through the center, a porch with dirt floor on the front with windows opening upon it, and chimney at each end of the building.

In this vicinity the Ingram brothers, Seth and Ira, had a store, with them being associated Hosea N. League, a lawyer by profession, who with his wife lived near by. League later formed a law partnership with David G. Burnet, their office being in the immediate vicinity. Ira Ingram later moved to Matagorda, of which municipality he was the first alcalde. He also drew up the first declaration of Texas independence, at Goliad, in 1835, was a member of the first Texas Congress and Speaker of the House. Seth Ingram, a surveyor, laid off the town of San Felipe. William Pettus, better known as "Buck" Pettus, who was later elected a member of the Ayuntamiento, also resided in a suburban villa in the "west end." Going on down to the town proper, which lay along the west bank of the Brazos, the first house on the left was my bachelor abode, and near it, on the same side, stood the "village smithy" over which I presided. Then came the Peyton tavern, operated by Jonathan C. Peyton and wife; the house was the regulation double log cabin. The saloon and billiard hall of Cooper and Chieves, the only frame building in the place, was next below the Peyton's. The first house on the right as you entered the town from above was Dinsmore's store, and next it the store of Walter C. White. The office of the "Cotton Plant," the first newspaper in the colonies, and near it the residence of the genial proprietor, Godwin B. Cotton, filled the space between White's store and the Whiteside Hotel, which differed from its companion buildings, only in point of elevation, it being a story and a half in height; through the center ran the regulation "passage," and at either end rose a huge stick and mud chimney.

It must not be understood that these rows of buildings presented an unbroken or even regular line of front; every fellow built to suit himself, only taking care to give himself plenty of room so that the town was strung along either side of the road something like half a mile—like Samantha Allen's funeral procession, "Pretty good as to length, but rather thin."

Professional men, as a rule, did not affect "offices."

The alcalde's office was in a large double log house standing back some distance from the main thoroughfare almost immediately in the rear of the Whiteside Hotel, which building it much resembled. By whom it was built, or for what purpose, I do not now remember, but my impression is that it was designed for a hotel. The walls of hewn logs were roofed in and abandoned at that stage. It was here the ayuntamiento held its sittings, and this windowless, floorless pen, through the unchinked cracks of which the wild winds wandered and whistled at will, was presumably the Faneuil Hall of Texas.

I regret that, having left Texas in 1831, I am unable to give any of the incidents or details of the conventions which decided the fate of the colonies, though many of the members were personally known to me. Strains of eloquence doubtless many times echoed through the old council chamber, but only on one occasion was I an auditor. Hearing loud talking in the alcalde's office one night, I concluded there must be something interesting going on, though there was no light save that which the bright moon poured in through the cracks and open door. Approaching warily, expecting every moment to hear the bullets begin to sing, I got near enough to make out that it was some one apparently delivering a speech. Curious to learn what it was all about, I quietly drew nearer, and, peering through a crack, perceived Whiteside, junior, a boy of sixteen, rehearsing the address of the Scythian ambassador to Alexander the Great to an appreciative audience composed of the negro boy Will; though doubtless the familiar lines, aided by the mystic light of the moon, brought up before the mental vision of the youthful orator an admiring circle of faces such as was wont to greet him on exhibition days in the old schoolhouse "back in the states."

Ludicrous as the incident was, there was something pathetic in it, occurring in that schoolless land, a relic of civilization which as yet had made but little progress there. The laws providing that two single men might constitute a family for colonization purposes, many of the so-called three hundred families consisted of a couple of old bachelors, a number of whom made their homes in town. Austin's colony being the mother colony, and San Felipe being the seat of government, the empresarios of the surrounding colonies naturally assembled there to take counsel together, and there was, of course, a floating population, some of whom tarried but a few days, while others remained indefinitely.

Among the men who were laying the foundation of a nation, Stephen F. Austin, the father of Texas, was of course, the central figure. He was at that time about thirty-six years of age, though care had left an added weight of years to his appearance. Dark hair and eyes, sparely built, and unassuming in manner, there was little in Austin's outward appearance to indicate the tremendous energy of which he was possessed. Though only mortal, he was far above the average of the mould, as his patience and perseverance under trials and difficulties that would have driven an ordinary man to despair abundantly testify.

His character often maligned, his motives impugned, the compact he had entered into with the Mexican government disregarded, thus impeaching his integrity, he yet extended his protecting care over the colonies, alone undertaking the doubtful mission to Mexico in 1833 to present the memorial of the colonists for statehood and exert the remnant of his influence to heal the ever-widening breach between them and the home government, his appointed colleagues refusing to take their share of the risk.

The story of his arrest and long imprisonment is well known. Returning home in broken health to find his labor and suffering thrown away, and the colonies already in the throes of revolution, he cast his lot with them, like his illustrious father, receiving his final summons in the hour of victory. Stephen Fuller Austin died at Columbia, December 27, 1836, a little over two months after the first regularly elected administration of the Lone Star Republic began its labors, Austin being Secretary of State.

Intimately associated with Austin was Samuel M. Williams, Austin's first secretary. An early advocate of independence, Williams, for his opposition to Santa Anna's centralization scheme, was one of the first five men proscribed by that tyrant. Associating himself with McKinney, the firm opened a store at Quintana, and patriotically purchased and equipped the first two vessels for the Texas navy. Williams and McKinney also opened the first bank in Galveston. When, in 1843, the British Ministers in Mexico and Texas arranged a peace conference between the two countries, Williams was one of the two commissioners appointed by President Houston to confer with the Mexican government, his colleague being George W. Hockley.

David G. Burnet, the first president of the republic, though having a colony of his own to settle, made his headquarters at San Felipe. A man of medium size, of no particular type of features, there was nothing in his general appearance to attract attention, unless it was a noticeable twist in his face. His father sat in the Continental Congress, and he himself was a delegate to the first convention of the Texan colonists; he it was who drew up the memorial to the Mexican government for statehood, of which Austin was the unfortunate bearer.

Francis W. Johnson, who afterwards distinguished himself in the revolution, I knew as a clerk in the store of Walter C. White, and later, a clerk of the ayuntamiento. Frank, as he was familiarly known, was of an inflammable temper and was consequently one of the earliest and most active supporters of the war, which course placed his name on the proscription list. Being second in command in the assault of San Antonio in 1835, Johnson was, on the death of Milam, raised to the full command and led the Texas forces to a glorious victory. Ambitious to achieve still greater renown, he joined Grant in his ill-advised scheme of a descent on Matamoras, which cost the struggling patriots so dearly, Johnson narrowly escaped the fate that befell nearly the entire force engaged in the undertaking, as well as Fannin's command, which but for the delay caused by waiting for detached bands, might have effected a safe retreat.

Godwin B. Cotton, the pioneer newspaper man in Texas, launched the "Cotton Plant," as he facetiously christened his paper, at San Felipe in '29. He was a genial old bachelor of fifty or thereabouts, his aldermanic proportions making him a conspicuous figure. His signature, G. B. Cotton, prompted an inquiring individual to ask the significance of the initials, "Why d——n it, can't you see? Great Big Cotton, of course," replied the owner of the name.

Judge Williamson was associated with him in the Cotton Plant, which after struggling about four years against conditions unfavorable to its perfect development, finally succumbed. The press was moved down to Brazoria and used to print the Texas Republic, the publication of which continued only about eighteen months; the editor, F. C. Gray, removed to California where he became wealthy, a circumstance so phenomenal to his craft as to unsettle his reason. Gray died in New York by his own hand.

Gail Borden whose name is more widely known than any of them and will perhaps outlive them all, had a blacksmith shop next door to me in San Felipe. He had an inventive genius, but strange to say it did not lean toward mechanics. His first venture was the soup biscuit which took quite a run, being very popular with seafaring men. He next embarked in the newspaper business, bringing out the fourth paper in the state at San Felipe in 1835. The Telegraph, as it was called, was devoted to the cause of independence, therefore when Santa Anna's invasion necessitated the evacuation of San Felipe, Borden thought it advisable to go along. The paper was accordingly removed to Harrisburg which was in turn abandoned, the plant being left in charge of a couple of printers who bravely stuck to their forms and had the paper in press when Santa Anna's invading host entered the town, captured the outfit and dumped the plant into the bayou. Not realizing, presumably, the strength of the weapons wielded by the harmless looking typos, they were not included in the sweeping decree of "death to every man taken in arms." The printers whose names do not appear though they should have been preserved, succeeded in saving a few copies of the paper, one of which, containing the account of the burning of San Felipe de Austin is still extant.

After the battle of San Jacinto freed Texas from Mexican domination, Gail Borden resuscitated the Telegraph and having purchased a new press set it up at Columbia; and subsequently at Houston where under new management with the name of the Houston Telegraph it flourished long after the civil war. Retiring from the newspaper business, Gail Borden turned again to invention, this time bringing forth the project which made him famous the world over; the Gail Borden Eagle brand condensed milk being a feature of every grocery store and every advertising medium.

Among the earliest and most ardent advocates of resistance to Santa Anna's usurpation of power was Judge R. M. Williamson, who being one of the first proscribed by the dictator, retreated to Mina, which district he represented in the Consultation which established the provisional government. To Judge Williamson nature had indeed been lavish of her mental gifts, but as if repenting of her prodigality in that line, she later afflicted him with a grievous physical burden; his right leg being drawn up at a right angle at the knee, necessitating the substitution of a wooden leg, which circumstance gave rise to the name by which he was familiarly known—"Three-Legged Willie." A member of a wealthy family, highly educated and an able lawyer, Willie was a living illustration of the aphorism, "'Tis but a step from the sublime to the ridiculous." Being appointed judge for the district of Washington, which office he filled with credit both to the state and himself, he would leave a court room over which he had just presided with all the grace and dignity of a lord chief justice, and within an hour be patting Juba for some nimble footed scapegrace to dance. The versatility of his genius was further evidenced by his success as a comedian. In the absence of support, he "went it alone," constituting himself a whole company. His strongest "cast" was the country school where all the urchins studied "out loud," the principal text book being Webster's elementary spelling book.

Beginning in the low diffident tone supposed to belong to the tyro, Willie plodded his way doubtfully through the tedious length of the alphabet and gaining courage from the successful termination of the journey, tackled the "a-b abs" in a louder tone passing on through the intermediate stages of "b-a ba, k-e-r ker, baker," thence to "c-r-u, cru, c-i cy, crucy, fi-x fix, crucifix," and so on through the successive increase of syllables gaining confidence with each rise till he finally arrived in triumph at in-com-pre-hen-si-bil-i-ty. To this succeeded the reading of the short proverbs at the bottom of the pages, the climax being reached when the star scholar shrilly piped out, "An old man found a rude boy up in one of his apple trees stealing apples, etc." So perfectly were the tone and manner varied to correspond with the successive stages, that one might almost imagine himself in an old fashioned country school. The Judge also conducted revival meetings by way of variety, in which he combined all the essential elements in himself. He was also a nimrod of no mean order, having accomplished a feat in that line which had no parallel in the history of the country. Being out alone on the prairie he espied a buffalo calf that had got lost from the band. Willie gave chase and coming up with the game, being otherwise unarmed, attempted to lasso it. Not being an expert with the lasso, however, he only succeeded in getting it on his own neck. The calf being pretty well winded, came to a stop and thinking to slip a noose over its head, Willie dismounted, when seeing its persecutor within its reach, the calf turned on him and before he could get out of its way the Judge received a blow in the stomach which sent him to earth, and no sooner had he risen to his feet than the vicious little brute gave him another. Willie retained his recumbent position till the calf being apparently satisfied that its foe was effectually disposed of, started on its way. The calf so far had the best of it, but the majesty of the law must be vindicated. Casting about for a weapon with which to avenge the insult offered to the state in the assault upon an officer who was attempting an arrest, the judicial eye fell upon the great clumsy wooden stirrups. Quickly unbuckling one of the straps, Willie grasped it firmly in his hand and again running upon his adversary dealt it a blow on the head with the stirrup which in turn sent it to earth, continuing the application till life was extinct.

I was aroused early one morning by hearing my name called by some one in the street. "O Smithwick; come here; here's a man with a broken leg." Recognizing the voice as that of Judge Williamson, I hastily donned my clothing, and, opening the door, found Willie sitting on the step with his wooden leg broken; he had been making a night of it with that result. I took the fractured limb to my shop and braced it up so that it was as good as new, and the Judge went on his way rejoicing.

The Mexican stirrup, usually made of oak and weighing about five pounds, encased in leather housings, the long ear-like tips of which almost touched the ground, is in keeping with his bridle bit and spurs, the outfit being aptly described by old Johnnie McNeal. Said he, "Their bridle bits look like steel traps, and the rowels of their spurs remind me of a cart wheel with the fellies knocked off, the piece that goes on the heel looking like a clevis."

Those old wooden stirrups made quite effective weapons, as I had occasion to demonstrate. Having business down at Columbia, I went to old Jose Riel to get a horse for the trip, telling him that I wanted a good animal. "O, si," said he; "buena, mucho buena." I expected to be away five days and old Jose exacted a dollar a day in advance; I paid the tariff and started. It was about sixty miles, and about midway was a wayside inn kept by Madam Powell, who had two attractive daughters; therefore it was not a source of concern to me that the horse began to flag toward night. The next day I went on to Columbia, where my business detained me one day, during which time my horse rested, but he had proceeded but a few miles on the homeward journey till he began to slow down. After working my passage a few miles further I dismounted and tried to lead him, but a Spanish horse will not lead, so I turned him loose and drove him. I wore out a good deal of timber on him and having got on the prairie, where I could not renew the supply, I took off a stirrup with which to urge the sulky brute along. The horse finally came to a dead stop and when I applied my persuader backed his ears and kicked at me. Exasperated beyond endurance I brought him a welt over the head that felled him to the ground; he lay quivering a few minutes and gave up the ghost. I took off the saddle and bridle and replacing the stirrup hid the outfit in the high grass and went on up to Madam Powell's, about ten miles, where I procured a horse for the remainder of my journey. I didn't go near old Jose Riel, but by and by he came around to know what I had done with his horse. After delivering him a lecture savoring strongly of brimstone for hiring me a broken down horse, I told him where I left it, also the saddle. The next day he came back and demanded pay for the horse. I threatened to wear the ground out with him; he then took his grievance to Thomas Dukes, the alcalde. Dukes came around to see me and after enjoying a hearty laugh over my adventure, advised that I pay the old fellow something, just to settle the controversy. We settled on $5 in addition to the five I paid for the hire of the horse.

An important personage was Padre Muldoon, not only in San Felipe where he made his home, but throughout the colonies, he being the only authorized agent of Cupid east of San Antonio. The father made a tour of the colonies occasionally when in need of funds, tying the nuptial knot and pocketing the fees therefor, $25 being the modest sum demanded for his services. But his visits were so much like an angel's, and his charges so much on the opposite extremity that the colonists had recourse to a plan of their own combining in itself the essential features of both marriage and divorce, the latter unknown in Catholic countries. When a couple concluded to join their fortunes they forthwith repaired to the alcalde's office and had him draw up a bond to avail themselves of the priest's services whenever he came around; both parties signed the bond and went on their way as man and wife. The plan had this advantage; that if they changed their minds before the priest got around, they had only to go together to the alcalde and demand the bond, which they tore to pieces and were free again.

Padre Muldoon was a bigoted old Irishman, with an unlimited capacity for drink. He found a congenial spirit in the person of "General" Walker, with whom he was one day "doing" the town. Stepping into Frank Adams' grocery just as the crowd were preparing to "lubricate" Frank politely invited the newcomers to join them. Old Muldoon elevated his nose. "No, I never drink with any but gentlemen," said he. Adams promptly drew back and dealt the Padre a blow between the eyes which had the effect of considerably modifying his ideas of gentility. The person of the priest being considered sacred by the Mexicans, Adams' assault came near involving him in a serious difficulty. Muldoon and his satellites demanded redress, and Austin, fearing that the government might resent the indignity offered its spiritual representative, would fain have made some show of compliance; but the sympathy of the populace was with Adams, regardless of consequences; Muldoon, who was no fool, seeing that he had few friends, apologized for his offensive language and accepted the proffered drink to assist him in swallowing his medicine.

Nestor Clay, the gifted nephew of a gifted uncle, though not a resident of the town, was an occasional visitor, at which times he was wont to imbibe rather freely; with the result that while he soon became unable to stand, his mental faculties seemed to expand in proportion to his loss of physical power.

Educated, brilliant, a perfect master of English and an adept at retort, I have seen him sit and talk politics when he could not rise from his seat, and not a man among us could begin to hold his own against him.

Thus he was sitting in Thomas Davis' saloon talking, and having his drinks brought to him, when Davis incautiously ventured into argument and getting the worst of it turned away saying:

"O, you're drunk, Clay."

"Ah! Is that so?" said Clay.

"Yes."

"Well, then are you not a fool to be arguing with a drunk man?"

A shout went up from the crowd which Davis drowned with free liquor.

There was nothing whatever to indicate that Clay's emigration had been compulsory, but with a family educated and refined and ample means, it was difficult to account for their presence in the colony on any other hypothesis.

Walter C. White, who kept the leading store, was associated with Colonel Knight, the proprietor of the trading post at Fort Bend; they had a little trading schooner, which ran up to Bell's Landing (Columbia), where they unloaded their goods, piling them up on the river bank and covering them with dry cowhides to protect them from rain while waiting for ox teams to take them up to their destination. Years afterward I met Colonel Knight at Bastrop. Out in front of a store lay a number of grinding stones with a chain passed through the eyes and fastened with a padlock. Colonel Knight cast a contemptuous look at the pile, and turning to me said:

"Gad, Smithwick, the 'better sort' must have got here. Do you remember how I used to pile my goods out on the river bank and leave them for days at a time? I never lost a pin's worth; we used then to hear fellows with 'store clothes' on lamenting the crude state of society and consoling themselves with the assurance that the 'better sort' would come after a little. I reckon they have arrived; there," pointing to the padlocked grindstones, "is indisputable evidence."

Colonel Knight was one of the earliest white settlers in Texas. Joining Long's expedition he assisted Mexico in throwing off the yoke of Spain, and also bore a gallant part in the Texas revolution. He had no family. Cooper and Sheaves, both single men, built the first frame building in San Felipe, using it for a billiard hall and saloon. The merchants were Walter C. White, Richardson & Davis, Clopper Bros., Cooper & Sheaves, Ira & Seth Ingram, and Thomas Gay, all single men, though Gay afterward married.

The legal profession was represented by David G. Burnett, Judge R. M. Williamson, Thomas M. League, Luke Lasacia and Holtham & Ewing; the last two bachelors.

Doctors Miller, Mosely, Rivers, Dayton, Gazley, Peebles and Phelps—the last three only having families—looked after the health of the people, the major part of their practice being devoted to the dressing of wounds and holding inquests.

The first preacher to venture into this stronghold of Satan was Thomas J. Pilgrim, a Baptist; but as the colonists were supposed to be Catholics, Colonel Austin did not deem it advisable to establish a Protestant church, so the preacher, willing to make himself useful, turned dominie, teaching the first English school in Texas, 1829. Comparatively few families resided in town, most of them going out on farms. On the farms, too, were to be found the wealthier portion of the colonists, who, having brought out slaves, were opening up cotton plantations.

Thus while there was a scarcity of ladies of any kind in San Felipe, single ladies were indeed few and far between. Occasionally one ventured into town to be almost immediately captured by some aspirant for matrimonial honors. Of the young ladies who were thus summarily dealt with during my sojourn I remember Miss Eliza Picket who a few days after my arrival married William C. White; Miss Westall married to Brown Austin; Miss Jane Wilkins, who was captured by the alcalde, Thomas Duke, and Miss Scott who became Mrs. Samuel M. Williams. Miss Pickett was the daughter of Mrs. Parmelia Pickett, a widow possessed of capital, and the bridegroom being a nephew of Jared E. Groce, the richest man in the country, the wedding was very select; social distinctions, it was alleged, having even then begun to develop. The leadership of the "ton" was accredited to Mrs. Jane Long, the widowed sister of Mrs. Alexander Calvet, and widow of General Long.

Miss Jane Wilkins with her widowed mother and younger sister maintained themselves by sewing; therefore the wedding was very quiet notwithstanding the high official position of the bridegroom. Miss Wilkins was an expert needlewoman and we old bachelors found much need of her services, almost all clothing then being made to order; consequently we felt that we had just cause of complaint against the alcalde when he selfishly appropriated our fair seamstress, leaving us with enough ready made clothing on our hands to stock a small clothing store.

A little incident connected with the marriage of Brown Austin and Miss Westall furnishes a sample of the annoyance and inconvenience to which the colonists were subjected by the religious restrictions imposed upon them. Anxious to show due respect for the law of the land, Austin had notified Padre Muldoon to be on hand; but the priest's residence being in San Antonio, and the distance and mode of traveling rendering intercourse uncertain, the padre failed to arrive at the appointed time. The bride was ready and so was the feast, but everything had to await the pleasure or convenience of the dilatory priest.

So great was the dearth of female society in San Felipe that during my whole residence there—'28 to '31—there was not a ball or party of any kind in which ladies participated. There being so little opportunity for social intercourse with the gentler sex, the sterner element should not be too severely censured if they sought diversion of a lower order. And if our stag parties were a bit convivial, they would probably compare favorably in that regard with the swell club dinners in the cities. Godwin B. Cotton was the host in many a merry bout; love feasts, he called them. Collecting a jovial set of fellows, he served them up a sumptuous supper in his bachelor apartments at which every guest was expected to contribute to the general enjoyment according to his ability. Judge Williamson was one of the leading spirits on these occasions. Having a natural bent toward the stage, Willie was equally at home conducting a revival meeting or a minstrel show, in which latter performance his wooden leg played an important part; said member being utilized to beat time to his singing. One of his best choruses was:
"Rose, Rose; coal black Rose;
I nebber see a nigger dat I lub like Rose."
a measure admirably adapted to the banjo which he handled like a professional.

Some sang, some told stories and some danced. Luke La Sascie, a Louisiana Frenchman, and by the way a brilliant lawyer, was our champion story teller; with Cotton and Doctor Peebles worthy competitors. I, being reckoned the most nimble footed man in the place, usually paid my dues in jigs and hornpipes, "Willie" patting Juba for me. Many a night was I dragged out of bed after a hard day's work in the shop to help out an impromptu "jag." The biggest time we ever had was on the occasion of a double wedding, the brides being a couple of grass widows who were domiciled together just out of town, their comfortable home and reputed bank account proving an irresistible attraction to a couple of good-looking young scamps who were hanging about; hence the wedding. The boys all got together and went out to charivari them. It was my first experience in that kind of a performance; and was unquestionably the most outrageous din I ever heard; cowbells, cowhorns, tin pans and in fact everything that contained noise were called into requisition; and with their discordant sounds mingled hoots, howls and caterwaulings enough to make the hair rise on one's head. But all our efforts to

[49]

bring out the happy quartette proved abortive. We overdid the thing and frightened them out of their wits; so after exhausting every device short of breaking in the door and dragging them forth, we adjourned to town to wind up. Austin never participated in these jamborees, nor did the Bordens. Sam Williams sometimes looked in, took a glass and cracked a joke.

A noted member of Austin's colony was Captain James B. Bailey, better known as "Brit" Bailey, his arrival even antedating that of Austin himself. But as up to that period foreigners could not procure title to land, Bailey had only a squatter's claim. Still he felt that the priority of his claim should be respected; therefore he rose in rebellion when notified that his claim was within the limits of Austin's grant and that in order to secure it he would have to comply with the regulations governing the real colonists. A compromise was effected, however, and Captain Bailey lived and died on his original claim. When he was in his last sickness, realizing that the end was near, he said to his wife:

"I have never stooped to any man, and when I am in my grave I don't want it said, 'There lies old Brit Bailey.' Bury me so that the world must say, 'There stands Bailey.' And bury me with my face to the setting sun. I have been all my life traveling westward and I want to face that way when I die."

His widow, in compliance with his request, had a deep hole dug like a well, into which the coffin was lowered, feet first, facing the setting sun.

Isaac McGeary was among the early settlers. He was a genial fellow with a passion for practical jokes in which he sometimes found a boomerang. While I was working down at Colonel Bell's, McGeary and a stranger one day rode up, their feet encased in moccasins and their heads covered with rude caps made of a green deerskin. The caps and moccasins so at variance with the balance of their attire, especially that of the stranger, whose name was Dickerson, at once suggested a misadventure. Inquiry elicited the remarkable story that they had camped out on the prairie the night before and the coyotes had stolen their hats and shoes. I saw by the twinkle in Mc's eye that there was a sequel to the story and as soon as he got a chance he unbosomed it to me. Dickerson was as verdant as a meadow in May and on their ride down from San Felipe, Mc amused himself by imposing on his credulity; telling him among other things of the penchant of coyotes for hats and shoes, cautioning him on retiring to put those parts of his apparel under his head, himself setting the example. After Dickerson fell asleep, Mc softly arose and stealing the hat and shoes from under his companion's head he carried them, together with his own, a little way aside and hid them in the high grass. Great was Dickerson's consternation when he awoke in the morning and felt for his hat and shoes. Mc felt for his and they too were gone. He commenced looking around, and when he had carried the joke far enough, he sauntered out to the place where he had deposited them intending to explain their disappearance, but behold they were not there; the coyotes had gotten them.

The hats they found torn to fragments; but the shoes were gone. McGeary dared not cheap then, so they went across to Captain Martin's on the river where they were fitted out in the manner above described. Dickerson often told that story as he understood it to illustrate the stealth of the coyote. McGeary played a worse joke on me, and that I should have liked to lick him for had I been physically able. Old Martin Varner had a lot of wild hogs running in the bottom and when he wanted pork, went out and shot one. Having occasion to replenish his larder, Varner invited McGeary and myself to go out with him. We all went out on foot accompanied by several dogs. The first game we flushed was a boar with tusks three or four inches long. The dogs caught him and Varner, seeing that he was not marked, took the opportunity of establishing his claim, an operation that somewhat riled his porcine lordship's feelings. McGeary and I held the struggling beast while his ears were being mutilated, and when I released my hold, McGeary, who had him by the hind feet, deftly slued him around with his head toward me, and shouting, "Look out, here he comes," turned him loose. With gnashing teeth and bristling hair the enraged beast sprang to his feet and made for me. I was considered fast on foot, and there seeming to be no other alternative, I took to my heels, the boar after me and the dogs after him. For about sixty yards I led them till, catching my foot on a stub, I fell flat. My pursuer was being too hotly pursued by the dogs to assault me. When the chase passed I rose to my feet; there was McGeary fairly rolling with merriment. I was mad for a few moments, and as before stated would have licked him had I been able. McGeary swore it was the fastest foot race he ever saw, and would want nothing better than to "travel" with me if I could run like that on a bet.

Old Vicente Padilla was running a monte game in San Felipe. Money was too scarce to bet more than a quarter at a time, and quarters—dos reales— were not plenty, so in order to provide enough such change, they cut a dollar in four pieces. When Mexico established her independence, one of her first acts was to change the stamp of her coin, the eagle dollar taking the place of the Spanish milled dollar. The latter being defaced by hammering was then worth only seventy-five cents. These hammered dollars were often cut into five pieces by a little extra hammering and made to pass as quarters. Old Vicente was getting the best of the game of course and nobody had any scruples about beating him in any way. One of the "buckers" was in my shop one day and seeing a lot of little triangular bits of iron lying around was struck with an idea. Gathering up the bits, he polished them up till they bore quite a resemblance to the quarters cut from the hammered dollars. He departed with his prize and after dark repaired to the monte bank where the dim light of the tallow candles enabled him to pass off his iron chips on the dealer without detection.

Nacogdoches was the gambler's heaven; that being the first town the newcomer struck after crossing the Sabine. Here there was a regular organization

[51]

for roping in the greenhorn and relieving him of his cash. Several of its members afterward took an active part in the revolution, one at least being a signer of the Declaration of Independence. This brave patriot having spotted a stranger who seemed to have deep pockets, steered him into a game and went out to look for another sucker. When he returned the game was over and the clique dividing the spoils. The steerer demanded his share. "Why you wasn't in the game," they contended. "The h——l I wasn't; didn't I find him first?" and backing his claim with a pistol he secured his share. So unscrupulous were they that they didn't even wait till the victim was out of the room to divide. Taking in the situation, a fellow that had been thus robbed, said to them, "I think it's a d——d outrage for the government to send old John H. Murrill to the state's prison and let such fellows as you go free."

Charles Falenash, one of the earliest settlers in Austin's colony, located on the river above San Felipe in territory now included in Burleson County. The family were well calculated for pioneers, fear having been left out of their makeup; its place being given over to cool, level-headed, self-possession, a quality invaluable on the frontier. This family trait came out conspicuously in an exploit performed by John, one of the little boys. The children were playing about a pond, into which a little chap incautiously waded. Hearing the child in the water scream, John was horrified to see that an alligator had him by the leg. The boy knew there was not a moment to lose as the alligator would make for deep water, so he wasted no time in trying to summon aid, but drew his knife and rushed to the rescue. Knowing, also, that the eyes were the only vulnerable points in an alligator's head, he directed his blows accordingly, getting in his work on both the creature's optics before it released its hold. Then, seizing his brother by the arm, John broke for the bank, which they reached in safety.

Old John Cummings, one of the Three Hundred, made his usefulness in the colony manifest by building the first mill in the state on a little creek to which he gave a name, a few miles above San Felipe. There was a sawmill, with corn cracker attached, all run by water. The saw was getting along in years and therefore a slow feeder. The old man, who was not in favor of wasting time, started the saw into a log and went home to dinner, and did up other little chores while it was eating its slow way through. He one day sat down on the farther end of a log to cast up his accounts, and becoming absorbed in the work, forgot the saw, stealthily creeping toward him with tortoise-like gait, till it seized him by the sleeve, and finding flesh easier to masticate than wood, proceeded to chew him up. Fortunately his assistant had the sense to stop the saw before it did more than lacerate his arm and head.

Down on the river below San Felipe, dwelt another of the original Three Hundred, old Joe Kuykendall. The old man was rather inclined to take life easy, a disposition which the superabundant energy of his thrifty helpmate,

Annie, together with his implicit reliance on her ability to manage the affairs of the house of Kuykendall, gave him ample opportunity to indulge.

Colonel Knight, getting down sick and having no family, Kuykendall took him home to take care of him. During the time one of Annie's milk cows came home, evidently having left a young calf hidden out. Annie put on her bonnet and followed the cow to find the calf. She was gone so long that Knight said he began to entertain fears for her safety, and suggested to Joe that he had better go and look for her, as she might have got lost.

"Annie get lost," exclaimed Joe, as if such a proposition were incredible. "O no! If it don't get cloudy, and a snake don't bite her, I'll be ———— if Annie don't come home." His confidence in her was fully justified when along toward sundown Annie came in driving the cow and calf.

Bob Matthews, a tinner, had a shop in San Felipe, the first enterprise of the kind in Texas, and probably the first on Mexican territory as the Mexicans had not progressed beyond the gourd and pottery. Bob had led a roving life, having been on a long trip to the Rocky Mountains before coming to Texas. He must have passed through some sanguinary scenes which left their tinge on his mind, one of his favorite adjectives being "bloody," sometimes using it in most incongruous connections. I was talking of going home.

"Ah," said he, "if you go home, you won't stay; they'll be all the time telling you of some bloody thing you won't want to hear. I went back once. I went to visit my sister, whose husband kept a hotel. On Sunday morning I was in the bar-room tossing pennies with the barkeeper when my sister passed the door. Going into her room shortly after, I found her crying over my wickedness. I was so disgusted with the bloody nonsense that I got up and left and never went back."

At another time he said to me: "You talk too much with your mouth. In a place like this it is best to keep your eyes and ears open and your mouth shut; and if you see something say nothing." Failure to heed the latter part of the admonition was really the mainspring of the trouble that befell me later.

Bob and I being the two crack shots of the place, where everybody was on the shoot, we often went gunning to see who could bag the most game. Our favorite sport was picking the squirrels from the tall pecan trees in the river bottom.

Colonel J. W. E. Wallace, United States Consul for the colonies, was anxious to pose as a crack marksman. He went squirrel hunting with us, and when we were dividing up the game asked to be allowed to take those that were shot in the head. We let him make his own selection and had many a sly laugh over his wonderful skill. Colonel Wallace used to go alone into the river bottom to practice, bringing back only proofs of center shots.

The boys used to come to my shop to get up shooting matches; every fellow putting up his dollar, the one who came nearest the center taking the pot. They came one day when I was very busy. I told them to go ahead, and when

[53]

they had all shot I'd take my turn. When it came to me, I shot and won. Just then old Joe Callahan staggered up, rifle in hand.

"See here, boys, can't Uncle Joe have a chance?" Willing to increase my winnings another dollar I replied, "O yes, Uncle Joe, you shall have a chance; go ahead." He anteed his dollar and raised his gun. He was too drunk to stand still, but after several lurches he made a supreme effort and blazed away. The ball struck the ground some ten feet short of the target and glanced, caught the lower edge of the target board, ploughed its way up through the center, tearing the paper to atoms. Uncle Joe won the money.

It wasn't always the man who hit the bull's eye oftenest that did the most effective shooting in an emergency. There were a couple of men in town, Moore and McKinstry, who fell out and agreed to settle their differences with pistols. They both came to me to train them. The course of training for dueling was to stretch a tape a man's height on a tree and shoot at the tape. Moore cut the tape oftener than he missed it, while McKinstry often missed the tree, seeing which, I looked on McKinstry as virtually a dead man. But when the duel was fought, Moore missed entirely, while McKinstry's ball struck him just above the ankles, breaking both legs.

Discussing the affair with Jesse Thompson, I expressed surprise at the result. "Ah," said he, "the tree had no pistol pointed at Moore when he was shooting at it."

And speaking of duels reminds me of another duel that took place, without the aid of seconds. There was a certain doctor who, when under the "influence," was always belligerent. He had a falling out with Colonel DeWitt and challenged him. "You can have your choice of weapons," said the doctor. "All right," said the colonel, "I accept your challenge, and this is my weapon." And with that, he raised his cane and gave the bellicose medico a drubbing that cured him of dueling.

There was a lawyer who had a penchant for dueling, to which men paid no attention. He sent a challenge to a merchant with whom he had trouble. The challenged party made no reply and the challenger proceeded to post him as a coward. A brother of the man who was being thus maligned, ordered him to take down the poster, and upon his refusal he was shot dead.

Nor were these San Felipeans indifferent to the claims of genius. The first public function after my arrival in the town being a demonstration in honor of a local bard, in which the distinguished gentleman, after having been made the recipient of a bran new suit of tar and feathers, was escorted through the whole length of the town seated on a rather lean Pegasus and bidden a long adieu at the further end.

The poetical flight which called forth this popular expression, had for its inspiration the banishment of a woman who, though posing as the wife of a prominent man, had previously sustained the same relation to an old circus manager, whom she deserted without the formality of a divorce when a younger suitor appeared. Her charms being already on the wane, the faithless lover soon wearied of his conquest and, in order to make room for a younger woman, to whom he could establish a legitimate claim, preferred charges against his whilom inamorita, which led to her banishment; an injustice which fired the poet's soul with indignation. The pen being mightier than the sword, the champion of the injured fair, chose the former weapon with which to avenge her wrongs, but unfortunately for him he neglected to put up his shield when entering the arena.

The verses as a whole, I do not recall, nor would their publication be admissible; the following couplets will be sufficient to establish their character. They were headed "Mrs. W———s' Lament."

> "The United States, as we understand,
> Took sick and did vomit the dregs of the land.
> Her murderers, bankrupts and rogues you may see,
> All congregated in San Felipe."

Then followed a long string of names including those of the most prominent men in the place, together with the cause which impelled them to emigrate. There was literally "more truth than poetry" in the argument, the master of ceremonies in the demonstration on the author, having been lighted on his journey thither by the moon's pale beams. As Dr. Rivers expressed it, "people were nearer on an equal footing socially in San Felipe than any place he ever saw; if one said to another, 'you ran away,' he could retort, 'so did you.'" Some wag fitted a tune to the doggerel rhyme, and the dare-devil spirit, which tempted the disinterested to sing it, was several times productive of blood-shed.

Many hard things have been said and written of the early settlers in Texas, much of which is unfortunately only too true. Historians, however, fail to discriminate between the true colonists—those who went there to make homes, locate land, and, so far as the unfriendly attitude of the Indians permitted, resided on and improved it—and the outlaws and adventurers who flocked into the towns.

To the lasting honor of Stephen F. Austin, be it said, that he conscientiously endeavored to comply with his contract with Mexico to settle none but respectable families on the land allotted to his colony. It being also stipulated that they should be Catholic in religion, Austin probably placed a liberal construction on the word "Catholic," which Webster defines as "universal," his colonists as a rule being of no particular opinion on religious matters. They were honest and kind hearted, never refusing to lend a helping hand to those in distress, and if that isn't universal religion it is near enough for all practical purposes. And in this connection it may not be amiss to state that though Austin was temporarily invested with discretionary power for the government of his colony, the founding of which was by special contract antedating the promulgation of the general colonization law by four years, his functions ceased with the establishment of a general system of government; after which the local conduct of affairs was vested in the ayuntamiento, the members of which were elected from the different sections of the colony. So that, at the period at which we have arrived, Austin had been divested of every semblance of authority; his colony being under the domination of a ring, the leader of which had skipped his bonds in Alabama to avoid prosecution on a criminal charge, bringing with him all of his personal property and leaving his friends to mourn his departure to the tune of several thousand dollars.

Faulty statutes in the United States sent many a man to Texas. Dueling was still practiced in many of the states, a trivial matter often ending in the death of one party, the other fleeing the country.

Another fruitful source of emigration was debt; and, while some absconding debtors took their portable property along, others gave up all and went to Texas to take a fresh start and grow up with the country. The law of imprisonment for debt was still in force in some states, and, as the Indian said: "How Injun goin to get deer skin in jail?" If an insolvent debtor really wanted to pay his debts, his only chance was to abscond.

Bob Stewart, a knight of the green cloth, whose capacity for contracting debts was only limited by his credit, had an original way of disposing of duns. When a creditor presented a bill, Bob would dismiss him with the rebuke, "Go and pay your own debts and don't come bothering me about mine."

It was the regular thing to ask a stranger what he had done, and if he disclaimed having been guilty of any offense he was regarded with suspicion.

There was one man in Texas—yes, two, though one, being only a slave, didn't count—whose title to honesty was above suspicion—Joseph Mims, who lived down on the San Bernard. The circumstances which gave Mims an opportunity to demonstrate his unimpeachable character, was one in which the Mexican Government would have been the only loser, which latter consideration makes his action all the more remarkable. The paymaster was on his way to Nacogdoches with a large sum of money, and in crossing the San Bernard in a dugout, the boat tipped over and the box of money went overboard and could not be found. Sometime later in a low stage of water, Mims' negro found the money, which he delivered to his master, who promptly notified the Government of the find.

I never killed a man, but I came so near it that I never felt the least inclination to repeat it; and can well understand how such a deed may poison a man's whole life, even though done under circumstances that entirely justify him in the eyes of the world; haunting him sleeping and waking, driving him to seek oblivion in the wine cup.

There were several men in San Felipe who labored under such a burden. I several times had to defend myself, but fortunately never had a fatal quarrel. The nearest I ever came to it was in the case above referred to. I had employed an old deserter from the United States army to cut a lot of wood to burn into charcoal for my shop. He came every morning for a bottle of whisky and then went off to the woods for the day. At length some one told me he wasn't cutting any wood, so I went out to see about it. I found him lying under a tree and very little wood to show for the whisky I had advanced him. The next morning when he came around for his regular bottle, I told him I would give him no more till he cut wood enough to pay for what he had already. Upon that he grasped his ax in both hands and, raising it above his head, came at me. I was working at the anvil with a heavy hammer, and, being quicker than my assailant, planted it between his eyes, felling him senseless to the ground. The blood gushed from his mouth and nose and I thought I had killed him, and, notwithstanding it was a clear case of self-defense witnessed by several persons, I began to feel very miserable over it; but he didn't die, though he was laid up for some time. I paid all his bills and was glad to do it. Yes, I know just how it feels to have killed a man.

But bad as many of the San Felipeans were, I was presumably the worst of the lot, I being banished from the colony in a "Star chamber" proceeding in which I was not allowed to participate; the indictment against me charging me with being "a dangerous person, having treated their authority with contempt." To the latter part of the charge I enter no demurrer, for I certainly felt the contempt, whether I evinced it or not.

The facts in the case were, that having in a difficulty with the alcalde at Gonzales (an overbearing man) killed the alcalde, the homicide, knowing there would be no chance of a fair hearing there, voluntarily came on to San Felipe accompanied by Henry Brown and gave himself up. As the case had to be tried in Saltillo the prisoner asked to be admitted to bail. This was refused and, there being no jail, he was put in chains and his trial delayed till the poor man was worn out. I knew there were frequent killings under less provocations for which no one was held accountable; but killing an alcalde was not an ordinary affair. The prisoner was a friend of mine, and, becoming incensed at the treatment to which he was subjected, I gave him a file to cut his irons off, also providing him with a gun and other essentials with which to leave the country. Instead of getting out of the way, however, he lay around in the hills, stealing in to the house of his brother-in-law at intervals to learn if his case had been decided. The minions of the law got wind of his proceedings and, going to the brother-in-law's house, took the latter out and whipped a confession out of him. They then went to the hiding place of the escaped prisoner and, upon his trying to elude arrest, shot him dead. The gun I had given him was rather a noted weapon, being all of my own make and the first rifled gun made in the colonies; hence the charge against me. But had I heeded the advice of my friend Bob Mathews and kept my mouth shut, I probably would not have been molested.

The first official notice I had of the case against me was when a squad of

militia under Captain Abner Kuykendall came to serve the sentence. I told them "they needn't make such a fuss about it, I thought, considering the character of the place, it was about the best thing they had ever done for me." Without allowing me even a day's time in which to wind up my business they put me in charge of a couple of my friends, who undertook to see me across the Sabine. When we were mounted to start, some one ran out with a bottle and glass and proposed that I drink to the health of Old San Felipe. I took the proffered glass, which I drained to the following toast: "If there is an honest man in the place may he be conducted to a place of safety, and then may fire and brimstone be rained upon the iniquitous town." That was my last farewell to San Felipe de Austin, my curse having literally been fulfilled before I was through that way again. This was in 1831.

I went on across the Sabine, there the authority of my escort ceased, and the next day recrossed the river, going up into the Redlands, as the country between the Sabine and Ayish Bayou was called. Here I sojourned for a short time, after which I drifted down to Alexandria, in Louisiana, where the next four years were mostly passed pleasantly and profitably among the wealthy planters, the most liberal and kind-hearted people in the world; and but for the unhealthy climate, which came near taking me off, I should probably never have returned to Texas. I had some rather interesting adventures in the Redlands, which I here relate. But first I want it distinctly understood that the disclosures I make are not to be construed as reflecting on the whole population of the Redlands, who were no more responsible for the evil emanating therefrom than it is that of any other section tyrannized over by a band of ruffians.

CHAPTER 6

The Redlands had a hard name, and there is no denying the fact that there were many hard characters there, its geographical position making it a convenient retreat for renegades, who infested the border along the Sabine, just as they do now along the Rio Grande. Worse, even, in that there was then no extradition treaty between the United States and Mexico, and the settlers, too weak to protect themselves, and having neither civil nor military protection, were completely at the mercy of these outlaws, who would not have hesitated an instant to put a bullet through any man who was foolhardy enough to resist them, or who was even distrusted as being so disposed.

This I discovered from the start. I suppose, on account of my having been banished from San Felipe, they looked upon me as a congenial spirit, and therefore took no pains to conceal their operations from me, even making overtures to me; but it was one thing with me to assist a friend to escape from prison, and quite another to become a bandit, counterfeiter, or land shark.

My first association was with a notorious counterfeiter, whom for the nonce we will call John Doe, in whose shop I worked, though not in his line of business. He offered me a partnership, proposing that we go over into Mexico and open up business. I never saw him manufacturing the "queer," but I saw his outfit, of which he made no secret. There was nothing of the desperado about him. On the contrary, he was pleasant and peaceable and generally liked, and, so far from being looked upon as a malefactor, was considered a public benefactor, in that he furnished the only currency to which the people had access. The country could not be said to be on either a gold or silver basis, copper being the basis of Doe's coinage, and, the supply failing, he sent out emissaries to rustle for the precious metal. Not finding any other available source of supply, they appropriated a copper still, which was converted into coin. His Mexican eagle dollars were as handsome coins as I ever saw, much finer in execution, in fact, than the genuine article, and passed current in the community until the plating began to wear off, when he gathered them in, and, treating them to a fresh coat, sent them out again.

Indian Bill, a Cherokee, was one day at a horse race, and, becoming thirsty, repaired to a booth where liquid refreshments were dispensed, and, calling for a drink, threw down a dollar. The proprietor picked up the coin, and, perceiving that the copper foundation was showing around the edges, handed it back to Bill with the remark:

"This is one of Doe's dollars. Take it back to him and tell him to plate it over again."

The Indian took him at his word, and, looking around among the crowd, espied the manufacturer of the rejected coin. Rushing up to him, Bill held out the dollar, saying:

"See here, Doe, this dollar no good; he no buy whisky. Take him, Doe, take him; skin him again, skin him again."

The crowd set up a shout, amidst which Doe calmly pocketed the dollar, handing Bill a brand new one, with which he returned to the bar and discharged his whisky bill, though the proprietor doubtless recognized its character as quickly as he had that of the first tender.

Doe also coined doubloons which, though perceptibly thicker than the genuine coin of that denomination, was still a trifle light, but as there were no scales to test them as they passed unchallenged as long as the plating was intact. Doe's currency furnishes a good example of the practical working of the populist idea: it was all right in domestic transactions, but when they attempted to discharge foreign obligations with it, it got them into trouble. Ambitious to extend his field of operations, Doe went over into Louisiana, where he was apprehended. The authorities failed to convict him, but his currency was depreciated to such an extent as to render the floating of it unprofitable. His die for dollars had a slight crack in it by which his coin soon came to be recognized, but his shrewdness turned it to account. Casting a pure silver dollar, he intrusted it to an accomplice, instructing him to go to a saloon and tender it in payment for drinks, and when it was refused, as it was sure to be, the mark being plainly visible, to feign indignation and offer to bet $500, which Doe supplied, that it was pure silver. The fellow did as instructed and had no trouble in placing his bet. The suspected coin was submitted to a jeweler, who, of course, pronounced it pure silver. By this coup Doe reimbursed himself for his losses on his venture and returned to the west side of the Sabine, where his efforts were more appreciated.

Another way in which Doe added materially to the wealth of the colonies was by restamping the old hammered dollars, a single blow of the hammer adding 25 cents to the value of each one. There were thousands of them thus rehabilitated. Indeed, it was a regular business collecting them.

A couple of years later his operations were thrown completely in the shade by what was known as the Owl creek money, counterfeit United States bank notes of different denominations, and so nearly a perfect reproduction of the genuine that they were even imposed on the banks. Paper and ink being cheaper even than copper, Doe's currency was given the go-by. The country was soon flooded with the Owl creek paper, and as everybody in the Redlands had more or less of it, and they were all interested in maintaining it at par, it, too, continued to circulate even after its true character was recognized. That, too, was practical populism. I was approached by one of the promoters of the scheme, who offered me any amount of the counterfeit paper at fifty cents on the dollar if I would take it into Louisiana and float it. Realizing that such secrets are dangerous, I told him that I would take the proposition under consideration. Said he, looking me straight in the eye, "Remember, if you 'cheep' your life won't be worth a snap." I told him I understood that, and would "see him later." I was alarmed lest some suspicion might attach to me, so I got away from there as fast as possible. Under such pressure it is not to be wondered that the paper passed, there being, as previously stated, no public protection accorded to the people of that section. The only semblance of government was the office of alcalde, presided over by old Ben Lindsey, a well-meaning old fellow, as ignorant of law as of grammar.

The only case, so far as known to the writer, that was ever tried before him was that of a man who was arraigned for shooting another man's dog, the complainant demanding damages therefor. Mace Cole was employed by defendant to conduct his case. There were no statute books available, the only book in court being the Bible on which the witnesses were sworn. Picking up the Bible, Cole asked the alcalde if, in the absence of other law, the old Mosaic code would be admissible. The alcalde, totally at a loss to know what to do with the case, consented to be governed by the primal statute. Turning to Deuteronomy xxiii, 18, Cole read: "Thou shalt not bring the hire of a whore or the price of a dog into the house of the Lord thy God, for even both these are an abomination unto the Lord thy God."

This appearing to be plainly against the plaintiff, the case was dismissed, the plaintiff paying costs.

Another swindling scheme that was being worked on a gigantic scale, and which was productive of more lasting evil, it will be necessary to go back to 1829 to explain. In that year Don Padillo came on from Saltillo as commissioner of the land office, to survey and make title to the claims of bona fide settlers outside the regular colonies, being provided with blanks for the purpose, on which were stamped the seal of the Republic of Mexico, lacking only the specifications and signature of the commissioner to complete them. Accompanied by T. Jefferson Chambers, surveyor general for the colonies, he established headquarters at Nacogdoches, but, unfortunately for the old don, he became enamored of the pretty young wife of one of his attaches, and to get the husband out of the way sent him on an errand from which he never returned alive. Suspicion at once fell on the commissioner and he was arrested as the instigator of the murder. He was thrown into prison and his papers all thrown into the hands of an unscrupulous gang, who at once proceeded to establish a land office of their own. Securing the services of an old Spaniard who had been a government clerk for years and was an expert penman, they had him forge the commissioner's signature to the blanks, and thus equipped set up business on a large scale, issuing floating certificates to any amount of land for an insignificant consideration. Any good plug of a pony would buy an eleven-league grant. James Armstrong, afterward a member of the legislature, told me how they conducted business.

"I had just come to the country," said he, " and, being broke, was looking around for a clerkship or other employment that might procure necessities. In this emergency I accepted a position in the office of the manager of the land-grabbers, and was set to work filling out the blanks. I worked a whole month, meanwhile running on 'tick,' and at the end of that time demanded my salary, which had been fixed at $50 a month. Imagine my disgust when, instead of cash, I was tendered a certificate for eleven leagues of land. The cool audacity of the thing fairly took my breath away. I told the boss that I preferred the money. 'You are a fool,' said he. 'Maybe I am,' I replied, 'but if it were land I was after I could have filled out a certificate for any amount that would have been just as good as yours.'"

I was also offered any quantity of these bogus land certificates to dispose of in Louisiana on shares, and no doubt I could have done so to advantage among the wealthy planters, whose slaves were becoming too numerous for their plantations, thus creating a demand for increased acreage. Perhaps it was only because I lacked the courage necessary to the making of a rascal; at any rate, I rejected all these alluring offers for fortune, not caring to run my neck into a halter by being made a cat's paw for these scoundrels. Of the effects of this wholesale land fraud I shall have occasion to speak hereafter. It was the foundation for all the land litigation that has vexed the souls of the settlers ever since.

To return to the lawless gang which infested the border, I will give an account of one of their outrages, which came near being the last one for some of them.

Over near Nachitoches, in Louisiana, there lived an old Frenchman, who had a mulatto wife and several quadroon children. These border ruffians went over there, murdered the old man, and seizing his wife and children, brought them over into Texas and tried to sell them. The family spoke but little English, but they managed to make the facts known, whereupon the people rose en masse against the perpetrators of the outrage, who, but for their timely flight, would have ended their careers at the end of halters. The unfortunate family were returned to Louisiana.

When the country began to settle up, circumscribing their field of operations, these outlaws disappeared. I found their descendants here in California when I came hither in '61, and was chagrined to find that such wretches had fixed the general character of the Texans in the minds of the people from other states. There were two gangs of them, and they at length had a falling-out and a vendetta ensued, and every time one was killed the mass of the people rejoiced. The darkest stain on the annals of the Redlands—and I only mention it here to illustrate the evil results of mob law—was the hanging of a man by the name of Luny by an excited populace. The victim, in company with one Connel, had served a term in the United States army, and on being discharged at old Fort Jessup, near Nachitoches, invested their savings in general merchandise, opening a store in the Redlands, where they were well liked, Connel marrying old Elisha Robins' daughter. Robins was one of the most prominent men in that section.

For some reason the partnership between Luny and Connel was dissolved. Luny went down on one of the lakes along Ayes Bayou and with another man, whose name I do not remember, opened a store there. As neither of the men had families, they bached together, having a half-witted boy for factotum. At length the partner was missing, and, on the theory that Luny was the only person that could have a motive in his disappearance, the people took the matter in hand and arrested Luny. He told them the last time he saw the missing man was early one morning, when he started out to hunt his horse.

The country was scoured without any trace, the people growing more excited as the subject was discussed. They took the boy in hand, and, through fright, induced him to tell that Luny had killed his partner and thrown the body in the lake. The lake was dragged without results, but the mob had worked themselves up to such a pitch of indignation that they determined to hang Luny anyway. In vain he protested his innocence, and, counsel of the more conservative element being thrown to the wind, poor Luny was strung up to a limb. Some time afterward the body of the missing man was found in the woods, sitting leaning against a tree, his bridle clutched in his hand, evidently the victim of heart disease.

With a number of other men I was standing on the porch of Elisha Robins' boarding house when a grotesque figure surmounted by a coonskin cap sauntered slowly past the group, scrutinizing each face as if in search of some one. Presently some one addressed me by name; the stranger turned quickly to locate the party answering. Stepping up to me, he inquired: "Is your name Smithwick?" "Yes, sir," I replied. His face lighted up. "You're the man," he exclaimed, extending his hand. "You're the man I've been hunting for." I involuntarily ran over in mind all the notable things, good and bad, I had ever done, but could recall none that seemed to fit my mysterious stranger. "You're the man," he again repeated, after the style of Poe's raven. "Well, what can I do for you?" I inquired, my curiosity being fully aroused by his queer introduction. "Just step this way," said he, eyeing my companions suspiciously. I felt a little timid about going with him, but, as his demeanor was rather friendly than otherwise, I walked out of earshot of the group on the porch. Looking all around to assure himself that there were no eavesdroppers, the old man drew from his pocket a small parcel tied up in a rag. Carefully untying the package he revealed a quantity of shining particles, which at first glance had quite a resemblance to gold. Said he: "My name is Brown. I live out in Tenehaw district, where we think we've got a fortune, but we heard you'd been out in Mexico and knew all about mining, so we want you to go in with us. You shall have an equal share. This is the stuff."

A moment's inspection satisfied me that there was no gold in the sample, but I saw that it would take stronger evidence than my word to convince him, so I took the parcel into the shop. I blew up the fire, and, putting the mass in a ladle, set it in the furnace. It bubbled and smoked and assumed the appearance of burnt leather. I then crushed it to a powder from which every semblance of gold had disappeared. The old fellow looked as if doubting the evidence of his own eyes, and glared at me as though I had been juggling with his specimen. Swallowing his disappointment, he departed, a sadder if no wiser man.

A few days later a friend of mine came over from Louisiana with a lot of jewelry which he proposed peddling out through the country. Being an entire stranger, he wanted someone to go out with him. Having nothing better to do, I acted as escort.

Colonel English, with whom I was acquainted, was quite an influential man in his neighborhood, and in trying to find his place we stopped at a cabin to inquire the way. The proprietor gave me a searching look and his brow darkened. Instead of answering my question he broke forth in a strain that savored of insanity: "I know what you're after, but you'll never find it, and if

you do it shall never do you any good," said he, in a menacing tone.

Completely mystified by such an unprovoked attack, I asked him to explain the meaning of it.

"You told Brown there was no gold in that stuff he showed you. We know better. Now you think you'll find it yourself; but if you do, it shall never do you any good." He looked savage, and, knowing something of his reputation, I didn't care to fool with him.

Finding it impossible to disarm his suspicions, and feeling sure that we would be under surveillance as long as we were in the neighborhood, and fearing for the consequences if we should by any chance get into the vicinity of the "mine," we were on the point of giving up the jewelry campaign. We succeeded in reaching Captain English's place, and to him related our encounter with his millionaire neighbor. The captain laughed heartily but we didn't feel as if it was altogether safe to be circulating promiscuously around in such an explosive atmosphere.

Captain English was head chief of the tribe, however, and he volunteered to straighten the matter up. He posted us on the location of the mine, and we were thus enabled to give it a wide berth. It was doubtless guarded as long as we were around. So strong was the delusion that it would have no doubt led to bloodshed had anyone attempted to examine the supposed gold mine. So can the glittering tempter conjure up the latent devil lurking in men's hearts; nor does it matter that the glitter is false.

One other story of the Redlands I must tell, only withholding the name of the principal actor therein. After I had been some time in Louisiana the cholera broke out, and there was a general stampede to escape its ravages. I had got hold of a pretty fast horse and concluded to take him over into the Redlands for the races. Away out in the piney woods, between Bayou Coti and Fort Jessup, lived a man by the name of Fox, who kept a hostelry for the accommodation of the few chance travelers on that lonely road. It was getting late in the day, and, seeing no signs of human habitation, I was growing apprehensive of having to make a dry camp, when I saw a little smoke rising some little distance from the road. Riding out to it, I perceived a pony staked near by and a man lying down. Upon my approach the latter arose to a sitting posture and greeted me pleasantly. In answer to my inquiries, he told me that it was but a short distance to Fox's, and I was going to proceed on my way when he asked me where I was going. I told him. Said he: "I am going there myself, and if you have no objection I would like to bear you company." Pleased with the appearance of my would-be traveling companion, I readily assented. The next morning we started on together, and I congratulated myself on my good fortune in having fallen into such pleasant company. He was an elderly man, decently and plainly dressed, seemingly well acquainted with that section. Surmising, perhaps, that I had some curiosity to know more of him, he at length said: "Perhaps you would like to know who your traveling companion is?" I confessed my curiosity. "Well," said he, "my name is H———, old John H———. I know you've heard of me; everybody has." Yes, I had heard of him, and was rather disconcerted to hear that my genial companion was a notorious horsethief. He probably anticipated my confusion, for he hastened to reassure me.

"You need have no apprehensions on that score," said he. "You'll find that when we get into the settlements everybody will be glad to see me."

I found that to be true, everybody shaking his hand and calling him "Uncle John." He then told me frankly that he was on his way home to the Redlands after being discharged from the Louisiana state prison, whither he had been sent for an alleged irregularity in horse trading.

"The jury that convicted me of stealing Nelson's horse were trying me on general principles. I clearly proved myself clear of that charge," said he; which was no doubt true on the face of it, but the jury had seen too much of that sort of thing to be deceived by outside appearances. They penetrated the disguise and unearthed the fact that he belonged to a regularly organized band scattered through different parts of the country, whose practice it was to meet as strangers in some town remote from their raids and trade horses in the presence of a crowd, and then each go his way on an animal which he knew perfectly well had been stolen, even if he were not the actual thief.

So old John went to the penitentiary, where his habits of thrift and enterprise enabled him to make the best of the situation. Said he: "I made money while there." I was interested in knowing how he did it. "Had some money when I went in, and I got some of the attendants to bring me in material for a cigar factory (convicts were not made to work in those days). By and by I enlarged my business, employing some of my fellow prisoners to help me, and by the time my term was up had quite a flourishing trade and saved money, after paying a go-between to buy my material and dispose of my wares. When I was leaving the prison I had the satisfaction of seeing Nelson, whose horse got me into trouble, just going in for having received a bale of stolen cotton from a nigger. I stepped up to him smiling, and, extending my hand, said: 'How do you do, Mr. Nelson? I am truly glad to see you.' Then, turning to the warden, I introduced him. 'This is a particular friend of mine, warden. Be kind to him for my sake.'"

We rode on until near noon, when I began to look around for some cabin where we might stop for dinner. There were no settlements, only just now and then a cabin in a little clearing where a few acres of corn were making a struggle for existence against the barren soil and dry atmosphere. Espying one of these, I suggested that we stop and try to get dinner.

"No use," said the old philosopher; "don't you see how black the smoke is? You can't get anything fit to eat there." We passed several with the same densely black pine knot smoke pouring out of the stick and mud chimneys. "No use," H——— persisted. By and by we came to an abandoned clearing, where the wild blackberries were grown up, full of the largest, finest berries I ever saw.

"I think we had better stop here," said he. So we took off our saddles, and while our horses dined on the luxuriant grass we did full justice to the blackberries. "I have been a bad man," he admitted, regretfully, I thought, "but I have a nice family, as you can see for youself if you will do me the honor to visit us, and for their sakes I am going to reform my ways."

"How is it," I asked, seeing the cordiality with which everybody greeted him, "that you seem to have no enemies in your business?" "Well," he replied, "I never speculated on my neighbors, and never allowed anyone else to. I always went outside."

I visited his home and found, as he said, that he had a nice family. I never again heard of his being engaged in shady transactions, and am therefore fain to believe that his reformation was genuine.

CHAPTER 7

Returning to Texas after an absence of four years, I landed at Matagorda in the fall of 1835, just at the time the growing dissension between Mexico and the colonists began to assume warlike proportions. There I met Dr. Fields, who was subsequently with Colonel Fannin at Goliad, and was only saved from sharing his fate by being a physician, his services being required for the wounded Mexicans. The doctor was preparing for a professional trip to Mexico and was in need of an interpreter. Having acquired some proficiency in the medical technique of the Spanish language during my attendance on "Dr." Webber, I undertook the office of interpreter for Dr. Fields. Packing our outfit on mules, we struck out. Arriving at Victoria, we found the whole place in commotion. A messenger had just arrived, bringing word that the government had ordered the disarming of the colonists, and that a detachment of soldiers was even then on the way to execute the order, thus leaving the defenseless families at the mercy of the Indians. Couriers were flying, committees of safety forming, volunteers enrolling, and the bustle of preparation for resistance resounding through the land. I came of a warlike race and all my life, like Norval, "had heard of battles." My father fought in the revolutionary war; one of his brothers fell in the battle of Cowpens, and there was a family tradition that my great-grandfather Bennet, when one hundred years old, knocked a man down for hallooing, "Hurrah for King George!" and when I, a little tot scarcely out of pinafores, saw my oldest brother march away to fight the British in 1812, I thought it was the grandest thing on earth and longed to be a man that I might don a bright new uniform and clanking sword and march away with flags flying, drums beating, and people cheering. My time had arrived, and I was destined to have more than enough of war, stripped, however, of all its magnificence. Ah! there was no glare and glitter in those life-and-death struggles of the Texas pioneers. It was useless to think of continuing our journey to Mexico, and rather preferring—at least I did—to kill Mexicans with bullets and powder than pills and powders, we laid off our packs and hurried on to Gonzales, the initial point of attack, to help repel the Mexicans, whose only ostensible purpose proved to be the recovery of an old cannon which the citizens had borrowed from the garrison at San Antonio some time before to defend the place against Indians, and which was practically useless, having been spiked* and the spike driven out, leaving a touch-hole the size of a man's thumb. Its principal merit as a weapon of defense, therefore, lay in its presence and the noise it could make, the Indians being very much afraid of cannon. But it was the match that fired the mine, already primed and loaded. Before we reached Gonzales the Mexican soldiers arrived on the opposite side of the river, which they did not attempt to cross, and made a formal demand for the cannon. Useless as it was, the Texans not only refused to surrender it, but crossed over and put the Mexicans to flight.

It was our Lexington, though a bloodless one, save that a member of the "awkward squad" took a header from his horse, thereby bringing his nasal appendage into such intimate association with Mother Earth as to draw forth a copious stream of the sanguinary fluid. But the fight was on. Not a man among us thought of receding from the position in which this bold act had placed us.

We failed to get into the initial scrimmage, but arrived on the scene the day following. Col. John H. Moore with a company of LaGrange men, Fannin with the "Brazos Guards," Coleman with the Bastrup company and a small company from the Colorado under Capt. Thomas Alley were already on the ground. Travis was there simply as a recruit. John A. Wharton and W. H. Jack were also on hand, though not in a military capacity. I can not remember that there was any distinct understanding as to the position we were to assume toward Mexico. Some were for independence; some for the constitution of 1824; and some for anything, just so it was a row. But we were all ready to fight. So, while trusty messengers "sped the fiery cross" on through the interior, we were preparing for the campaign, which we intended should be quick, short and decisive. Our plan was to rush on to San Antonio, capture the garrison before it could get reinforcements, and then—on to Mexico and dictate terms of peace in the capital of the Montezumas. The Sowells had a blacksmith shop at Gonzales, and, being a gunsmith, I set to work to help put the arms in order. There was no coal, so some of the boys were set to burning charcoal. We brushed the old cannon (an iron six-pounder), scoured

---

*Probably one of those spiked by Lieutenant Magee's army in 1813. If so, it would possess double value as a relic.

it out, and mounted it on old wooden trucks—transverse sections of trees with holes in the centers, into which were inserted wooden axles—and christened it "the flying artillery," making merry over it as if it were some holiday sport we were planning for. We had no ammunition for our "artillery," so we cut slugs of bar iron and hammered them into balls; ugly looking missiles they were I assure you, but destined to "innocuous desuetude," as I shall relate in due course. We were going to do things in style, so we formed a company of lancers and converted all the old files about the place into lances, which we mounted on poles cut in the river bottom. While some were busy with the arms and ammunition, others were devising a flag. I cannot say who designed it nor who executed the design, as that was not in my department, and history is silent on the subject. Hubert Bancroft devotes some space to the origin of the Lone Star flag. Had he consulted me, I could have given him a pointer, for to my certain knowledge the first Lone Star flag used in the revolution was gotten up at Gonzales for Austin's army and consisted of a breadth of white cotton cloth about six feet long, in the center of which was painted in black a picture of the old cannon, above it a lone star and beneath it the words, "Come and take it," a challenge which was lost on the Mexicans. It was not called the Lone Star, however, but the Old Cannon flag. I doubt if there is another man living who rode out of Gonzales behind it that October morning near sixty-four years ago. What days those were! So full to the brim with busy preparation, excitement and eager anticipation, without one misgiving as to the outcome. Looking back on it now, from the snow crowned summit of my ninety-one years, it seems a piece of egregious foolhardiness, and I find it hard to identify myself with the hotheaded youth who entered into it with such ardor. Our whole available force could not have amounted to more than 250 men, while Mexico had an organized army of several thousand, and there were thousands of Indians eagerly watching for an opportunity to swoop down on us and wipe us from the face of the earth and thus regain their lost hunting grounds, which they had always been able to maintain against the Mexicans. That one old bushed cannon was our only artillery, and our only arms were Bowie knives and long single-barreled, muzzle-loading flintlock rifles, the same that our fathers won their independence with, and that the famous Kentucky brigade used with such telling effect in the battle of New Orleans; while all the powder in the colonies would scarce have sufficed to charge one of the big guns now in use. But the Mexican soldiers had not shown themselves brave; the army, indeed, being largely composed of peons and convicts—men who had no incentive to patriotism or bravery, and over whom it was necessary to keep a strong guard to prevent them from deserting. Then, too, the seat of war was a long way from the Mexican base of supplies; a weary waste of desert infested by hostile Indians intervening, and no means of communication except by courier. Perhaps, too, we unconsciously relied on the active sympathy of the United States, whose offspring we were; still, as a rule, I do not think we apprehended the remotest possibility of such assistance being necessary. It is needless at this date to discuss the rights or wrongs of that revolution. This much, however, I will say, that though I was opposed to the revolution, yet it is not in the nature of things for the superior race to long remain under the domination of the inferior, and as to Mexico's claim to the territory, it is doubtful if she ever could have maintained it against the Indians. The Spaniards overcame the effeminate Aztecs and the blended races subdued the California rabbit hunters, but the Texas Indians were of a different mold, and it was mainly because of Mexico's inability to hold the territory against them that it was thrown open to the Anglo-American. It was he who beat back the savage and converted the wilderness into civilized homes. Why then should he not control its destiny? Meanwhile the fortress of Goliad, containing valuable stores, had surrendered to a mere handful of Texans with scarcely a show of resistance. No prophet had arisen to warn us of disaster and experience had not yet taught us that a cowardly foe might also be a cruel foe when opportunity offered. Recruits were constantly arriving, singly and in squads, each squad being duly officered if there were men enough to go round, and we soon had more officers than men. When we came to organize companies, however, there were few jealousies or murmurings among the officers who were necessarily reduced to the ranks; realizing, as we did, that in that army military titles were empty honors. Capt. Alley's company—there was no alphabetical order—was the first company organized; his company absorbing that of Capt. John Hensley who, by way of compensation was made first lieutenant. An election for second lieutenant, in which Dick Woodard and myself were the contestants, resulted in victory for me.

What, with burning coal, brushing cannon, repairing rifles, molding bullets and making flags, lances and cannon balls, there was little time for military tactics, but it was necessary that we learn to act in concert, the most important maneuver being to fire by platoons and fall back to reload. We had neither swords nor bayonets and few of us had pistols, and we knew that, if we all fired at once, the Mexican cavalry would be upon us with sword and lance before we could reload, and then our only resource would be to club our rifles, a very effective mode, however, as was demonstrated in the battle of San Jacinto. By the way of variety we went out one day to do up a band of Comanche braves who, scenting trouble, had already begun to hover round like vultures. They showed fight, but seeing our force, they scattered and fired from hiding. At last they all left but one, who proved to be a white boy some eighteen years old. He could not or would not speak a word of English; but, in common with all Texas Indians, had learned some Spanish, the only visible effect of the old Spanish missionaries' labor. He said he was very small when taken and remembered nothing of the circumstances and the Indians would tell nothing. He evinced no disposition to leave, and we were quite

[73]

disposed to lionize him, but one morning he was missing, and so were several of the best horses in camp. A thorough Indian to all intents and purposes, he had rejoined the tribe, and no doubt joined in many a massacre of his own race and dangled their reeking scalps from his belt. Soon Austin, accompanied by Moses Austin Bryan, arrived and at once addressed himself to the work of unifying the volunteers and stimulating them to adhere to the course to which they had committed themselves. To this end he made a speech in which he said: "Retreat is now impossible; we must go forward to victory or die the death of traitors." And, referring to the enfeebled condition in which his long imprisonment and suffering had left him, he said: "I will wear myself out by inches rather than submit to Santa Anna's arbitrary rule." In his efforts Austin was ably seconded by Wm. H. Jack, who also made a speech, well calculated to arouse us to enthusiasm. The same sentiment pervaded both addresses, but the one was a calm statesmanlike review of the situation, the other a fervid appeal to passion and chivalry.

Colonel Milam joined us at Gonzales after having assisted in the capture of Goliad. The Colonel cut rather an unmilitary figure. Having recently escaped from a Mexican prison his clothing was in tatters when he reached Goliad, where he replenished his wardrobe from the stores taken from the Mexicans. Milam's stature being near six feet, the pantaloons thus acquired were at least six inches too short and his sleeves ditto. We rushed our preparations with all possible dispatch and in about ten days were ready to take the field with about 600 men.

There were a number of aspirants for the office of commander, among them Col. J. W. E. Wallace, lately United States Consul at San Felipe. There was, however, little active opposition to Austin whose claim was generally conceded, though I do not think he had any personal desire for the position. John A. Wharton was especially active in his advocacy of Austin, on the ground of expediency. Said he: "Austin can come nearer uniting the people than any other man, and, furthermore, it will give us better standing abroad." So Austin was elected by acclamation. Captain Dickenson, who fell in the Alamo, and whose wife and infant daughter were the sole American survivors of that awful massacre, commanded the "artillery."

Major Bennet presided over the commissary department, but his duties were not arduous. When we ran out of meat we went out and drove in as many beef cattle as we wanted. The harvest was abundant and from the adjacent fields we gathered corn, grinding it on steel mills or pounding it in mortars. Wharton and Jack returned to San Felipe to attend the pending convention, and, having completed our organization, we broke camp on the morning of the 13th of October, with the understanding that we were to proceed direct to San Antonio de Bexar.

Words are inadequate to convey an impression of the appearance of the first Texas army as it formed in marching order. Nothing short of ocular demonstration could do it justice. It certainly bore little resemblance to the army of my childhood dreams. Buckskin breeches were the nearest approach to uniform, and there was wide diversity even there, some being new and soft and yellow, while others, from long familiarity with rain and grease and dirt, had become hard and black and shiny. Some, from having passed through the process of wetting and drying on the wearer while he sat on the ground or a chunk before the camp fire, with his knees elevated at an angle of eighty-five degrees, had assumed an advanced position at the knee, followed by a corresponding shortening of the lower front length, exposing shins as guiltless of socks as a—Kansas Senator's. Boots being an unknown quantity; some wore shoes and some moccasins. Here a broad-brimmed sombrero overshadowed the military cap at its side; there a tall "beegum" rode familiarly beside a coonskin cap, with the tail hanging down behind, as all well regulated tails should do. Here a big American horse loomed up above the nimble Spanish pony ranged beside him; there a half-broke mustang pranced beside a sober, methodical mule. Here a bulky roll of bed quilts jostled a pair of "store" blankets; there the shaggy brown buffalo robe contrasted with a gaily checkered counterpane on which the manufacturer had lavished all the skill of dye and weave known to the art—mayhap it was part of the dowery a wife brought her husband on her wedding day, and surely the day-dreams she wove into its ample folds held in them no shadow of a presentiment that it might be his winding sheet. In lieu of a canteen, each man carried a Spanish gourd, a curious specimen of the gourd family, having two round bowls, each holding near a quart, connected by a short neck, apparently designed for adjusting a strap about. A fantastic military array to a casual observer, but the one great purpose animating every heart clothed us in a uniform more perfect in our eyes than was ever donned by regulars on dress parade. So, with the Old Cannon flag flying at the head, and the "artillery" flying at the heels of two yokes of long-horned Texas steers occupying the post of honor in the center, we filed out of Gonzales and took up the line of march for San Antonio. Our pride in our artillery soon began to wane. We had to take turns riding in its rear, and the slow pace of the oxen ill accorded with our impatient zeal. Sometimes, when the forward column opened a rather wide gap, we prodded up the oxen with our lances (the only use that was ever made of them) until they broke into a trot and the old trucks bumped and screeched along at a lively gait till the gap was closed. But rapid locomotion was not congenial to them; they protested by groans and shrieks and at length began to smoke; we poured on water, but our way lay across a high prairie where no water was obtainable and our supply was limited to the contents of our gourds, a quantity totally inadequate to quench their insatiable thirst. We tried tallow, the only lubricator at hand, but that failed of relief, and finally, after all the trouble we had brought upon ourselves in its defense, the old cannon was abandoned in disgrace at Sandy Creek before we got half way to San Antonio, and the Mexicans might have taken it with impunity. It had played its part, that of inaugurating the revolution. I never saw nor heard of it again, and am unable to ascertain what became of it, though I scarcely think it was destroyed, and I herewith call the attention of the Texas Historical Society to the desirability of gaining possession of it. The old cannon having thus been thrown out, the flag lost its significance; but whether it accompanied the march or was left to keep the "artillery" company, I cannot say. At the Cibolo, Sam Houston came up with us. It was my first sight of the man who more than all the others was destined to win enduring fame from the struggle we were inaugurating. I have a vivid picture of him before my mind's eye as he rode into our camp alone, mounted on a little yellow Spanish stallion so diminutive that old Sam's long legs, incased in the conventional buckskin, almost touched the ground. He made a speech to us, urging the necessity of concerted action among the colonists: arguing that it should be for independence, otherwise we could expect no assistance from other powers. He also advocated the enlistment of the Cherokees as allies, and, owing to his great influence with them, he could no doubt have used them to advantage. They were Uncle Sam's wards, however, and he said "no." Houston immediately returned to San Felipe to take part in the convention. While camped on the Cibolo our scouts brought word that a strong picket force was stationed at the crossing of the Salado. A squad of twenty-five men was dispatched under cover of night to dislodge them. We crossed the creek some distance below the ford, and, dismounting, crept along under the bank on foot. Occasionally a dry twig would snap with a report seemingly as loud as a pistol shot, and we would pause and hold our breath to listen; but we heard no other sound save the rustling of the fallen leaves, with now and then the dismal hoot of an owl, or long, hungry howl of a wolf—uncanny sounds at any time, and certainly not calculated to cheer us in our critical situation. We knew not how many of the enemy there were, but we knew there were just twenty-five of us and no reinforcements at hand. At length, when we were nearing the site of the supposed camp, one fellow began to weaken. "Boys," he said in a shaky whisper, "I don't like this. Ef thar's a big force of 'em they'll whop us." Thereupon Conrad Rohrer, a big Pennsylvania Dutchman who never realized the meaning of the word fear, hissed half under breath: "Shet up; don't say they'll weep us; you're weeped already!" The logical inference, so forcibly expressed, provoked a smothered laugh despite the peril in which we stood. A careful reconnoissance failed to discover any enemy, so with lighter hearts—if somewhat heavier steps—we returned to our horses, mounted and galloped back to camp. Among the small parties joining us at Cibolo was Jim Bowie, who, accompanied by Joseph Hamm, ——— Donahue and several other Louisianians, all spoiling for a fight, had posted on at the first intimation of trouble. Bowie's prowess as a fighter made him doubly welcome, and Austin at once placed him on his staff. Without further incident worthy of mention we reached the San Antonio river at the old San Jose Mission, eight miles below Bexar. Here the main body halted while Col. Bowie with the companies of Fannin and Coleman went on up to reconnoitre and select a position from which to direct operations against the garrison. Being a personal friend of Bowie's, the writer was permitted to accompany the expedition. The only opposition we encountered was from a party of Mexican soldiers who came up and fired on us at long range. We returned the compliment and they retired, leaving the road clear. We went on up, made our observations, and camped in a bend of the river on the east side, about a quarter of a mile above the old mission of Concepcion and distant some two miles from San Antonio, expecting the main army to follow right on, but for some reason Colonel Austin did not do so. Just about sundown we were startled by a dull boom and, ere we had time to frame a question as to its import, a cannon ball, shot from a gun mounted in the church tower two miles away, shrieked through the air overhead and buried itself in the earth a few rods beyond our camp. With a horrible hiss that no language can describe, another, and another followed, to the number of half a dozen; then, all was still. At dawn we were roused by the discharge of musketry, and directly our pickets came running in. One man had his powder horn shot away. Another fell as soon as we got into camp, and we thought he was killed; but, on examination, found that his only injury consisted in a sick stomach caused by a bullet striking and breaking a large Bowie knife which he carried stuck under the waistband of his pantaloons directly in front. The knife saved his life, but he was incapacitated from taking part in the fight. The dense fog masked the strength of the enemy. They crossed the river, which was very low, down at the mission and moved up on the open plain fronting our camp. We got our horses down out of range and, drawing close under the bank, which was five or six feet high, took up positions on both arms of the bend so as to get in a cross fire; Fannin's company occupying the lower arm and Coleman's the upper. When the fog lifted we found ourselves pretty well surrounded; though the bluff and heavy timber on the west side of the river secured us against attack in the rear. In front was a field piece flanked by several companies of infantry; and across the river, to cut off retreat, were two companies of cavalry—but retreat formed no part of our programme. The Mexicans now opened on us with cannon, but we lay low and their grape and canister crashed through the pecan trees overhead, raining a shower of ripe nuts down on us, and I saw men picking them up and eating them with as little apparent concern as if they were being shaken down by a norther. Bowie was a born leader; never needlessly spending a bullet or imperiling a life. His voice is still ringing in my deaf old ears as he repeatedly admonished us, "Keep under cover, boys, and reserve your fire; we haven't a man to spare;" and, had he been obeyed, not a man would we have lost. The Mexicans moved up till they came within range of Fannin's men, when, upon the Texans opening fire, they halted and begun forming for a

charge. Seeing this, Bowie ordered Coleman to the support of Fannin, and, in executing the movement, the foolhardiness of some of our men caused the only casualty of the engagement. We scarcely waited, really, for orders, but broke for Fannin's position. Excited and eager to get a shot, some of the boys mounted the bank and cut across, exposed to the fire of the whole Mexican army. They got there before we did, who went around, but the first man I saw as I came around was Dick Andrews, lying as he had fallen, great drops of sweat already gathering on his white, drawn face, and the life blood gushing from a hole in the left side, just below the ribs. I ran to him and attempted to raise him. "Dick," I cried, "are you hurt?" "Yes, Smith," he replied, "I'm killed; lay me down." I laid him down and put something under his head. It was the last time I saw him alive. There was no time for sentiment. There was the enemy, outnumbering us four to one, charging our position, so I picked up my gun and joined my comrades.

"Fire!" rang out the steady voice of our leader, and we responded with a will. Our long rifles—and I thought I never heard rifles crack so keen, after the dull roar of the cannon—mowed down the Mexicans at a rate that might well have made braver hearts than those encased in their shriveled little bodies recoil. Three times they charged, but there was a platoon ready to receive them. Three times we picked off their gunners, the last one with a lighted match in his hand; then a panic seized them, and they broke. They jumped on the mules attached to the caisson, two or three on a mule, without even taking time to cut them loose, and struck out for the fort, leaving the loaded gun on the field. With a ringing cheer we mounted the bank and gave chase. We turned their cannon on them, adding wings to their flight. They dropped their muskets, and, splashing through the shallow water of the river, fled helter skelter as if pursued by all the furies.

Our pickets, who had been stationed at the old mission and cut off, now climbed upon the roof and gave them a parting volley as they ran past. I don't think it was ten minutes after we opened fire till the last Mexican who was able to run was across the river. The cavalry took no part in the fight, but joined the wild race for the fort, and, no doubt, came down the homestretch in the lead. They left about sixty killed and a number wounded, while our casualties were one mortally wounded and one slightly wounded; less than usually results from a bicycle race, or a football game.

Having no knowledge of civilized warfare, the poor wounded wretches thought they were to be summarily dispatched, and it was pitiful to hear them begging for the miserable lives that no one thought of taking. We had no means of relieving them, even if we had had an opportunity. We knew not what turn affairs at the fort might take, and where Austin was we had no idea. The utmost we could do was to give water to those who asked for it, which no one was brute enough to refuse. How our humanity was repaid, let Goliad and the Alamo testify. About an hour after it was all over, Austin came up with the main body. Had their arrival been a little more timely, our most sanguine expectations might have been more than realized; for the whole force of the garrison was out, and, being mostly infantry, while our men were all mounted, the enemy might have been cut off and well nigh annihilated. As it was, we who were in the fight were satisfied, but the other boys were loud and bitter in their denunciations of the course that had deprived them of a share in the glory. Soon the padre came out with a train of carts and attendants, and, after a parley with Austin, carted the dead and wounded Mexicans away to San Antonio, leaving us in undisputed possession of the field.

Poor Dick Andrews lived long enough to know that the fight was won. He recklessly, foolishly threw away his life, but his was the first freeman's life blood that wet the soil where the germ of the young republic was just bursting into life. We buried him at the foot of a pecan tree on the battlefield, where his bones were left to mingle with the silent dust,
"With not a stone to mark the spot."
The tree has no doubt long since gone to decay, the battlefield been converted into a cotton field, whose snowy fleece bears no trace of the crimson tide which that day soaked its sod. Thus the first gun, the first flag and the first martyr have all gone down to oblivion together.

CHAPTER 8

The Texans, flushed with the easy victory obtained over the Mexicans at the battle of Concepcion, wanted to make an immediate assault on Bexar, but the council of war decided otherwise, Austin and Ben Fort Smith being the only officers favoring an immediate assault. Some military men had said that siege guns were necessary to take the town. As later events proved, artillery was not essential from the standpoint of the frontiersmen, who consequently became dissatisfied with the delay, and, there being no power to prevent, they began to leave for home. It was given out that a cannon had been landed at Velasco, and whenever a man decided to leave, he facetiously remarked that he "was going after that cannon."

I was not in robust health and, not being equipped for winter campaigning, went through the formality of getting a furlough and went into Bastrop to fit myself out. I was taken down with fever while in Bastrop, but was convalescent when Crockett came on, and wanted to return with him to San Antonio, but, seeing that I was not in condition to do so, he persuaded me to wait for another party to arrive a few days later. But the expected party did not come that route, and there were too many risks for a lone man to start out. In the meantime the Alamo was successfully stormed, and, considering the fun all over, I cursed my ill-luck, though it was doubtless fortunate for me, as otherwise I should probably have been with some of the parties who were exterminated the following spring.

The Indians, taking advantage of the disturbed condition of the country, were committing depredations, and the army, numbering not more than 500 or 600 men, rank and file, was preparing to invade Mexico and bring her rulers "to a realizing sense of their situation;" having no time therefore for such trivial matters as the murdering of the citizens by the Indians. So, the government provided for their protection as best it could with the means at its disposal, graciously permitting the citizens to protect themselves by organizing and equipping ranging companies.

Captain Tumlinson was commissioned to raise a company on the Colorado, and early in January, 1836, he reported for duty with a company of sixty mounted men, myself included. We were assigned to duty on the head waters of Brushy creek, some thirty miles northwest of the site of the present capital, that city not having been even projected then. The appointed rendezvous was Hornsby's station, ten miles below Austin on the Colorado, from which place we were to proceed at once to our post, taking with us such materials as were necessary to aid us in the construction of a block house. We were on hand at the appointed time and, just as we were preparing for our supper, a young white woman, an entire stranger, her clothes hanging in shreds about her torn and bleeding body, dragged herself into camp and sank exhausted on the ground. The feeling of rest and relief on finding herself among friends able and willing to help her, so overcame her overtaxed strength that it was some little time before she could give a coherent explanation of her situation. When she at length recovered, she told us that her name was Hibbons; that, in company with her husband, brother and two small children, she was journeying overland up to their home on the Guadalupe, when they were attacked by a band of Comanches; the two men were killed, the wagon plundered, and herself and children made prisoners; she being bound onto one of their mules and her little three-year-old boy on the other.

The other child was a young babe, and the poor little creature, whose sufferings the mother could not allay, cried so continuously that at length one of the Indians snatched it from her and dashed its brains out against a tree.

The scene of the attack being a lonely spot on a lonely road, the cunning redskins knew there was little risk of the outrage being discovered till they were beyond the reach of pursuit; so, when a cold norther met them at the crossing of the Colorado about where the city of Austin stands, they sought the shelter of a cedar brake and lay by to wait for it to subside. Confident that Mrs. Hibbons could not escape with her child, and trusting to her mother's love to prevent her leaving it, the Indians allowed her to lie unbound, not even putting out guards. It was bitterly cold, and, wrapping themselves in their buffalo robes, they were soon sound asleep. But there was no sleep for Mrs. Hibbons. She knew, as did her captors, that there was small hope of rescue from the discovery of her murdered relatives, and, realizing that the only hope lay in herself, she resolved to escape and to rescue her child. There was no time to lose, as another day's travel would take her so far beyond the reach of the settlements that it would be impossible for her to procure help before the savages reached their stronghold; so she waited until assured by their breathing that her captors were asleep, then, summoning all her courage, she carefully tucked the robe about her sleeping child and stole away, leaving him to the mercy of the brutal barbarians.

She felt sure the river they had crossed was the Colorado, and knew there were settlements below; how far down she had no idea, but that seeming to offer the only means of escape, she made straight for the river, hiding her tracks in its icy waters, hurried away as fast as the darkness would permit.

Once she thought she heard her child call, and her heart stood still with fear that the Indians would be awakened and miss her. She momentarily expected to hear a yell of alarm, and, not daring to leave the shelter of the bottom timber, she meandered the winding stream, sometimes wading in the shallow water along the edge, and again working her way through the brush and briers, tearing her clothing and lacerating her flesh, never pausing in her painful journey till late in the afternoon, when she came upon the first sign of civilization in some gentle cows feeding in the river bottom.

Perceiving that they were milk cows, she felt that she must be near a white settlement, but she dared not attempt to call assistance lest the Indians be in pursuit; so she secreted herself near the cows, which she surmised would soon be going home, and, waiting till they had finished their evening meal, followed them to the station, having spent nearly twenty-four hours in traveling a distance of only ten miles on open ground.

Fortunate, beyond hope, in finding the rangers there, she implored us to save her child, describing the mule he rode, the band of Indians, and the direction they were traveling.

Hastily dispatching our supper, we were soon in the saddle, and with a trusty guide (Reuben Hornsby), traveled on till we judged that we must be near the trail, and fearful of crossing it in the darkness, we halted and waited for daylight. As soon as it was light enough, our scouts were out and soon found the trail, fresh and well defined as if the marauders were exercising neither haste nor caution in their retreat; having no doubt spent a good portion of the previous day in a fruitless search for their escaped prisoner. They did not seem to be at all alarmed as to the consequences of her escape, and it was about 10 o'clock in the morning when we came upon them, just preparing to break camp. Taken completely by surprise, they broke for the shelter of a cedar brake, leaving everything except such weapons as they hastily snatched as they started. I was riding a fleet horse, which, becoming excited, carried me right in among the fleeing savages, one of whom jumped behind a tree and fired on me with a musket, fortunately missing his aim. Unable to

control my horse, I jumped off him and gave chase to my assailant on foot, knowing his gun was empty. I fired on him and had the satisfaction of seeing him fall. My blood was up and, leaving him for dead, I ran on, loading my rifle as I ran, hoping to bring down another. A limb knocked my hat off and one of my comrades, catching a glimpse of me flying bareheaded through the brake on foot, mistook me for a Comanche and raised his gun to check my flight; but, another ranger dashed the gun aside in time to save me. The brave whom I shot, lay flat on the ground and loaded his gun, which he discharged at Captain Tumlinson, narrowly missing him and killing his horse; when Conrad Rohrer ran up and, snatching the gun from the Indian's hands, dealt him a blow on the head with it, crushing his skull.

The other Indians made good their escape into the cedar brake, where it was worse than useless to follow them; but, we got all their horses and other plunder and, to crown our success, we achieved the main object of the expedition, which was the rescue of the little boy, though the heedlessness of one of our men came near robbing us of our prize in a shocking manner. The Indians, careful of the preservation of their little captive—they intended to make a good Comanche of him—had wrapped him up warmly in a buffalo robe and tied him on his mule preparatory to resuming their journey. When we rushed upon them they had no time to remove him, and the mule, being startled by our charge, started to run, when one of our men, not seeing that the rider was a child, gave chase and, putting his gun against the back of the boy, pulled the trigger. Fortunately the gun missed fire. He tried again with like result. The third time his finger was on the trigger when one of the other boys, perceiving with horror the tragedy about to be enacted, knocked the gun up, it firing clear, sending a ball whistling over the head of the rescued child. Providence seemed to have interposed to save him. The boys held an inquest on the dead Indian and, deciding that the gunshot wound would have proved fatal, awarded me the scalp. I modestly waived my claim in favor of Rohrer, but he, generous soul, declared that, according to all rules of the chase, the man who brought down the game was entitled to the pelt, and himself scalped the savage, tying the loathsome trophy to my saddle, where I permitted it to remain, thinking it might afford the poor woman, whose family its owner had helped to murder, some satisfaction to see that gory evidence that one of the wretches had paid the penalty of his crime. That was the only Indian I ever knew that I shot down, and, after a long experience with them and their success at getting away wounded, I am not at all sure that that fellow would not have survived my shot, so I can't say positively that I ever did kill a man, not even an Indian.

The scene of the rescue was on Walnut creek, about ten miles northwest of Austin. Gathering up our booty, which was inconsiderable, we started on our return, and late in the afternoon rode into the station in triumph. There was a suspicious moisture in many an eye long since a stranger to tears, when the overjoyed mother clasped her only remaining treasure to her heart, and I could not help stealing a glance at Rohrer, and trying to imagine what his feelings would have been had not his gun refused to obey his murderous behests. The little one was too much dazed and bewildered by the many strange scenes through which it had passed so rapidly, to even know its mother.

Poor Rohrer; he was as brave a soul as ever drew the breath of life, but his excitable temperament rendered him as dangerous to friend as foe; in fact, I got to be more afraid of him than of the enemy, when we went into an engagement. He was finally ambushed and killed by an Indian in Thomas Moore's yard.

We went on up to our appointed station, where we built the old Tumlinson blockhouse, making it our headquarters till the invasion of Santa Anna necessitated our recall, after which it was burned by the Indians and never rebuilt. And, save this old dismantled hulk, there is not, to my knowledge, one of those old Tumlinson rangers now living.

CHAPTER 9

Somewhere about the first of March we were called in to Bastrop. Santa Anna, with a large force, was marching upon the poorly protected frontier, and all advanced positions were ordered abandoned, and the forces to concentrate at Gonzales, whither every available man was urged to repair forthwith; thus leaving the frontier settlements exposed to both Mexicans and Indians. Families were gathering at Bastrop, preparatory to a general hegira before the ruthless invaders, who were said to be waging a war of extermination, and we were ordered to cover their retreat, and afterwards join General Houston. Turning the command over to Major (Judge R. M.) Williamson, Captain Tumlinson and his first lieutenant, Jo Rodgers (afterward killed by Indians) went to remove their families to a place of safety.

People were poorly prepared for moving, and, in order to give them all the time possible, it was decided to put a picket guard out on the San Antonio road, beyond Plum creek, to give notice of hostile approach. A squad of eight men were detailed for this duty, of which I was given command. Taking supplies for a two-days' sojourn, we started on our mission; but, before we reached our station, a courier overtook us with an order to send all the men back but two.

The Alamo had fallen and its brave defenders been put to the sword. Houston was in retreat, and families fleeing for their lives. Here was a situation to try men's souls. I had no kith nor kin in the country, was young and active, well armed and mounted, and so didn't blame others, less fortunately circumstanced, for hesitating when I read the dispatch aloud and said: "Well, boys, you hear the order. I've got to stay. Now who is going to stay with me?" They looked blank, and some of them swore they weren't "going to stay there to be murdered." "Then up spoke brave Horatius" in the person of little Jim Edmunson, a lad not more than 16 years old. "By gumie, Cap, I ain't afraid to stay with you anywhere." "Very well, Jim," I said. "You can all go back, boys. Jim and I will keep watch."

We both had good horses, and I knew that, with a fair start, no Mexican plug could catch us; so we took leave of our companions, who, to do them justice, were reluctant to leave us to our perilous mission; for there was even more danger from Indians, who were hovering on the outskirts, than from Mexicans who would come by the highway.

We kept a sharp lookout for Indian signs, but were relieved to find none. On reaching our station we carefully reconnoitered the country in every direction, selecting a position on a rise overlooking the road for several miles. We loosened our saddles without removing them, only slipping the bridle bits to allow our horses to eat corn we had brought with us. By that time it was growing dark, and, not daring to light a fire, we ate a cold bite. I then told Jim to lie down, and I kept watch with eye and ear all night long, unwilling, under such circumstances, to trust a growing boy to keep awake.

Morning came at last, and, no foe being in sight, we kindled a fire, made some coffee, attended to the needs of our horses, and then, instructing Jim as to his duties, I lay down and slept, but you may well imagine it was not a very sound slumber.

Thus another night and another day passed, and our lonely vigil was ended. There was no sign of a foe, so, late in the afternoon, we tightened up our saddle girths and set out on our return, going as far as Cedar creek, where we stopped for the night. The residents were all gone. There were chickens and eggs to make a preacher's mouth water, and we helped ourselves, feasting right royally, considering that we had earned the right to do so.

The next day we rode into Bastrop, which the brief interval of our absence had served to depopulate, excepting our company of twenty-two men. There being nothing more to detain us, we sunk all the boats and started down on the east side of the river, but had only gone about ten miles when we met a courier with orders for us to remain at Bastrop and get as many of the cattle over to the east bank as possible. So back we went.

The river was up swimming and all the boats were sunk; but, as no Mexicans had appeared, we concluded that they were not coming that way, and, knowing that there was a dugout up at Webber's place, four of us went up for it. It proved to be a new one, unfinished, and very heavy and clumsy, but we hitched on to it with our lariats and snaked it down to the river, where we launched it, Ganey Crosby, otherwise known as "Choctaw Tom," and myself manning it, while the other boys took charge of the horses.

Our craft proved rather unmanageable, spilling us into the river and wetting our guns, which we hung on to, however, being good swimmers. We righted our boat, bailed it out with our hats, re-embarked and went on down to old Marty Wells' place, when, being hungry and wet and a cold norther blowing, we landed and tied up for the night. The place was, of course, deserted. So we took possession and made ourselves comfortable. There was plenty of provender, and we made a roaring fire in the kitchen, cooked a sumptuous supper, dried our clothes and laid down to sleep.

By and by we were aroused by a roar and glare; our first thought being that the Indians had crept upon us and were trying to cremate us. A second look assured us that it was only the old stick and mud chimney, which had succumbed to our fire. Tom ran out and, snatching a fence rail, thrust it between the house and the chimney, throwing the latter down. We scattered the blazing sticks around, throwing water on them, and then lay down and finished our nap.

Next morning we again set sail, and at Caldwell's place, lower down, found a better canoe, of which we availed ourselves, reaching Bastrop without further mishap.

There was no chance of getting any cattle across; but, not knowing where our army was, and feeling no apprehension of the Mexicans coming that way, we stayed on, becoming so careless that we didn't even keep guards out, except one sentinel down at the ford. But one morning we woke up and saw the Mexicans, six hundred strong, on the opposite side of the river, they having captured our boat. We didn't "stand on the order" of our going, but went at once, and in such a hurry that we came near leaving the sentry, old Jimmy Curtice, on duty. We had got away when I happened to think of him, and rushing up to Major Williamson, said: "You ain't going to leave Uncle Jimmie on guard, are you, Major?"

"Good God! No; ride back and tell the old man to come on." I galloped back and found Uncle Jimmie sitting leaning against a tree, with a bottle of whisky beside him, as happy and unconscious of danger as a turtle on a log. "Hello, Uncle Jimmie," I cried, "mount and ride for your life. The Mexicans are on the other side and our men all gone." "The hell they are! 'Light and take a drink." "There's no time for drinking. Come—mount and let's be off. The Mexicans may swim the river and be after us any moment." "Let's drink to their confusion," he persisted, and, thinking it the quickest way to start him, I drank with him and we struck out.

"Well, we can say one thing; we were the last men to leave," said he, not in the least disturbed. He was one of the first white settlers in the colony and had had many brushes with the Spanish authorities.

We had two old men—old Andy Dunn and Jimmie Leach, who had lost their horses, and we younger men walked alternately, letting them ride our horses. The ground in the pine woods through which we were traveling was so boggy that we could not quit the road, and, thus hampered, our situation was not an enviable one. We traveled on all night, and, as hungry and tired we floundered on through the mud, we heard a signal shot from the advance guard.

They had discovered two men in the road ahead, who, on being hailed, dropped their bundles and ran. We examined the contents of the packs and were satisfied the owners were only runaway negroes who would keep out of the Mexicans' clutches, and so give no information.

At that juncture, Major Williamson, "being a little lame," concluded not to wait on our enforced slow pace, and accordingly went on, accompanied by "Choctaw Tom" and old Jimmie Curtice. The command then devolved on Lieutenant George M. Petty, a man destitute of experience, and possessed of a large amount of that "discretion" which is popularly esteemed "the better part of valor."

For some reason the Mexicans did not pursue us. They probably didn't know how we were situated, and doubtless were all busy gathering up plunder, it being their first opportunity, Gonzales having been burned when Houston left. It was said they gathered up everything of value and stored it carefully away before they left, thinking to return and possess the land from which they thought the Texans were expelled for good. Their expectations were doomed to failure for more reasons than one. The Comanches came next, and after taking all they wanted, set fire to the town.

The desolation of the country through which we passed beggars description. Houses were standing open, the beds unmade, the breakfast things still on the tables, pans of milk moulding in the dairies. There were cribs full of corn, smoke houses full of bacon, yards full of chickens that ran after us for food, nests of eggs in every fence corner, young corn and garden truck rejoicing in the rain, cattle cropping the luxuriant grass, hogs, fat and lazy, wallowing in the mud, all abandoned. Forlorn dogs roamed around the deserted homes, their doleful howls adding to the general sense of desolation. Hungry cats ran mewing to meet us, rubbing their sides against our legs in token of welcome. Wagons were so scarce that it was impossible to remove household goods, many of the women and children, even, had to walk. Some had no conveyance but trucks, the screeching of which added to the horror of the situation. One young lady said she walked with a bucket in hand to keep the trucks on which her mother and their little camping outfit rode from taking fire.

And, as if the arch fiend had broken loose, there were men—or devils, rather—bent on plunder, galloping up behind the fugitives, telling them the Mexicans were just behind, thus causing the hapless victims to abandon what few valuables they had tried to save. There were broken-down wagons and household goods scattered all along the road. Stores with quite valuable stocks of goods stood open, the goods on the shelves, no attempt having been made to remove them.

When we reached Cole's settlement (Brenham) we found a notice which Major Williamson had stuck on a tree, reporting the surrender and subsequent massacre of Fannin's men. We then understood the precipitate flight of the inhabitants, and realized the fate in store for us should we fall into the hands of the enemy.

There was an old fellow, John Williams, in our squad, who had been through several revolutions, from which he had derived a holy horror of Spanish methods of warfare, and he so worked upon the natural timidity of our commanding officer, that he saw a Mexican soldier in every bush. He actually tore up his commission, lest it be found on him, and condemn him to certain death. I cursed him for a coward then; but, looking back at it now and remembering that Houston was bitterly denounced as a coward for pursuing the only course that could have saved Texas, I am fain to confess that what we hotheads sneered at as cowardice in Lieutenant Petty, was really commendable caution. Had Grant and Ward and King been of the same temperament, the lives of themselves and their followers would not have been so uselessly sacrificed. Ignorant of the whereabouts of either friend or foe, knowing that Gaona was behind us, and surmising that Santa Anna was between us and Houston, we had good reason to feel timid.

Two of us who had the best mounts, Felix W. Goff and myself, offered to go on to Washington and see who was there; but, that not being considered advisable, we made for the Brazos bottom above Washington, where we lay concealed till night, when we sent out scouts to reconnoiter. There was a full moon just rising, and by its rays the scouts discovered a large body of moving figures coming down the road to Washington, which they supposed, of course, was Gaona's division of the Mexican army. With two of our men flat afoot and several others not much better off, the enemy close upon us in the rear and the Brazos river booming full in front, there was nothing for us but to try and keep out of the way. The only course open was up the river, and this we accordingly took, going up to Tinoxtitlan before we effected a crossing.

At that point we fell in with Colonel Bain and Captain Bob Childress, who, with their rangers, had been convoying the families from their district. They had two men without horses, who, with our two, constructed a raft and started down the river; poor old Andy Dunn and Jimmie Leach getting drowned on the way down. Thus reinforced we struck down the river in search of our army, the first intimation of its locality being conveyed to us by the guns of San Jacinto, while we were still some miles away. Uncertain what course to pursue, we halted, and soon a messenger came with the tidings of victory.

It was then my turn to swear; but, notwithstanding I had added the Spanish list to my vocabulary of "cuss words," I couldn't begin to "do the subject justice," especially when we learned that the Mexican army that had sent us racing off up to Tinoxtitlan, was only a drove of cattle, which had been abandoned and were roving over the prairie. I felt mean and ashamed to go on to Houston's camp, as if we ought to be drummed out; but, the battle was fought and won just the same without us, and perhaps, had I been there, I might not now be writing the story of it.

If ever I did thirst for gore it was when we reached San Jacinto and found the army jubilating over the glorious victory, of a share in which only the timidity of our commanding officer had deprived us. The ferry at Washington having, by Major Williamson's order, been kept open for us, the way was absolutely clear.

The dead Mexicans lay in piles, the survivors not even asking permission to bury them, thinking, perhaps, that, in return for the butchery they had practiced, they would soon be lying dead themselves. The buzzards and coyotes were gathering to the feast, but it is a singular fact that they singled out the dead horses, refusing to touch the Mexicans, presumably because of the peppery condition of the flesh. They lay there unmolested and dried up, the cattle got to chewing the bones, which so affected the milk that residents in the vicinity had to dig trenches and bury them.

The battlefield bore testimony to the desperate hand-to-hand struggle our men had maintained—rifles broken off at the breech, the stocks besmeared with blood and brains, told but too plainly how foes had met their death. One of the few Mexicans who escaped to carry the news of the disaster, accounted for their defeat on the hypothesis that "the Americans were all drunk." He said the Mexicans had them whipped, when a boat loaded with whisky came up. The Americans then all filled up with corn juice, and, yelling "Alamo, Alamo," made a wild rush for the Mexicans, falling upon them with clubs, and beat their brains out. The latter part of the statement was literally true, and it was equally true that many a poor wretch was brained while on his knees. But with the blood of relatives and friends butchered in the Alamo and at Goliad crying for revenge, the Texans did not stop to reflect that these abject creatures were only tools.

Old Jimmie Curtice had a son-in-law, Wash Cottle, slain in the Alamo, whom he swore to avenge. San Jacinto gave him the opportunity and he made the most of it. The boys said he clubbed his rifle and sailed in, in Donnybrook fair style, accompanying each blow with "Alamo! You killed Wash Cottle!"

The arms and ammunition captured were brought into camp. No one wanted the muskets, so they were stacked; and, as the cartridges wouldn't fit our guns, they were thrown into a heap. By some means fire got among them and there was a stampede, such as they never could have created shot from muskets in the hands of Mexicans. "Pop!" "Fizz!" "Bang!" The enemy was charging every point of the compass! The air was full of bursting shells! The proud victors of San Jacinto dropped their guns and fled. Trees were at a premium. The rout was complete. The blind enemy held possession of the camp until the last cartridge was exhausted.

We luckless wights who failed to get into the fight got no share of the spoils, which were quite considerable. Santa Anna's horse and accoutrements were, by common consent, given to General Houston, whose horse was shot under him in the fight. The saddle fairly glittered with gold, which Santa Anna said was solid and valued at $600, but it was subsequently ascertained to be only plated. The horse, a magnificent black stallion, had been taken from Allen Vince, which, coming to Houston's knowledge, he promptly restored it to its owner.

There were said to have been a number of United States soldiers, from General Gaines' command, in the battle of San Jacinto. Deserters, they were called; but, after the battle, they all "deserted" back to the United States army, and no court martial ensued. General Gaines, it will be remembered, moved his command over to Nacogdoches, ostensibly to protect the families against the Indians.

The only one of our killed with whom I was acquainted was Lemuel Blakey, a boy about eighteen, whose father died of fever at Brazoria within a few weeks after setting foot in the promised land for which they left their old Kentucky home in 1832. Thus left with a large family, the older ones daughters, Mrs. Blakey went on up to Bastrop, "Austin's little colony" it was then called, locating her headright on the west side of the Colorado, where her descendants still reside. When Houston issued his call for volunteers, Edward, her oldest son, enlisted, but, when it became evident that the families would have to leave, his mother's claims were strongest, and his brother Lemuel went in his stead. Edward was afterward killed by the Indians in the battle of Brushy. Of the humble private, who falls at his post, history is oblivious; but, there were bitter tears mingled with the rejoicing, in that refugee camp over beyond the Trinity, for the son and brother who would return no more. Their tears have all been shed, not one of all the family remaining to tell the story of that terrible flight, as indeed there are few now living who participated in it.

It was a time to try the souls of all, even the little children realizing something of the situation, which must have left such a vivid impression on their minds that time has not effaced it. Years afterward I was in Bastrop when a little Italian Jew came along playing on a hand organ. Old Sampson Connell, somewhat the worse for "booze," sat nodding in the sun outside a store. By and by he straightened himself up and said: "——— ——— that thing, it makes me think of the runaway scrape. I had nothing but a pair of old trucks to get my family away on, and whenever they got dry they went 'cru-uchy, cru-uchy," just like that thing does." The "runaway scrape" marked an epoch from which Texans were wont to date all events up to the time of the late war,

which, of course, obliterated old landmarks, so that the rising generation probably knew but little about it; but, that they may know something of the hardships of those who wrested their heritage from the savage, I would that every survivor should lend his experience to swell the volume of history.

Though our loss at San Jacinto was trifling, we had paid dearly for our victory. Two hundred brave men who fell fighting with Travis, Bowie, and Crockett in the Alamo, 390 butchered in cold blood with Fannin at Goliad, and the parties of Grant, Ward, King and Johnson, about 150 in all, who perished with their leaders at Agua Dulce, Refugio and San Patricio; aggregating nearly as many men as fought under the Lone Star at San Jacinto. A needless sacrifice, too. Had the policy of Houston and Governor Smith been sustained, all of these tragedies might have been averted. The defenders of the Alamo fought to the last gasp. All the other parties surrendered when the contest became hopeless, and were disarmed, marched out and shot to death, in violation of the rules of war. Such are the methods of Spanish warfare. And yet, Santa Anna alone is responsible for the atrocious deed, his officers pleading in vain for the lives of their prisoners. When General Urrea heard of the massacre at Goliad he exclaimed, with tears in his eyes: "Thank God, I had nothing to do with the murder of those brave men."

When the unfortunate men were being made to kneel, Fenner, having a presentiment of what was intended, sprang to his feet, calling to his comrades: "Turn! don't let us be shot in the back." With his warning some fell over on their faces and escaped the first volley, but it was only to prolong their agony. I personally knew one man who fell on his face and lay perfectly still. A Mexican came along and thrust a lance through his neck, leaving him for dead; but, after night he crawled away to a Mexican house where the mistress of it took him in and kept him concealed till he recovered.

When Santa Anna unfurled his black flag in front of the Alamo, Travis assembled his little band in the court and drawing a line across it with his sword requested all those who were resolved to die fighting to step across the line. There was a rush to get across; Jim Bowie, who lay helpless in bed, asking to be carried across, and, true to his word, he had his loaded pistols laid beside him, and, when the murderous fiends burst into the room, he opened fire on them and had the satisfaction of seeing several of his assailants fall before he himself was overpowered.

Though slightly acquainted with many of the victims of Santa Anna's barbarous policy, Bowie was the only one for whom I entertained a personal regard. My relations with him dated back to 1828, when he made his appearance in San Felipe de Austin (about a year after the famous encounter which established his character as a fighter and made the reputation of the Bowie knife). The encounter referred to was a free-for-all fight on a sand bar in the Mississippi river fronting Natchez; the initial skirmish being a duel in which the principals, Major Wright and Dr. Maddux, after having vindicated their honor by the exchange of harmless shots, shook hands across the blood-less chasm.

This tame ending of an affair which had promised to be an exciting event, all the parties having come up from Louisiana, bred dissatisfaction among the crowd, which brought on a general engagement; and, when the smoke of battle cleared, there were two dead men and two wounded. The details of the fight as I remember them were that General Cuney, with Jim Bowie as his second, personally challenged Colonel Crane; whereupon, Crane whipped out two pistols, discharging them simultaneously, killing Cuney and wounding Bowie, after which he turned and ran. Bowie drew his knife—all the weapon he had—and started in pursuit but fell, and before he could rise Major Wright rushed up and attempted to stab him with a sword cane. Bowie caught the cane and, jerking Wright toward him, with a tremendous sweep of his knife cleft him clear through the abdomen to the back-bone, the mangled bowels pouring out upon Bowie, who was sitting on the ground. Seeing the horrible fate that had befallen his friend, Alfred Blanchard, also armed with a sword-cane, ran up to avenge him. Shooting out his long arm Bowie slashed Blanchard across the abdomen, disemboweling him.

The blood christened weapon which had saved its owner's life twice within a few seconds, was an ordinary affair with a plain wooden handle, but when Bowie recovered from his wound he had the precious blade polished and set into an ivory handle mounted with silver; the scabbard also being silver mounted. Not wishing to degrade it by ordinary use, he brought the knife to me in San Felipe to have a duplicate made. The blade was about ten inches long and two broad at the widest part. When it became known that I was making a genuine Bowie knife, there was a great demand for them, so I cut a pattern and started a factory, my jobs bringing all the way from $5.00 to $20.00, according to finish.

Bowie went on out to San Antonio where he married the daughter of ex-Governor Veremendi. I never met his wife, but was told that she was of a pure Castilian type and very handsome. I know that she had a deep hold on Bowie's affections. Strong man that he was, I have seen the tears course down his cheeks while lamenting her untimely death, which occurred while I was in Louisiana, where I again met him after his bereavement. In 1831 he again displayed his fighting qualities in an all-day fight near the old San Saba mission, which himself and brother Rezin with seven other white men and two negro boys maintained against 164 Indians, many of whom had firearms; the whites losing but one man, while the Indians lost a third of their number.

When I renewed my acquaintance with him in Louisiana he, with Rezin P. Bowie, his brother, were prosecuting a claim to a large amount of land in Louisiana under an old Spanish grant. The case was in all the courts and became celebrated as the "Bowie claim." They won their suit and had a fortune, but Jim was prodigal with his money, though he was no gambler, and soon let his share slip away from him. In the same way a fortune which he was said to have made out of the slave trade, carried on in connection with Lafitte, filtered through his fingers.

As previously related, it was under his leadership that we fought the battle of Concepcion; after which I transferred my services to the rangers and we never met again. James Bowie was a fine specimen of physical manhood and by nature calculated to be a commander of men. Whatever faults he may have had, infidelity to friends was not one of them; he stood up to them right or wrong. There was a story told of him that, getting into a fracas in San Antonio, and failing to receive the support of a friend who was present, he afterwards called him to account for it. "Why, Jim," his friend exclaimed, "you were in the wrong." "Don't you suppose I know that as well as you do? That's just why I needed a friend. If I had been in the right, I would have had plenty of them," retorted Bowie.

Colonel Travis, who previous to the opening of hostilities was simply "Bill Travis" and lived below San Felipe, was a good fighter; but, had not the qualities necessary to a commander, else he never would have allowed himself to become penned up in the Alamo. He, however, made the same fatal mistake to which Col. Barnard E. Bee attributed the defeat of Santa Anna. In talking with Colonel Bee about the battle of San Jacinto, I asked him how he accounted for the utter rout. "Why, sir," said he, "Santa Anna despised his enemy. It's a dangerous thing to despise your enemy."

The fate of Fannin's command was due to his solicitude for the detachments under King and Ward whom he had despatched to Refugio to bring off the families; and for whom he waited three days after all was in readiness for retreat, not knowing that they had been cut off.

In striking contrast to the campaign just closed was that of the previous fall in which we expelled the whole Mexican force from the territory, with a loss to the Texans not exceeding half a dozen men, all told. Among these latter was Ransome Graves, a youth about eighteen years of age, who lived with his widowed mother at Matagorda. Ransome did not thirst for glory, but was rather ambitious to shine with the girls; a weakness of which I took advantage to kindle a martial flame.

"Now," said I, "here's your opportunity. There is nothing a woman so despises as a coward; but, if you will go bravely to the front and fight for freedom, when you come back you will be a hero, and the girls will be proud of your attentions." Ransome remained silent for a moment as if contemplating the alluring picture.

"Yes," he dubiously interposed, "but what if your Uncle Fuller was to get thrust through?"

That was a proposition which I had no argument to combat. But when the test came, Ransome did not fail. He was among the first in the field and—was "thrust through."

[98]

It was a terrible baptism, that of the Lone Star republic; but, we had triumphed and it was to the future that our eyes were now turned.

Houston's ankle having been shattered by the ball that killed his horse, as soon as the treaty of peace was signed and the Mexican army in retreat, he turned over the command of the army to General Rusk (who, though secretary of war, had joined the army and bore a soldier's part in the battle of San Jacinto), and sailed for New Orleans for repairs.

Sam Houston made his debut on the stage of Texas politics in 1833, when, as the representative of Nacogdoches in the convention that convened at San Felipe to take measures to secure statehood, he, as chairman of the committee on constitution, drew up the document which accompanied the petition to Mexico.

The convention having finished its labors, Houston disappeared from public view until 1835, when he again came to the front in the council which declared war and established the provisional government. Houston being elected commander-in-chief of the Texas army, his name thereafter is indissolubly intertwined with the history of the state. Though his peculiar bent did not incline toward the founding of a nation, every instinct of his nature prompted him to resistance when the life and liberties of the nation were threatened.

He was a living exponent of the natural law alluded to by him in Congress when the West Point Military Academy bill was under consideration. Said he, "You might as well take dung-hill fowl's eggs and put them in eagle's nests and try to make eagles of them, as to try to make generals of boys who have no capacity, by giving them military training."

With no previous military training, he enlisted as a private in the Creek war, from which he emerged with the rank of lieutenant; after which his military pursuits were limited to the militia. This was his military record up to the time he debouched on the field as commander of the Texas army.

Like the Duke of Wellington, Houston was great on retreat; his much anathematized retreat alone making possible the glorious victory of San Jacinto. With no adequate force to oppose the invading army, the only hope of success lay in dividing it and taking it in detail; a consummation that, whether Houston foresaw it or not, was practically attained when Santa Anna, finding the Texas army in retreat, sent General Gaona across by Bastrop, and General Urrea down along the coast to sweep the country clean, while he himself hurried on after the retreating army, confident of his ability to annihilate it if only he could overtake it. Thus we find the Texans at bay at San Jacinto with less than one-third of the Mexican army confronting them; and while Santa Anna is snoozing away the time waiting for his scattered forces to rejoin him, the bridge behind him is burned, cutting off help and retreat alike, and the gallant little band is upon him dealing death to his surprised and routed army. He had not dreamed of attack. "Why," said he after his capture, "such a thing as assaulting breastworks without either bayonets or swords was never before known." The Texans had established a precedent, and, could the men have gotten hold of him after his identity was revealed, they would have established another one for him. "Why," he enquired of Houston, "didn't you attack me yesterday before General Cos came up?" "Oh," replied Houston, "I didn't think it worth while to make two bites of a cherry."

Nor was Houston's policy in dealing with Santa Anna as a prisoner productive of less happy results. Had the bloody wretch been hanged, as the army demanded and as he richly deserved, the Mexican army under General Filisola would have made a combined attack on the Texans and probably have overwhelmed them; but, with the president in hand, the Texans held the key to the situation. Like Washington, Houston proved himself equally as competent to guide the helm of the ship of state as to command its army.

Captain George Erath, one of San Jacinto's heroes, being a man of action, condensed the whole code of military tactics into one word. The marked success attending his campaigns against the Indians at the head of a company of minute men suggesting military training, he was asked if he had not received a military training. "No," said he, "I knows but vone vord of command, und dot ish, 'Sharge, poys, sharge.'"

CHAPTER 10

When the Texas army, under General Rusk, moved up from San Jacinto to Victoria in the wake of the retreating Mexicans, the rangers were detailed to guard the baggage. The country being deserted, we helped ourselves to anything in the way of provisions we found lying around loose; but, the Mexican army having marched and countermarched through that section, there was little, except livestock, left to forage on. Camping for the night at Squire Sutherland's place on the Colorado, the only thing in the way of commissary we could find, was a number of fat hogs lying around the gin house. They jumped up and "booed" at us when we came up, and, our military honor forbidding us to allow such an affront to pass unnoticed, we charged upon the saucy porkers, bringing down a 200-pounder. Dressing our prize, we soon had pork chops to broil. The odor arising therefrom wasn't exactly what we could have wished; but, as we sniffed the air rather doubtfully, familiarity with the peculiar odor served to lull our suspicions, and by the time the meat was cooked, we had persuaded ourselves there was nothing unusual about it. One bite served to dispel the fond delusion. Having been fattened on cottonseed alone, the meat was so strongly impregnated with the flavor that it was impossible to eat it.

All danger from the Mexicans being over, our men were strung out across the prairie, sometimes a mile ahead of the wagons. The sedge grass, which in many places was waist high, was getting dry, furnishing material for a terrible conflagration if by chance a spark should light among it. So when a column of smoke suddenly rose up some little way ahead, realizing the danger to which we were exposed, we put spurs to our horses and hurried to the spot to prevent its spreading. On reaching the scene of the incipient fire we found a man lying half unconscious in the midst of the smoke, his face blackened and burned, his clothing on fire and his right arm almost torn from his body. The fragments of what had a few moments before been a powderhorn and a pipe accounted for the poor fellow's condition, but there was no time to waste in speculation, as the fire was making such headway that a few moments more would put it beyond our control. The fire being extinguished, we resuscitated the unfortunate victim, who, to our inquiries as to the cause of the explosion, said he had lighted his pipe for a smoke, but the tobacco didn't burn well, so he turned up his powderhorn to add a few grains of powder for kindling. The experiment was entirely successful, and but for our prompt arrival on the scene, he might have burned himself and the wagons and possibly other men. Thus the Texas rangers demonstrated their ability to cope with the devil in his natural element as well as when incarnated into a Comanche.

Arriving at Victoria, we erected a lot of cowhide sheds, which we dignified by the name of barracks, a mile or so above town. General Rusk then issued an order for all the smiths and wagon-workers to form an armorers' corps and go into town to work. My trade put me in the corps, having for my assistant a stalwart son of the Blue Grass state, Lang by name. General Rusk, had he been inclined to enforce strict military discipline, knew too well the disposition of the men to attempt it, so we were given, or took, the largest liberty possible to any kind of regulations. One order, however, it was necessary to enforce, that those dealing in intoxicating liquors should not sell their goods to the men except in the presence of an officer. The boys naturally resented any such infraction on a time honored custom, and laid their heads together to devise some plan to circumvent the general. One day a little Frenchman came up with several goatskins filled with vena mescal, for which he charged the exorbitant price of fifty cents a wineglass—five dollars a bottle. Half dollars were scarce, but we determined to test the virtues of the Frenchman's wares, officer or no officer.

There was an old sailor in the crowd who had served in the navy, and it was said was one of Lafitte's men. Be that as it may, he was up to all the tricks to outwit officers. He devised a plan whereby we might get the better of the commandant and the grasping Frenchman also. Among the plunder taken at San Jacinto was a captain's uniform. Into this we inducted Lang and commissioned him captain. He looked every inch of it. After rehearsing his part we staked him with fifty cents, and after dark he sauntered into the French-man's shanty. Swaggering around with an air of importance, he called for a glass of liquor, for which he threw down the half dollar. Directly the boys began to drop in, each one saluting "Captain" Lang. When the initiated had all got in, Lang looked around patronizingly.

"Well, boys," said he, "if I had known I was going to meet so many of my company here I'd have put some money in my pocket to treat you."

The Frenchman's face fairly shone with delight.

"Ah, monsieur Captain, zat is no matter; suppose you like for treat ze men, never mind ze money; you pay me to-morrow."

"All right," said Lang. "Step up, boys."

We obeyed the order with alacrity, emptying our glasses with military pre-cision, first to Captain Lang and then to the smiling vendor of the villainous liquid. By that time the stock was exhausted and we didn't tarry.

"Come around to my quarters to-morrow," said Lang, as we departed.

Returning to camp, we court martialed Lang and broke him of his com-mission. Bright and early next morning the Frenchman was on hand inquir-ing for Captain Lang's headquarters. Up and down he went, but, it is need-less to state, he never found them.

The complex character of the army rendered the position of commanding officer an extremely difficult one to fill. The citizen soldiers, having proved the worth and wisdom of their leaders, were disposed to acquiesce in their decisions; but, as other parties, under their own officers and actuated by dif-ferent motives, came on, there was unavoidably some friction. The citizens had taken up arms in self-defense; another class had come through sympathy with their struggling countrymen; others, still, from love of adventure, and, as is always the case, there were some who seemed to be actuated by no higher principle than prospective plunder, and in the pursuit of their object were no respecters of persons. These latter, so far as I know, were not en-gaged in any of the battles, and acknowledged no authority, either military or civil. At Victoria they did not even camp with the army; still General Rusk was held responsible for their misdeeds.

They foraged the country round, gathering up horses and mules, ostensi-bly preying upon the unfriendly Mexicans; but I knew of their taking a pair of mules from the widow of Martin De Leon, whose family were always friendly to the Texans. Her son complained to General Rusk, who went with him to the captain of the thievish band, but that worthy refused to surrender them, and Rusk was not in a position to force their release, inasmuch as the men were not regularly enlisted and a conflict with them was not advisable. They did not tarry long after that, but, gathering up everything of value they could lay their hands on, left for their stronghold.

Our men all liked General Rusk, whose native good sense would not allow any assumption of superiority over the men under his command. The dignity of his position demanding a "staff," he appointed a couple of young striplings, sons of old friends, as aids, with the rank of major. One day a bluff old citizen called on the general, and, being well acquainted with him, walked into his tent without any ceremony, ignoring the presence of the youthful aids until Rusk formally introduced them as "Major Dexter and Major Hoxie, my aids."

"Aids, h——l!" said the old fellow, looking the boys over contemptuously; "when I was their size I went in my shirt tail."

When General Green came on he requested a quarter guard. Rusk, who had never had anything in his quarters worth stealing, pretended to misunderstand.

"Why, bless your soul, General," said he, "there isn't a man in the army that would hurt you."

Pretty soon Green had a ten-gallon cask of wine sent to his tent, an outrage the boys were not disposed to submit to. So they located the cask and after night the general was called out on some pretense, when Cy Gleason, a sturdy New York boy, raised the flap of his tent, rolled the cask out, and, raising it on his shoulders, marched off to the river, where he sank it, raising it as occasion required.

Captain H——, the only officer who ever had the temerity to try to enforce strict military discipline, paid for his folly with his life. There came up a violent thunderstorm one night, and when it was over the poor fellow, whose only offense was a little youthful vanity, was found in his tent with his brains blown out.

James P. Gorman, well known in the vicinity of Bastrop, was appointed wagonmaster. He picked up a Mexican sword, for which he made a cowhide sheath. With that strapped to his side and his head surmounted with a fox-skin cap, the ears standing erect on top and the tail hanging down behind, he cut a grotesque figure. The boys called him General Gorman. He was sent down to Linn's Landing on the bay to bring up a cannon that had been landed there. On the way up he was tempted to try the merits of the piece on a drove of deer that were feeding some distance away. He put in a charge of grape, and, bringing the gun to bear on the deer, touched it off. Hearing the report and suspecting that Gorman had been attacked, General Rusk hurried off a detachment to his relief. We made all possible haste to reach him, and imagine our disgust when we came up and instead of the enemy we were prepared to engage, saw only a herd of harmless deer, upon which the shots had taken no effect except to make them bound into the air when the bullets cut the dirt under their feet. General Rusk placed Gorman under arrest for his escapade, but he swore "the show was worth it; he never had so much fun in his life."

Sauntering up through camp one day I came upon another character well known to most old Texans along the Colorado—Peter Carr—seated on a dry cowhide, the center of which was doing duty for a table. Another hide laid on a framework of poles served to keep off the summer sun. Peter was engaged in dealing 21 with a deck of cards so ragged and begrimed that their faces were scarcely decipherable.

"Hello, Pete; what's your limit?" said I.

"Oh, bet as much as you please," he replied.

I "sized his pile" and knew I could beat it, and with an unlimited game was sure to win in the long run, so down I sat. The other players soon "went broke" and dropped out, leaving the issue to Peter and myself, and it wasn't long till I had the game "busted." He accepted his defeat good naturedly, often referring to the incident in after years as the "unkindest cut" fortune had ever dealt him. He had had many reserves and was at that time flat broke, and had just succeeded in getting up a little game whereby he hoped to make a "raise," when along came a friend and "scooped the pot."

The detailed adventures of Peter Carr would make an entertaining narrative. Briefly stated, Peter Carr, a native of Pennsylvania, I think, first made his advent into Texas with a little schooner loaded with merchandise, about 1824. Chartering his vessel to another party, he took his goods up to Victoria, and after a short sojourn there, during which time he contracted a matrimonial engagement with a daughter of an old Spanish family, packed up his stock and went on a trading expedition among the Indians, who robbed him of his outfit. Returning to Victoria, the mercenary old don refused to allow his daughter to consummate her engagement. About that time Carr got word that his vessel (which he had taken the precaution to insure in New Orleans) had been wrecked. He went back to New Orleans, collected the policy, and invested it in a fine hack and span of horses, with which he proposed to run between San Antonio and Matamoros. On his first trip out he drove into one of those bottomless water holes to water his team. The horses went down, taking the hack with them, and, being unable to extricate themselves, were drowned, Peter narrowly escaping the same fate. Again he was broke, but with undaunted courage he made his way down to the gulf and from there round to New Orleans, thence home to Pennsylvania. His family being well-to-do, he got another stake, with which he bought a distilling outfit in New Orleans, shipping it on the vessel which brought me back to Texas in 1835. After getting his property safely aboard, seeing he had an hour or two to spare before the sailing of the schooner, he went back up town to take leave of his friends. When the hour of starting came, Peter was still absent, but the steam tug hitched on to our vessel and away we went. Before we were out of sight Peter came rushing down to the dock, shouting and waving his hat, but the captain didn't go back, so he had to hunt up another vessel, and I did not meet him again till I returned with the army to Victoria. In the meantime his attitude on the political situation not seeming satisfactory to General Houston, he had Peter arrested and his property confiscated, which left him stranded for the third time. After many unsuccessful attempts to retrieve his fallen fortunes, he finally got in with some cattle buyers and with them went out to the

Rio Grande, where his knowledge of the language and "peculiarities" of the Mexicans enabled the buyers to make much more favorable terms than they could otherwise have made. For his services he received a share of the stock, which he drove in on the Colorado below Austin. From that time on Peter prospered, and many a poor family blessed the day when Uncle Peter, as he came to be known in later life, brought his herds into the country. Anyone was welcome to take up the cows and milk them. He was the first mail carrier from Austin to LaGrange. Whether the heartless desertion of the senorita chilled his heart, rendering it impervious to the smiles of her sex, I cannot say, but he lived and died a bachelor. Before his death, which occurred some years back, he bequeathed a large tract of land in Burnet County for the founding of a university. The will, I believe, was broken. Thus the last hope of his eventful life, like most of its predecessors, was doomed to disappointment. Faults he had, as who has not? But his good deeds counterbalanced them.

One of our new recruits, Jimmie Snead, a Pennsylvanian, was out on the prairie one day when he found a Mexican bridle-bit. Thinking it some kind of a trap, he procured a stick and tried to spring it. He failed to touch it off; but, not daring to put hand on it, he got it on the stick and brought it into camp.

One other incident of army life and I am done. The Mexican army in its retreat left a number of heavy baggage wagons on the east side of the Colorado, being unable to cross them. These some of us were sent back to bring up. Before we could cross them the river began to rise, and having no ferry, we went up to Sutherland's gin and collected a lot of bale rope, of which we constructed a cable of sufficient strength to tow the wagons over, crossing back and forth in a "dugout." We had an old sailor along who was engineering the work, and, like many another old salt, he couldn't swim. He was crossing the river (which by this time was pretty full) with the tow-line when the canoe fouled and capsized. Fortunately there was a stranded tree near, some of the limbs of which were above water. This he succeeded in reaching, and, climbing upon a limb which bent under his weight, he hung on for dear life. The river was rising fast and the current caused the tree to sway and tremble and almost start from its anchor. Every now and then a wave would submerge the limb on which the old fellow had taken refuge. The canoe was gone and the situation becoming critical.

"Bear a hand there!" he shouted frantically, "Bring me a hawser. Don't you see the river is rising?" We procured a rope and one of the boys swam in with it, making one end fast to the tree and the other to the shore. The sailor was all right then, he had a rope in his hands. We then swam in and got the canoe and succeeded in getting all our wagons across.

When it was definitely ascertained that the Mexican army had retired beyond the Rio Grande, there seeming to be no further need of their services,

the citizens were anxious to return to their homes and we were accordingly ordered down to Columbia (where congress was then sitting) to be mustered out. Passing through Matagorda, en route, my acquaintances, who had seen me leave there a year before in company with Dr. Field, gazed on me as one risen from the dead, believing that I had fallen with Fannin, a fate from which Dr. Field's profession saved him.

No man in Texas was oftener called upon, nor in more capacities, to serve his adopted country, than Thomas Jefferson Rusk: First, and that within a year after his arrival, as a delegate to the first revolutionary convention—1835—and again to the convention that promulgated the declaration of Texas independence, which convention conferred upon him the office of Secretary of War; leaving this office to take care of itself, joined Houston at the front and as a member of the general's staff participated in the battle of San Jacinto, taking the command after Houston was wounded; when the constitutional government was established, was again chosen Secretary of War; afterwards conducted several campaigns against the Indians; served as a member of the Texas congress; was chief justice of the supreme court of the republic; president of the convention that consummated the annexation of Texas to the United States; and, with Houston, first represented the new state in the national senate, a position to which he was twice re-elected, being at the time of his death—1856—president pro tem. of that body. As chairman of the committee on postoffices and postroads, he took an active interest in the establishment of the overland mail route to California.

General Rusk's military education had progressed no farther than Captain Erath's, but he had the esteem and confidence of his men to such an extent that an attempt to replace him with General Lamar stirred up such a spirit of mutiny that Lamar was constrained to withdraw. The only complaint against Rusk (having its origin among the upstart subs who wanted to set up a military aristocracy) was his easy familiarity with the privates. Meagre as was the honor attaching to the office of commander of the Texas army, it must have been that which brought forward so many aspirants for the position, which was by no means lucrative, and fraught with difficulty, often mortification—the army going on the principle that "the majority should rule."

But whatever the inducement, it was sufficient to engender bitter animosity between the rival candidates, which in one notable instance culminated in a duel, the parties to which were Generals A. Sidney Johnston and Felix Huston.

Johnston was appointed by President Lamar to supersede Huston. Feeling aggrieved over his displacement, Huston visited his displeasure on Johnston, whom ostensibly, on account of discourtesy on the part of the latter, he challenged. Johnston was seriously wounded, but he held the place.

CHAPTER II

The settlers gradually regained confidence and by this time were pretty much all back in their homes. The Indians were committing many outrages, making it again necessary to garrison the frontier. As neither Captain Tomlinson nor his lieutenants reported for duty, Colonel Coleman was instructed to proceed up on Walnut creek, six miles below Austin, and build the Coleman fort, consisting of a cluster of log cabins enclosed with a heavy stockade. All of the Tomlinson rangers were ordered to report to Coleman, their term of enlistment (one year) not having expired. Bastrop country suffered more from Indians during the year 1836 than for any other year of its history. I could mention numbers of its best men who were killed during that time. The return of the rangers, however, checked hostile incursions for a time, and people began to scatter out from the forts, in which they had been compelled to take refuge, and settle down to the business of preparing for the next season's crops; few of them having made anything that year.

Mechanics were rather scarce in the frontier settlements, and there was so much need of blacksmith work that I did not stop at the fort all the time, but worked in the settlements. It was while thus employed that I received an invitation down to old Sammie Craft's, below Bastrop, the occasion being the marriage of his stepdaughter, Candice Thompson, to David Holderman, Bastrop's principal merchant. Mr. Craft had a more commodious house than was ordinarily found in that section, having also a good "plank" floor, a luxury that most of the settlers were forced to forego. These advantages taken with the genial hospitality of the family, insured a full attendance at a social gathering within its walls. This being an extraordinary occasion, all the elite in the country round were invited, and few regrets were sent. I being a pretty fair Arkansas fiddler had the entree of all social functions, where dancing was a feature. The bride needed not the aid of artificial lights to make her appear lovely, therefore the marriage ceremony was performed in broad daylight. I can't tell you just how the bride was dressed. The bridegroom, being a merchant, had on "store clothes," but that kind of apparel was not de rigueur. There were many homespun suits and the old reliable buckskin was also in evidence. Among the ladies, the rustle of silks was not wanting, if the styles were somewhat varied according to the period at which the wearer migrated thither.

The writer was resplendent in a brand new buckskin suit, consisting of hunting shirt, pantaloons and moccasins, all elaborately fringed. It was on this occasion that I first met the lady who afterwards became my wife, and I used to tell her that it was my picturesque attire that won me her favor.

There was neither gas nor kerosene to light the dancing room, but the tallow candles beamed on the assembly from highly polished tall brass candlesticks, such as now are carefully treasured as heirlooms by the descendants of old families.

Among the guests was the Rev. Hugh M. Childers, who, though a Methodist minister, was also an expert with a violin, and even "tripped the light fantastic." For an all around useful man he had few equals, always bearing his full share of anything that came along, from a prayer meeting to an Indian fight. A preacher who could only talk found himself out of a job in those parts.

Dr. Fentress also wielded the bow and, between us three, we kept the dance going all night. We were not versed in the giddy measures of the dances in vogue nowadays, but,

"Hornpipes, strathspeys, jigs and reels
Put life and mettle in our heels."

There were a couple of strangers present who attracted a good deal of attention—an elderly man, with a professional handle to his name, and his son, a lad of twenty or thereabouts. They had money for which they were seeking investment. Both of them were well dressed, sporting gold watches and shirt studs, and the young man was cutting a wide swath among the girls, laying us buckskin boys quite in the shade. But by and by old Aunt Celie, a mulatto woman who was looking on through the open door, beckoned to her young mistress, Miss Harriet Craft, and, taking her aside, said:

"Miss Ha'it, wat you in dar dancin' wid dat niggah fo?"

"Hush, Aunt Celie; that isn't a nigger," said Miss Craft.

"He is niggah, Miss Ha'it; he jes' as much niggah as I is. Look at his ha' and his eyes," urged the indignant old woman.

Commanding Aunt Celie to hold her peace, Miss Harriet returned to her guests, but the furtive glances bestowed upon the young stranger betrayed the doubt Aunt Celie's warning had awakened. Later developments proved the keenness of the old woman's perception. She was not easily deceived on the color line. Our host spared no pains to make the time pass pleasantly, himself going through the evolutions of a hornpipe to show us clumsy young fellows how they danced in his youth.

There was a bountiful feast, the table remaining spread and the coffee pot kept boiling all night, those who chose repairing to the dining room for refreshments at any time.

We literally "danced all night to broad daylight and went home with the girls in the morning," the unsafe condition of the country rendering such escort absolutely indispensable. We didn't neglect to take our rifles along either.

We didn't always have boards to dance on. Sometimes there were puncheons (split timbers), and sometimes only the ground, but we enjoyed any respite from the wearing cares that beset us, and overlooked all minor discomforts.

My term of enlistment expiring about the beginning of 1837, I substituted

a man who had a family, to whom he was desirous of returning, and again took up my quarters in the fort. The weather was cold and wet and our men suffering for clothing. Buckskin was sufficient while the weather remained dry; but, a story my wife used to tell on Jimmie Manning will best illustrate the objection to which buckskin was open as a wet weather garment. Jimmie, who had not then been long in the country, was out with a surveying party when there came up a drenching rain, and before they could reach shelter the buckskin breeches of the party were thoroughly saturated. The widow Blakey's house opened its hospitable doors to receive the dripping, shivering surveyors. Mrs. Blakey had two grown up daughters and it could generally be depended on to find one or more visiting young ladies there, making it a favorite stopping place at all times, especially so on a rainy day.

The hero of the story being unacquainted with the vagaries of buckskin, on alighting from his horse and finding his feet enveloped in the slimy folds of his pantaloons, which had lengthened a foot or so and become as unmanageable as a jelly fish, took out his knife and cut off the extra length. Men didn't keep extra suits of clothing those days and, as there were no dry garments to offer the party, there was a rousing fire built in the great open fire place and the boys drew up in front of it to dry their clothing. When the fire began to make its influence felt, Jimmie's breeches began a retrograde movement, perceiving which he reached down and stretched them out again to the ill concealed amusement of the girls, who had witnessed the amputation. But the pantaloons were on the retreat, and by the time the buckskin reached its normal condition had put a safe distance between them and the tops of his shoes. Jimmie didn't wait for the rain to stop, but struck out for Bastrop to procure clothing of a more stable character.

The government bought a lot of United States army clothing, consisting of pantaloons and runabouts, which were sent up to Coleman for the rangers. As it was all rather under size, we agreed to distribute it by lots, an arrangement which was productive of some laughable results.

Isaac Casner, who tipped the beam at 200, got a suit that would have been a snug fit for a man of 140. As the old fellow couldn't begin to get into them he took them on his arm and went round among the boys trying to effect an exchange. We all liked Uncle Isaac and the largest suits in the lot were brought out. He tried them one after another, but like the "contraband's" song, "they didn't go half way round," and but for the ingenuity of Mrs. Casner the old man's suit would have been a total loss. Clothes were scarce, though, so Mrs. Casner ripped open the outside seams of the pantaloons and set in stripes to extend them to the necessary dimensions, also setting a stripe down each sleeve and in the center of the jacket, with a false front to expand it over his aldermanic proportions. A stranger would have taken him for commanding officer on account of his stripes.

Wolfenberger, who would have measured six feet barefooted, got a suit of which the bottoms of the pantaloons struck him about half way to his knees, the jacket failing to connect with them by full six inches, and his arms protruding a foot beyond the end of the sleeves. He presented a ludicrous appearance as, amid shouts of laughter, he stalked up and down like an animated scarecrow, trying to negotiate a trade. Failing in that, he pieced them out with strips of blanket and was quite as comfortable as the rest of us.

The Indians were not depredating in our beat, probably because they found better game elsewhere. In the meantime Coleman had been relieved of command and Captain Andrews appointed.

Coleman was not popular with the settlers, his men were allowed too much license in the way of foraging, and, when one of his inferior officers inhumanly murdered one of the enlisted men, the settlers and the comrades of the victim preferred charges against Colonel Coleman, on which he was relieved from command and ordered to report to the war department at Columbia. While the investigation was pending, Coleman was out in a boat hunting, when the boat capsized and he was drowned.

The circumstance which led to his removal was this: There was in Coleman's company a man who had been a United States regular; some said a deserter. However that may be, he was, by virtue of his military knowledge, raised to the rank of lieutenant, upon which he proceeded to visit upon his subordinates the abuses which he may have undergone at the hands of some upstart cadet. Among the men was one poor fellow who had a weakness for intoxicants, which he would indulge whenever an opportunity offered. Having imbibed too freely, Lieutenant R. ordered him tied up to a post all night to sober off. The man was so completely under the influence as to be unable to maintain an upright position; his limbs gave way, and he sank so that the cord about his neck literally hung him. The outburst of indignation frightened R. and he skipped out, leaving Colonel Coleman to bear the odium of the inhuman deed.

One evening early in the spring of 1837 we were out on the parade, which was lighted by the silvery rays of a crescent moon, whiling away the time between supper and taps. The soft night wind regaled our nostrils with the mingled fragrance of the millions of wild flowers with which nature so lavishly adorned the hills and prairies ere the advent of the white man forced them, like their contemporaries, the Indian and the buffalo, to give place to prosy corn and cotton.

The older men were smoking and spinning yarns, the younger ones dancing, while I tortured the catgut. The festivities were brought to a sudden close by a bright flame that suddenly shot up on a high knoll overlooking the present site of Austin from the opposite side of the river. Fixing our eyes steadily on the flame, we distinctly saw dark objects passing and repassing in front of it. Our scouts had seen no sign of Indians, still, we knew no white men would so recklessly expose themselves in an Indian country, and at once decided they were Indians.

Hastily summoning Captain Andrews, we held a consultation as to the measures to be adopted for their capture. We surmised they had but just struck camp, otherwise they would have known their camp fire could be seen from the fort. The Indians, being on the other side of the river near the regular crossing, Captain Andrews suggested that we take an early start and intercept them at the ford. My plan always was, when there was a momentous job on hand, to go right at it and get it over with. So I urged that we start at once and surprise them in camp.

"Well," said the captain, an easy-going old fellow, "I hate to order the boys out after night."

"No need to order them," I replied; "just call for volunteers."

To this he assented. A call for volunteers was responded to by almost every man in camp. Lieutenant Wren offering to lead the expedition. Selecting fifteen of the best mounted men, we were soon ready to start. The moon was getting low, and having the river to cross, we made all haste to get across before it went down. With the disappearance of the moonlight clouds blew up, obscuring the stars and making it difficult to keep on our course. We had the river to guide us, however, and, having scouted the country till we were familiar with every hill and ravine, we moved slowly forward. Lieutenant Wren, Jo Weeks and myself formed the advance. Picking our way through the brush, and stumbling over rocks, we watched and listened for any sign that might indicate discovery, and, satisfying ourselves on that point, returned to bring up our comrades.

In this way we consumed the greater part of the night. Away on toward day, when we knew we must be nearing the locality of the fire we had seen the evening before, and were therefore proceeding with extreme caution, we suddenly found ourselves in the midst of a caballado, which, startled by our sudden advent among them, sprang to their feet, snorting and stamping. There were a number of mules in the drove, which at once set up a friendly braying. Fully expecting the commotion would arouse the Indians, who we knew must be in the immediate vicinity, we kept perfectly still till the horses and mules, having recovered from their fright, began to feed. We knew the animals had been stolen and, as the Indians always traveled night and day after having made a haul till sure they were beyond the reach of pursuit, we surmised they were tired when they struck camp, which accounted for their sleeping so soundly. Wren, Weeks and I then dismounted and, leaving our horses with the other boys, started out to locate the marauders.

Their fire had died out, leaving no trace to direct us in our search. I had eyes almost equal to an Indian's then, and, after carefully reconnoitering the ground, led off toward a clump of cedars. After going a hundred yards we descried several dark objects lying motionless under a spreading live oak. We were close upon them before we discovered them. There was something suspicious about them, so we crouched low and waited for some sign by which to determine their character. At length one of them turned himself and grunted. That was sufficient.

We stole back to our waiting companions and arranged the plan of attack. Securing our horses behind a clump of trees, we divided our force into parties, Wren taking one division and going up to the right under cover of a ravine, while I led the other up in front.

In making the detour Wren mistook the tree under which our game was sleeping, getting away beyond. I could hear the boys stumbling over obstructions, and momentarily expected the sleeping savages would be awakened thereby.

By this time the twittering of birds announced the approaching day; still the Indians lay wrapped in slumber, unconscious of the enemy only waiting for the signal to pour a deadly fire upon them.

I had just raised my gun to see if I could draw a bead on the Indian nearest me, when he raised himself to a sitting posture, and began to sing his matin lay, "ha ah hah."

Upon hearing the song, Wren perceived his mistake and, hastily retracing their steps, the boys made noise enough to wake the dead.

The Indian's ear caught the sound and, springing to his feet, he turned his face in the direction whence it proceeded, his back presenting such a good target Jo Weeks could not resist the temptation, and, without waiting for the word, raised his gun and fired, bringing down his game. The other Indians rose running. We fired a volley after them, but they got into a ravine, from which they fired back, one ball striking Philip Martin in the head, killing him instantly. I had stepped over Jo Weeks' Indian when we charged the camp, supposing him dead, but when we went to look for him he was gone. So we didn't get a scalp to show for our night's work; but we got all their horses and camp equipage, and, but that we had a dead comrade to carry home, would have been very well satisfied with our raid.

Poor Philip Martin was one of the best men in camp; a genial, warm-hearted son of old Erin. We carried him back and buried him with the honors of war outside the fort on the north side, beside the victim of Robel's cruelty.

CHAPTER 12

The Indians were worsted for the time being, but they played for even and won hands down. Not long after our unceremonious call upon them Lieutenant Wren, with half a dozen men to assist him, took the horses out to graze.

The government didn't furnish feed for the horses, nor to any extent for the men either. It was quite early in the morning, and, there having been no recent irruptions of the Indians in that vicinity, we had grown careless. So little apprehensive were we of a raid, that the guards were not even mounted.

The horses were feeding towards the creek, and when near the timber, half a dozen Indians suddenly dashed out blowing whistles and yelling. The horses snorted and started to run, when an Indian mounted on a quick horse rushed in ahead of them, leading off up the creek, the other Indians following, still yelling and whistling.

It was all so quickly and neatly done that the guard only fired at them without effect. A number of the horses, however, broke away and started back towards the fort, and the Indians, no doubt realizing that "a bird in the hand was worth two in the bush," didn't stop to recover them. My horse, a fine American, of which I was very proud, buying corn for him, struck straight out for the fort. I threw the gate open, and he ran in.

Felix McClusky, a wild Irishman, had just saddled his horse to go out and herd the caballado while the men on duty came in for breakfast. I hastily saddled my horse and we two started after the horses that had escaped from the Indians and were tearing madly off down towards Hornsby's station.

Old Isaac Casner, who had left the service and was then living at Hornsby's, had been up to the fort and was jogging along leisurely on his return. He had crossed the creek and gained the open prairie when he heard the clattering of hoofs coming in his rear. He turned in his saddle and took one look behind. The frightened animals pursued by McClusky and myself were bearing right down on him. We had lost our hats in the wild race, and our hair flying in the wind gave us much the appearance of Indians. Uncle Isaac, who, as previously stated, weighed about 200 pounds, laid whip to his horse, which was a good animal, and led off across the prairie to Hornsby's station, about a mile distant, the horses following in his wake and we trying to get in ahead of them. McClusky's sense of fun took in the situation. "Be Jasus," said he, "look at him run!" and the reckless creature could not refrain from giving a war whoop to help the old man along.

Hearing the racket the men at Hornsby's fort ran out, and seeing the chase, threw the gate open. Breathless from fright and exhaustion, Casner ran in, gasping, "Injuns."

Before the inmates of the fort had time to do anything we dashed past, running down into the bend, where I succeeded in getting ahead of the fleeing horses and stopping them. As soon as I got breath enough I took McClusky to task for yelling at poor Casner. With ready Irish wit he promptly explained: "Be Jasus, I was thryin' to stop him." We drove the horses back to the fort, pretty well tired out ourselves and the horses so badly winded that we were obliged to let them rest till the next morning before we could pursue the Indians.

The crafty marauders had laid their plans well, having marked out the trail they proposed taking by bits of white rags, which they didn't stop to remove. We followed them three days and never found where they had stopped long enough to make a fire.

We came across the remains of a horse from which they had cut portions of the flesh, which they must have eaten raw as they ran.

On the third day we got out on the head of the San Gabriel, where there were a great many mustangs, and their tracks having obliterated the Indians' trail, we were forced to abandon the pursuit, returning home empty-handed.

The rascals were doubtless gratified to find some of the very same animals among their haul that we took from them a short time before.

President Houston suspended Lieutenant Wren, but we all liked him and knew that no power on earth could have held those terror stricken animals after the Indians made their dash. So we unanimously petitioned the president to reinstate him, a petition which was granted. After that, however, we didn't go out on foot to herd the horses, but just the same the Indians again stampeded the caballado and got away with a portion of it.

There was no braver or better man in the service than Lieutenant Nicholas Wren. I know not whence he came nor whither he went, but had I been sent on a perilous mission I know of no man I would have chosen before him to bear me company. When his term expired he left, and I never knew where he went.

The Indians, apparently satisfied with their reprisal, gave us a respite and we had an easy time of it at the fort, hunting being now our principal occupation. I was out alone in the river bottom one day riding along a narrow trail through the thick underbrush, when I heard my dog, which had run ahead of me, baying something out in the brush. As it was impossible to ride through the tangle I dismounted, and, tying my pony, started to see what kind of game the dog had flushed. I had proceeded but a few steps when I hear a snort and then a crash of brush coming in my direction, so near that there was no time to untie my horse and mount; the brush was so thick there was no chance to get out of the trail, but there was fortunately a fallen tree across the path, which had lodged so as to rise some four feet above the ground. Catching a limb, I hastily swung myself upon the tree just as an old buffalo bull rushed into view, closely pursued by the dog. On seeing me the dog redoubled his attack, bringing the bull to bay right under my perch, the bull snorting and fending him off, sometimes striking the tree in his angry lunges, almost jarring me off. The tree was a mere sapling and afforded a very insecure footing, but I clung to another sapling with one hand and to my rifle with the other. Watching my opportunity, I put the muzzle of my gun right over his loin and fired, breaking him down, after which I finished him at my leisure. There are a good many things I would rather face than an angry buffalo bull.

Reuben Hornsby and Jacob Harrell were out on the prairie together, and seeing a band of buffalo, concluded to replenish their stock of meat. They shot a buffalo, which, not being immediately disabled, made toward them. There was a small mesquite tree near, the only tree around there. Hornsby was quite agile in spite of his years and 180 pounds weight. He sprang for the tree, which bent under his weight.

"Climb, Harrell, climb!" he shouted. Jake was busy loading his gun. Just before the wounded animal reached them it fell, and Jake gave it another shot before it could rise.

"How did you expect me to climb, Hornsby, when the only tree near was bending with you?" "O, by guinie, that was your own lookout," Hornsby replied. The saying became proverbial.

Jake Harrell used to tell a story about some negroes who were talking about buffalo.

"What you do Pomp, if buffalo git arter you?" asked one.

"I'd climb," said Pomp.

"Ah, boy," said an old blind sage, "you 'pend on dat, you pend on broken stick; buffalo climb, too."

Another time a squad of us were out scouting on the head of Gilleland's creek. The country was mostly open, but here and there were motts of chaparral and prickly pears, forming a veritable stronghold for any animal that chose to avail himself of it. In passing one of these motts we saw a large panther run into it by a narrow pathway. We immediately circled his lair, and whenever a fellow caught sight of the game he blazed away, regardless of those on the further side.

One or more shots taking effect, the panther assumed the offensive. We had a green fellow along, Butler by name. Not being able to handle a rifle, we armed him with a musket. Anxious to distinguish himself he dismounted and started into the jungle on foot to "beard the lion in his den."

Just then the enraged beast came into view from my position, making straight for Butler, its hair turned the wrong way, its tail erect, and eyes like balls of fire.

"Look out, Butler, he's coming!" I shouted. Just then Butler caught sight of the panther.

"The Jesus!" he cried, "look at his eyes!" And dropping his musket he crashed through the brush and prickly pears, regaining the open just as the infuriated animal made a spring for him. Fortunately the panther was so crippled that his spring was rendered ineffectual, and before he could collect himself for another I shot him dead. It took Butler some time to get rid of the cactus needles, and he never got rid of the joke while he remained in the service.

When Coleman went up to build the fort he recruited a company from the men who were mustered out at Columbia. Generally speaking they were as little fitted for the position as men jobbing around cities usually are. Colonel Coleman himself was a lawyer, commanded a company at the battle of Concepcion, and was a staff officer to General Houston in the brief but glorious campaign of '36.

Many of his company were not mounted—in fact, didn't know how to ride, and so unskilled in the use of fire arms that the only possible way in which they could have killed an Indian would have been a la Fitzsimmons; their fists were big enough and there was "beef" enough behind them.

On one occasion a couple of men came in from the fort on Little river to get ammunition. Captain Andrews, fearful of an attack being made on them, sent an escort back with them, most of the men detailed being these raw recruits, who were on foot. When we reached the San Gabriel without having seen any signs of Indians, we dispensed with the "infantry," myself and one other man going out to Little river and returning the next day, leaving the boys to take care of themselves during our absence.

Game, which was the principal source of food supply, was so abundant that we never thought of taking anything along but salt when we went out on duty. So these bold soldier boys camped without grub, and when we returned next day were half famished, with droves of buffalo and deer all around them. Their stock of ammunition was nearly exhausted and they hadn't even drawn blood. Remembering my own failure in that line when I first came to the country, and therefore heartily sympathizing with them, I at once started out to relieve their distress, bidding them all remain in camp, but their gnawing hunger would not admit of their quietly biding the time and they must perforce accompany me. Several times I was in the act of shooting when "bang" went a musket and away went the buffalo. Becoming exasperated, I at length turned on the crowd and swore roundly that if they didn't immediately return to camp I would, and they might starve.

This gentle admonition had the desired effect and, relieved of their presence, I succeeded in killing a nice fat cow, packing my horse with the meat and walking back to camp.

It was about sundown when I got in, and the ravenous crew couldn't wait for the meat to cook; they snatched it off the fire before it got warm through, bolting it like hungry dogs; I left them eating when I went to sleep, and there was scarcely enough left for our breakfast next morning. I fully expected they would be sick from the effects of the gorging, but perhaps the long tramp back to the fort saved them. A conspicuous member of the company was Cy Gleason. His father being a well-to-do merchant in New York, Cy had been accustomed to living on the fat of the land, and being a good eater, was consequently a good forager, ranging the country over in search of chickens, eggs, etc. I was passing his mess one day when he called to me to "come in and eat something."

"Why, Cy, I'm not hungry," I replied.

"Well, goll darn it all, eat for fear you do get hungry."

When he first went into the ranging service he had a fine horse, but he had probably never had a horse before—certainly never had the care of one, for he seemed totally oblivious to the fact that there was a limit to the endurance of a horse. He chased every coyote and jack rabbit he came upon, never giving his horse a grain of corn and not even changing his stake pin once a week. The horse soon began to show the effect of such treatment. He came to me one day and in his peculiar drawl said:

"See here, Cap, I wish you'd come and look at my horse; I gol, there's somethin' the matter with him; he grows poorer."

I laughed outright. I told him it didn't need a doctor to diagnose the case, and gave him a prescription that was warranted to cure. Not satisfied that I had proved the trouble, he offered to trade horses with me, and having great faith in my prescription, I traded. Under my regime the horse soon began to recuperate and I was quite proud of him. By and by, however, he developed unmistakable signs of fistula, a disease which was beyond my skill. Some one told me that old Natty Moore cured fistula, so I got leave of absence and rode out to his place. The old man said oh, yes, he had cured many cases. I unsaddled the horse and the old man took up an old, rusty hatchet, and, taking the bridle, started to lead him away, bidding me remain. After a time he returned without the hatchet.

"Now," said he, "don't do anything to it; just let it alone and it will go away."

I was curious to know what he had done to it.

"Well," said he, after a moment's consideration, "I'll tell you if you will keep it to yourself. Just take a horse that has fistula to where two roads cross, stand his fore feet right in the center of the cross, and with some old, rusty hatchet or knife mark three times lengthwise and three times crosswise of the afflicted part and throw the instrument behind you without looking round, and the fistula will go away."

I was completely nonplussed, not to say mad, to think I had gone all the way out there on that fool's errand, but the old gentleman was so kind and friendly and evidently believed so implicitly in his remedy that I concealed my chagrin and offered to pay him.

"Oh, no," said he, "that would break the charm." Well, I concluded I would wait a few days and see how the charm worked, but I saw that the fistula was growing, so I applied to Reuben Hornsby and he gave me a practical prescription, which proved so effective that I will repeat the formula for the benefit of any one who may be in need of it.

Take the root of the poke weed and boil it till it becomes soft, then mash it into a pulp and apply it hot, also bathing the afflicted part with the water.

The next time I saw Uncle Natty he inquired how my horse was getting on. "Finely," I told him. "O, I never knew it to fail," said he, gratified at the success of his conjuring. I never did tell him how I cured that horse, and he was wont to cite that as an instance of his skill. Some time after one of his sons came to me and asked how I cured the horse, as he had one that he wished to treat.

"Why," said I, "didn't your father cure it?"

"O, h——l, no; he can't cure it; now, I want to know how to cure mine."

I then told him, stipulating that he shouldn't tell his father, and he kept his word.

Natty Moore and his sons formed a strong link in the cordon of frontiersmen, which, after all, was the most effective barrier to the incursions of the hostiles. Revered by all who knew them, the old man and his worthy helpmate lived to see their posterity in the fourth generation settled comfortably in the prairie which bears his name.

Meanwhile the Comanches seemed to have withdrawn to their stronghold and what councils were there being held can only be conjectured from what subsequently transpired.

Early in the summer of 1837 a band of Comanches, consisting of two chiefs—Quinaseico (eagle) and Puestia—and six warriors, came to the fort waving a white flag. They had not yet learned to speak English, but all Texas Indians understood more or less Spanish. I, being the most expert in the use of the latter language, went out, though not alone by several, to ascertain their business.

They stated that their tribe was desirous of entering into a treaty with the whites, and to that end requested that a commissioner be sent out to their camp to talk the matter over with the head men. I thereupon conducted them into the fort, where they laid their request before Captain Andrews.

The white people, weary of the perpetual warfare which compelled them to live in forts and make a subsistence as best they might, hailed the proposition for a treaty with delight, and would have been willing to purchase even a cessation of hostilities at almost any price; but, the Indians were so treacherous that the office of commissioner was not one to be coveted.

For reasons above stated, the chiefs selected me to undertake the business, pledging themselves that no harm should befall me. Knowing that there is a degree of honor even among Indians touching those who voluntarily become their guests, I yielded to the stress of circumstances and agreed to accompany them back to their camp, only about thirty miles distant, on Brushy creek.

One man was really safer than several, as the Indians would naturally have been suspicious of conversation they could not understand, and if treachery were intended numbers would not avail against it.

I bade adieu to my comrades, many of whom thought it would be the last time they would see me, and, putting my life into hands red with the blood of my race, proceeded to the camp where old Muguara, the head chief, received me with every mark of friendship, conducting me to his lodge, where I was

[123]

made the recipient of every attention known to their code of hospitality. The camp was not nearly so large as I had expected, there being only about fifty lodges and not over one hundred warriors. There must have been more of the tribe somewhere, as they could, on occasion, muster a much larger force. They were exceedingly chary of information regarding their strength, however. There were six prisoners in camp: one white woman and two white boys, and one Mexican woman and two Mexican boys. The Mexican woman was the only one of the lot that evinced any desire to return to her people. She was not permitted to talk to me in private, and policy prevented her giving vent to her feelings in the presence of her captors. After I had been some time among them, they relaxed their espionage somewhat, and she managed to tell me that she was very homesick, having been captured after she was grown. The poor woman cried bitterly over her situation, she having been appropriated by one of the bucks. The white woman said she was very small when taken, and remembered nothing of the circumstances. She had an Indian husband and several children.

None of the boys remembered anything of their homes. One of the white boys, a youth of eighteen or thereabouts, I recognized as a prisoner we had twice recaptured, once at Gonzales and again at Victoria. Each time he stayed a few days, apparently quite satisfied with his surroundings, but, when he got a good chance, decamped, taking several of the best horses along.

The other white child was a bright little fellow, five or six years old. Loath to leave him to grow up a savage, I tried to buy him, offering a fine horse in exchange, but the squaw who had adopted him gathered him close to her bosom with every show of affection. "No," said she, "he is mine; my own child." That was plainly a falsehood, but the love she manifested toward the hapless boy was some palliation therefor.

The Indians would give no information about any of their captives except one little Waco, which Quinaseico had adopted, and I should not have known he was a Waco but that the old chief himself told me. Observing that the other members of the family were all grown up, I asked the old man if that little boy was his child.

"Yes," said he, taking the child in his arms, "mine now." He then told me that during the war between the Wacos and Comanches, the latter surprised an encampment of the enemy and killed all the occupants except that one little child. Said he:

"After the fight was over I went into a lodge and found this boy, about two years old, sitting beside its dead mother crying; and my heart was sorry for him, and I took him up in my arms and brought him home to my lodge and my wife took him to her bosom, and fed him, and he is mine now." And the little orphan Waco, as well as the little white boy, was petted by the whole tribe.

"Smithwick" being too much of a tongue twister for the average Comanche, old Muguara called the chiefs together in council, when it was decided to bestow upon me the name of an illustrious chief, who had previously departed for the happy hunting ground.

Old Muguara then communicated the decision to me and in a voice that might have been heard a mile proclaimed to all the camp that the white brother's name was henceforth "Juaqua." The name was taken up and repeated by every separate member of the tribe, the men pronouncing it with loud jocularity, the women shyly lisping it half under breath, and the children, with an expression that reminded me of nothing in the world so much as the little bark or squeak of the prairie dog as he disappears into his burrow at the approach of an enemy.

"Juaqua!" The name clung to me years after. I use the Spanish alphabet in spelling these Indian names, it seeming better adapted to the soft sound of the Comanche tongue. I tried to get some knowledge of the latter language, succeeding fairly well with the nouns and adjectives, but when it came to the conjugation of the Comanche verb I gave it up.

The Indians were very skeptical about the utility of writing, but when they told me the names of different objects and saw me write them down and afterwards refer to them, giving the names correctly, they concluded it was "buena."

CHAPTER 13

I have often regretted that I did not preserve the notes I made of the Comanche tongue, very little of which I now recall. I do not think they followed the rule adopted by the northern tribes in their nomenclature, few of their names seeming to have English equivalents. Of the six chiefs, Mugua-ra, Quin-a-se-i-co, Pote-se-na-qua-hip, Ca-ta-ni-a-pa, Pa-ha-u-co and E-sa-nap, only the second and third appeared interpretable—Quin-a-se-i-co (eagle) and Pote-se-na-qua-hip (buffalo hump). My adopted name, Juaqua or Wah-qua, had no special significance that I knew of. One of the Spanish boys who, though having lost all other traces of his identity, still remembered that his name was Juan, was called by the Indians Un-ar-o-caddy, but whether it was considered the Indian equivalent of John or merely like Juaqua, the name by which he was adopted into the tribe, I could not determine. I presume the squaws had names suggestive or otherwise, but I failed to catch them. About the only common nouns that I remember were tuhaya (horse), ait (bow), pock (arrow), wood-ah (bear) and quasack (a coat or covering for the body). The last word I am inclined to think an adaptation from the Spanish.

The study of the Indian tongue was fraught with many difficulties. Many of their nouns bore so strong a resemblance to the Spanish as to suggest a common origin. This, however, may have been but a natural sequence to the long intercourse between the Mexicans and Indians, the latter having adapted the Spanish to their peculiar vocalization. But even on this hypothesis it was sometimes difficult to account for the remarkable resemblance. One striking example was found in the Indian word bee-sone (buffalo), which is the Spanish pronunciation of bison; the Mexicans, however, using the word "cibola" in speaking of the American buffalo. There were also many words used in common by Mexicans and Indians, which, while certainly not Spanish, were possibly relics of the Aztec tongue; "wah-ho-lo-te" (turkey) for instance, the Spanish for which is "pavo." "Tuhuya" and "woodah" were presumably pure Indian, being totally unlike anything in any civilized language. Their numerical system, perhaps, offered the most promising field for philological research. My achievements in that line were limited to the first ten numbers, the last four of which are all I remember: mammiwassett, seven; semimami-wassett, eight; seminot, nine, and samot, ten.

I could never discover anything analogous to written language; the nearest approach to it being diagrams, or more properly maps, which they sometimes marked out on the ground to convey an idea of locality. They were peculiarly expert in sign language, however. Some idea of drawing they had acquired, their work at times evincing a remarkable degree of skill. Any smooth surface—a board, a flat stone, or smooth-bark tree, served for canvas, while charcoal furnished pencils. Colored chalks were sometimes substituted; but, whatever the material used, the subject was always the same—Indians chasing buffalo. When on a scout, out to the old Tumlinson block house, we found the walls covered with these Indian drawings; every loose board being similarly ornamented. The block house was burned by the Indians shortly after. Whether there may have been some special significance attached to the drawings, or whether they were but the expression of a vague longing after the ideal, I could not even conjecture.

Nor did they seem to possess any method of computing time; and though there were some very ancient looking people in the tribe, I could form no idea of their age.

I have known several deaf mutes among the Indians, but never a blind one. It is quite likely, however, that if a babe were born blind it would be put out of the way. And, really, aside from deafness, I never knew of any natural physical defect in an Indian. Nor were there any maimed or lamed in battle, though, like warriors of all times, they were very proud of battle scars, particularly those made by bullets, bringing them out more conspicuously by tattooing lines around them.

The utmost harmony prevailed among the various divisions of the polygamous families. The oldest wife seemed to be the mistress of the harem. There was one large central lodge used in common by all the families, each squaw having a smaller one for herself and children, the latter never numerous.

The family meals, consisting of meat alone, generally roasted on sticks, were all served together on the flesh side of a dried skin, each fellow helping himself. Their drinking vessels were made of buffalo horns and terrapin shells, and some had even become possessed of a tin cup.

The vessels for carrying water were made of deer skins "cased"—stripped off whole—the legs and necks tied up tightly with sinews. Sometimes the smaller stomach pouch of a buffalo was used.

Not wishing to give the least occasion for offense, I ate with them, but I laid in a supply of coffee before I went out, which I boiled myself, drinking it from the cup in which it was prepared. In order to be sociable, I offered old Chief Muguara some coffee, for which he soon contracted quite a liking, thus cutting my supply short.

The Indian mode of cooking meat—roasting it on sticks—was excellent, but they had become so far civilized as to possess a pot in which, perhaps out of deference to me, they sometimes boiled their meat; but I much preferred the roasted, that seeming a little less filthy.

So far as my observation went, the Texas Indians were unlike those of any other section of the country, subsisting entirely on meat. The northern tribes raised corn, beans and several kinds of vegetables. Those of Arizona and New Mexico raised wheat and beans, and the California Indians in their primitive state gathered vast quantities of acorns, pine nuts, and grass nuts, which constituted their staple food.

Perhaps, though, it was owing to the unfailing supply of game that the Comanche eschewed vegetable food, which required more labor than did the meat. Another peculiarity of the Comanche was his abstinence from whisky, few of them even venturing to taste it; old Muguara alone showing signs of dawning civilization by occasionally indulging.

On one of our several visits into Bastrop, when we were about starting on our return, he said to me:

"Juaqua, hadn't we better get a bottle of fool's water? We might meet hostile Indians on the road and it would make us brave."

Chief Muguara was also bald-headed, the only instance of the kind I ever knew; that may also have been attributable to his over-civilization.

There were some of the dishes set before me that my stomach absolutely declined to do honor to; for instance the curdled milk taken from the stomachs of suckling fawns and buffalo calves, which they esteemed a rare delicacy.

They were also very fond of tripe, which they broiled without even taking the trouble to wash it, merely dragging it over the grass to wipe off the thickest of the filth.

They had some kind of religious belief which seemed akin to sun worship. Judging from outward manifestations there was some power which it was

necessary to propitiate by offerings. When out on a hunt as soon as game was killed they struck fire and roasted meat, and always before eating a bite the chief would cut off a morsel and bury it; the first fruit of the chase, I suppose.

A similar ceremony was observed when the chief lit his pipe; the first puff of smoke was blown toward the sun and the second to the earth after the manner of incense offering; the substance used for the purpose being a mixture of tobacco and dried sumach leaves. The pipes were made of soft stone generally, though sometimes hard wood was substituted. They were not seemingly anxious to make proselytes to their religion, therefore were reticent about their tenets, all I gathered concerning which being from observation. They evidently believed in a hereafter, but whether the conditions thereof depended on their conduct in this life was uncertain. One thing I know, that though they would fight desperately to rescue the body of a fallen comrade so long as his scalp was intact, the moment he lost it he was abandoned; they would not touch the body, even to bury it. Whether, like the Chinamen, the cue was considered a necessary passport to the other world, or perhaps only because they thought that the enemy having secured the coveted scalp there was no use in hiding the body in the ground, remains a mystery to me. Another point on which they seemed to be superstitious was in never touching the heart of an animal. They would strip off every particle of flesh, leaving the skeleton entire and the heart untouched inside.

Although it was customary for the first fellow who woke in the morning to announce the fact in song, the act seemed rather a spontaneous outpouring akin to that of the feathered songsters than a religious rite; the song itself resembling the lay of the birds in that it was wordless save for the syllables, ha ah ha, which furnished the vehicle on which the carol rode forth to the world; the performance ending in a keen yell.

Theories and conjectures are not evidence. I therefore spare the reader mine, simply stating facts, from which all are at liberty to draw conclusions. Perhaps some of the old Comanches in the Indian territory might be prevailed on to throw some light on the subject.

But taking them all around they were the most peaceable community I ever lived in. Their criminal laws were as inexorable as those of the Medes and Persians, and the code was so simply worded there was no excuse for ignorance. It was simply the old Mosaic law, "an eye for an eye and a tooth for a tooth." "Whoso sheddeth a man's blood, by man shall his blood be shed."

In cases of dispute, a council of the old men decided it, and from their decision there was no appeal. And when one died, all his belongings were destroyed, precluding all possibility of a family quarrel over the estate.

During the whole period of my sojourn among the tribe—three months—I did not hear a single wrangle among the adult members. The youngsters had an occasional scrimmage, which they were allowed to fight out to the amusement of the onlookers.

Notwithstanding their inhuman treatment of the helpless prisoners that fell into their hands, I never saw a woman or child abused. The women, as in all savage tribes, were abject slaves, but their inferiority was their protection from the chastisement which "civilized" husbands sometimes visit on their wives.

An Indian brave would have felt it a burning disgrace to strike a woman. I don't think they ever resorted to corporal punishment within the tribe. Like the ancient Jews, however, tribal law didn't apply to "the stranger without the gates," nor within, either, when the stranger was a captive.

There was a distinct line dividing the provinces of men and women, the mother having complete control of the children.

When an Indian girl arrived at a marriageable age, it was the mother who arranged the match; the suitor generally winning her favor by gifts, or barter of skins, and sometimes horses, if the girl was a belle.

The women, of course, performed all the labor, aside from killing and bringing in the game; stripping the skins from the animals, dressing and ornamenting them with beads or paint, a process which interested me very much. The skins were first staked down to the ground, flesh side up. With a sharp bone the squaw then scraped off every particle of flesh; next the scraped surface was spread with lime to absorb the grease, after which the surface was spread with the brains of the animal, rubbing it in and working it over till the skin became soft and pliable, the process requiring days and days of hard work.

Then with paint, which they manufactured from colored chalks, and brushes made of tufts of hair, the artist, with the earth for an easel, beginning in the center, drew symbolic designs, the most conspicuous of which was the sun, executed with a skill truly remarkable.

A multitude of different colored rays commingling in a common center and radiating out in finely drawn lines, the spaces made by the divergence again and again filled in, taking as much time as a work by the old masters. Time was no object, life having nothing to offer beyond the gratification of this single vanity.

These painted robes were worn over the shoulders like shawls, the fur side underneath.

The old people of both sexes were treated with deference, another sign of their benighted state. Little notice was taken of the female children by either parent, all their pride and affection being centered on the embryo warriors, fitting them out with bows and lances, with which they fought imaginary foes and "mimic frays," much after the fashion of the old school days commemorated in the lines—

> "O were you ne'er a school boy,
> And did you never train;
> And feel that swelling of the heart
> You ne'er can feel again?"

The little Indian girls, brought up in the way they should go, played at dressing skins, setting up lodges, etc. Yes, and they played with dolls, too. I was never allowed to inspect those Indian doll babies, so I can't tell how they were made; but the little Indian maids bound them on pieces of bark, setting them up against trees, swinging them in hammocks or carrying them on their backs just as their mothers had done with them.

The small boys went entirely nude, but the girls always wore some covering. When not hunting, the bucks whiled away the time in telling marvelous stories of the fight and chase—the former for my benefit, I presume—running races, sometimes on horseback, sometimes on foot. I sometimes ran with them, and in a 50-yard dash could beat most of them, that distance only serving to limber them up. They always insisted on running at least a quarter of a mile, in which case they could have distanced me, so I declined to run over my limit.

They were inveterate gamblers and would sit out in the broiling sun for half a day with the perspiration streaming down their faces intent on a game, the merits of which I failed to penetrate, though I watched them by the hour. The game, which seemed a combination of dice throwing, five corns, marbles and all other games pretty much, was played on the flesh side of a buffalo robe, marked into sections with chalk lines. The implements with which it was played were two smooth sticks, about four inches long, flat on one side and oval on the other, an inch or so in width on the flat side. These they placed face to face, and, holding them between the thumb and forefinger, struck them endwise on a flat stone in the center of the chalk lines, at the same time releasing them, when the rebound threw them in various directions, the points scored depending on the position in which they fell, both as to the sticks and the marks on the robe. They would bet their last deerskin on the game, and of course some one had to lose; still, I never knew of anything even approaching to a quarrel over the outcome.

Occasionally they had visitors from other tribes with whom they swapped lies, sometimes conversing entirely by signs, not seeming to understand each other's language at all, though it all sounded the same to me.

Among other things they told how on one occasion they had been down to Gonzales and collected a fine drove of horses and mules—they didn't hint that the animals were stolen—with which they were returning to their camp, when they were surprised by cowardly white men who stole upon them while they slept and chased them into the cedarbrake, wounding three of their warriors, one of whom died before they got home—a piece of information gratifying to me, as we didn't know we killed any of them—capturing all their horses and camp equipage. I didn't chirp about my part of the raid.

I often accompanied the bucks on their hunts, and rarely saw an animal killed in wanton sport, old buffalo bulls then being the victims. Having killed what they wanted for meat, they sometimes singled out an old bull, shooting arrows into his hump until he became irritated to the fighting pitch; then, as he charged one of his tormentors, another would run up beside him and jerk an arrow from its position in his hump. The pain thus produced would impel the now thoroughly angered brute to turn on his daring foe, and I have seen them, clumsy as they look, wheel so quickly that it would be all the Indian's pony could do to get out of the way of his horns; but then another Indian would create a diversion by running up and snatching an arrow. And so they kept it up till the bull was too much fatigued to make the sport interesting; when they would despatch him to recover their arrows. This sport was doubtless an adaptation from the Spanish bull fight.

Another one of their sports, though in this case combined with business, was the lassoing of turkeys, deer, mustangs, and buffalo calves.

When a drove of turkeys ranged out on the prairie in pursuit of grasshoppers, the Indian would follow at a distance until the birds were a mile or more from timber; then he would dash upon them, causing them to rise. Putting spurs to his horse he would then keep right under the flock, keeping them on the wing until they fell to the ground from exhaustion, when he ran among them and lassoed all he wanted.

When he wanted venison the Indian secreted himself near a watering place till the deer came in to drink, after which they become stupid and any good mustang could run upon them with ease. The same tactics were pursued in the capture of mustangs, which often fed away ten or twelve miles from water, remaining until thirsty, when they would start on a run, keeping it up till water was reached, by which time they were tired and thirsty, imbibing such quantities of water as to render them incapable of exertion, thus falling easy prey to the Indian's lasso. If veal was his desire, the Indian would start a band of buffalo, crowding them so closely that the calves could not keep up, and, falling behind, were cut off and lassoed.

One of the Indian's principal grievances against the white men was the wholesale slaughter of the buffalo, which the Indians claimed were their cattle, placed there for them by the Great Spirit. White men would run upon a band of buffalo and shoot them down in wanton sport, sometimes not even taking the hides, though they were a marketable commodity.

Some years later Michael Ziller, in Austin, contracted with Captain Merrill to furnish him a flatboat load of buffalo skins. Merrill came to me to fix his gun. This contract called for a boatload regardless of number, and his aim, therefore, was to secure as many bulls as possible, they being so much larger than the cows, and it was a sheer waste of time and ammunition to shoot at them with an ordinary rifle. So he bought the largest bore rifle he could find, and, not finding it effective, wanted it bored out till twenty of its bullets would weigh a pound. I bored it out and fixed him with a splendid gun, with which he was well satisfied till some one told him that old Bobby Mitchell had one that carried ten balls to the pound. Determined to have the biggest gun in the country, he brought it back and wanted it enlarged to the capacity of eight balls to the pound. I bored it anew, the tremendous charge causing a rebound that almost dislocated his shoulder. Nothing daunted, he padded the butt and created consternation among the buffalo with his artillery. He hired two men to take care of the hides and shot down hundreds of the animals, leaving the bodies for the wolves; but the Indians came upon them over on Little river and took revenge on them, just as white men would have done had they caught Indians killing their stock. Two of the men, Dr. Kinney and ————. Castleberry, were killed, and Merrill narrowly escaped by having a good horse.

He filled his contract, however, and Ziller started the boat down the Colorado, but at Rabb's shoals, just above LaGrange, it was swamped, and the cargo, which had directly cost two men their lives and goodness knows how many indirectly, was a total loss.

CHAPTER 14

I had many long, earnest talks with those old Comanche chiefs, and I could not but admit the justice of their contention.

The country they considered theirs by the right of inheritance; the game had been placed there for their food. In the true poetry of the simple child of the forest old Muguara said:

"We have set up our lodges in these groves and swung our children from these boughs from time immemorial. When game beats away from us we pull down our lodges and move away, leaving no trace to frighten it, and in a little while it comes back. But the white man comes and cuts down the trees, building houses and fences, and the buffalos get frightened and leave and never come back, and the Indians are left to starve, or, if we follow the game, we trespass on the hunting ground of other tribes and war ensues."

I suggested allotting them land and furnishing them with means to cultivate it like white men.

"No," said he emphatically, "the Indians were not made to work. If they build houses and try to live like white men they will all die. If the white men would draw a line defining their claims and keep on their side of it the red men would not molest them."

They had learned the import of surveying and never lost an opportunity of manifesting their hostility toward it. While I was in their camp they stole upon a party of surveyors at Brushy creek and ran off their horses. The Comanches disclaimed the theft, alleging that it was done by some other tribe.

And just here I will speak of another delusion of the Indians which I found it hard to dispel. They thought the white people were divided into tribes, those of one section constituting a tribe, and could not understand why hostility toward the whites in one section necessarily implied hostility toward all, nor why a treaty made with the people of the Colorado, for instance, should extend to the whole country.

Before the advent of the white man the Indians held full sway. They drove out the Spanish missionaries who attempted to take possession of the country as they had done in Mexico and California, and inspired the Mexicans with such a holy horror of them that they (the Indians) went into the Mexican towns and helped themselves to whatever they wanted, no one daring to oppose them. They tried that game on the Americans, and to their dismay found it would not work. Then, too, the northern Indians came among them, telling how they had been despoiled of their homes and hunting grounds by the pale face, and warning the Texas Indians that it would be the same in their case.

They were becoming uneasy and wanted some kind of an agreement by which their hunting grounds would be secured to them. I really felt mean and almost ashamed of belonging to the superior race when listening to the recital of the wrongs the redmen had suffered at the hands of my people. Nevertheless, when they made hostile incursions into the settlements I joined in the pursuit and hunted them as mercilessly as any one.

That the Comanches were brave, no one who had occasion to test their courage will deny. I never knew a warrior to submit to capture; they fought to the death. On two different occasions, noted elsewhere, I saw a wounded buck lie flat on his back and fight till dead. And in spite of all that has been told of their treacherous nature, I have good reason for asserting their claim to some noble traits of fidelity.

During my sojourn a band of Wacos one day came to the camp. They had been on a horse stealing expedition to the white settlements, some of the braves thereby being precipitated into the happy hunting ground, a sin which demanded blood atonement.

Upon learning of the presence of a white man in the Comanche camp they came in all the hideousness of war paint to demand him for a sacrifice. I could not understand the mongrel jargon in which they carried on their conference, but from the few words of Spanish I caught, I knew it concerned me, and judging from the vindictive looks they cast upon me, I surmised it boded no good to me, so calling one of the Spanish boys to me I made him interpret the conversation. The Comanches and Wacos were for the time being allies and I can assure you that I felt as if my chances for life hung on a slender thread, and I made up my mind then and there that if the Comanches yielded to the demand of the Wacos I would fight to the death; I would not be taken alive to be slowly tortured to death by the merciless fiends.

But old Muguara stood up for me like a man and brother. Drawing his naturally tall form up till he literally towered above the Waco chief, he replied in tones of thunder:

"No! This man is our friend, and you must walk over my dead body to reach him! Hurt but one hair of his head, and not one of you shall get away to tell the tale!"

His warriors gathered around him, bow and lance in hand, and it looked for a time as if there would be a pitched battle over the possession of my carcass—for such it would have been e'er it fell into the Waco's hands—but the Comanches were too strong and the baffled Wacos finally withdrew muttering vengeance against the paleface. I breathed free again, but I had no assurance that my wily foes would not attempt to accomplish by stealth that which they had failed to do by force.

Old Muguara, however, took every precaution to guard against such an outrage, giving me certain signs by which to distinguish friend from foe, warning me to keep close with the Indians when out hunting and when I visited the settlements, which I had occasion to do several times during my sojourn with him, he sent a strong body guard with me; the only times I was ever so honored.

Assuming that I would remain with them indefinitely, the Indians instructed me in various signs which I afterward treacherously turned to account. Old Muguara, the chief medicine man of the tribe, exhibited the contents of his medicine pouch, among other things a yellow substance resembling ochre, which he assured me was possessed of a power to turn aside any missile which might be directed against a body on which it had been rubbed.

I wanted very much to try my hand at breaking the charm, but felt constrained to treat his assertion with respect. I failed to learn where the substance was procured, but it must have been rather scarce, as only the chiefs availed themselves of its protective agency, and they must either have exhausted the supply or neglected to anoint themselves with it before going into the council house at San Antonio some years later, as not one of them came out alive.

I had several times conducted parties of Comanches into Bastrop, which was then the outside town, where the citizens, anxious to conciliate them, made them many presents, both useful and ornamental. On one memorable occasion Mother Muguara—the old chief and his head wife always called me "son"—accompanied us. I escorted her into Palmer & Kinney's store and was assisting her in bartering her buffalo robes and buckskins for calico and tobacco, when in came a couple of young ladies of my acquaintance. Pleased to meet them, epecially one of them, I deserted Mother Muguara and went over to the majority. The old woman eyed the "paleface squaws" critically, and said in Spanish:

"Wahqua, are both these your wives?"

Amused at the perfect sincerity of the question, I answered, laughingly, "No."

"Then," persisted she, "which one is?"

I assured her that neither of them sustained that relation to me.

"Och," shaking her finger in my face, "you lie."

At this, I laughed so heartily that my friends were devoured with curiosity to know what was being said of them, surmising that the conversation related to themselves. Not being selfishly inclined I shared the joke with them. Fortunately Dame Muguara was not versed in the language of the female blush, otherwise I fear the glow that suffused the face of one of our fair auditors would have hopelessly compromised my character for veracity in her estimation. Had the astute dame interrogated me on the subject later I would have proudly vindicated myself from her imputation.

At length, after many long talks with the wise men of the tribe, I induced five of the chiefs to go with me down to Houston, then the seat of the government, Palmer accompanying us to get his pay for goods advanced to the Indians.

On our way down we crossed the Brazos river at the site of old San Felipe de Austin. I left my curse on the town when its ayuntamiento banished me, and it was therefore with grim satisfaction that I contemplated the heaps of ashes that marked the historic spot; a few isolated cabins only having escaped the torch applied by Mosely Baker to prevent its stores falling into the hands of the Mexicans in '36. Its illustrious founder, who might have instilled the phoenix spirit into the ashes, himself had returned to dust. Later I met the man who was the leader in the movement against me. Said he:

"I was the best friend you had; it I hadn't got you away from there some of those fellows would have killed you."

Perhaps he was right.

President Houston, having spent many years among the Cherokees, was fully alive to the situation, sympathizing with the native races, as I had also learned to do, for the wrongs that had been done them from the time Columbus, totally ignoring their inherent rights, took possession of the western hemisphere in the name of Spain, and knowing that he was powerless to prevent it, that in spite of treaties, the conflict must go on till the Indian was exterminated or forced into exile. When I explained the Indians' desire for a definite line of division between them and the whites, the president sadly shook his head. Said he:

"If I could build a wall from the Red river to the Rio Grande, so high that no Indian could scale it, the white people would go crazy trying to devise means to get beyond it." And I knew that he was correct.

We neglected no opportunity to impress our guests with the prowess of the pale face, showing them through our armory and ostentatiously exhibiting our cannon. There was a steamboat lying at the wharf in which the savages were greatly interested, it being the first one they had ever seen. We conducted them on board and were showing them over it when the whistle blew, and, thinking there was some trick being played on them, they scuttled for shore. I explained the significance of the whistle, thus reassuring them.

President Houston told me to tell them we had hundreds of steamboats and Americans could make them to run on land just as easily as on water, a statement which the Indians accepted with a large pinch of salt.

We finally fixed up a treaty, the provisions of which I do not remember, nor is it essential since they were never complied with by either party. One article of the treaty stipulated that a trading post should be established on Brushy at the site of the old Tumlinson block house, where the Indians could come and get supplies. They were fast becoming civilized in that respect, bartering buffalo robes and buckskins for blankets and clothing.

V. R. Palmer agreed to take charge of the post. The Indians also requested that a resident commissioner be appointed, and, as I had won their confidence, they wanted to have me return and take up my permanent abode with them. The president, too, was anxious to have me accept the office, but I had had enough of it; in fact, had formed far different plans for the future, in which another's interests were bound up, so I declined to become a Comanche by adoption, recommending A. P. Miles for the position.

Having collected all the gifts they could conveniently carry, the Indians set out on their return. At Bastrop I parted company with them. There were horses stolen before they got out of the settlements, and the theft was laid to their charge, whether justly or not I can't say.

Open hostilities ceased for a time, however, and gave the settlers a chance to quarrel among themselves. Dissensions arose, and, lulled by the fancied security, the more venturesome spirits pushed further out, exciting anew the distrust of the Indians. Then, when the time in which the trading post was to have been established passed, and they came in with their skins to trade and found no trading house, they came to call on me to know why the treaty had not been complied with. As there was no plausible excuse for the failure, they held me responsible, saying I had lied to them, which, of course, destroyed any influence I might have previously exercised over them, and the irrepressible conflict recommenced with redoubled vigor. Thus my honest endeavor to bring about an adjustment of difficulties was worse than thrown away, for my enemies asserted that because of the sympathy I had conceived for the Indians, I was disposed to screen them, but I had illustrious company, for there were like charges preferred against both General Houston and General Burleson, and in such company I am content to let my name go down to posterity. We were crucified between thieves, the usual fate of mediators. I have often thought that I might have been able to exert a pacific influence over the Comanches, had I done as they entreated me to do; but, aside from my aversion to their mode of life, I did not feel justified in ignoring the rights of her who had consented to share my lot in life. And perhaps had the trading post been established according to contract, I might have still had influence with them. They would probably have seized on the first pretext, however, to rob the trader. Jack Palmer had had a little experience with the Comanches which may have caused him to hesitate about opening a trading post. He came out to the camp during my sojourn there, bringing with him, as presents to old Muguara, a fine military cloak and plumed cocked hat, expecting, of course, a present in return. But old Muguara didn't seem to value his gift so highly as Palmer thought he should, and only tendered one old mule in return. That didn't suit Jack, and, seeing a large fine mule in the caballado he asked to be allowed to take that. "O, yes," said old Muguara. Now it so happened that that particular mule was the property of Madame Muguara, and by her used to move her camp equipage. I accompanied Palmer on his return, we camping one night on the way. The next morning Jack's mule was gone and no trace of it could be found. We went back to the camp but it was not there. After a few days' absence I returned to the camp and there was the mule. "It got away and came back," old Muguara said.

So far as I know there were no overt acts committed on the Texans by the Comanches during my stay with them, but they were too restless to remain long in inactivity, so they got up an excursion, or incursion rather, over into Mexico to "get" horses, they said. They made elaborate preparations for the expedition, holding councils and war dances several nights before they set out. As they had not returned when I left the camp, I never knew what success they had, but if the Mexicans along the border had anything the Indians wanted they doubtless got it. They facetiously spoke of the Mexican ranchero as their "majadomas."

I still retain some vivid recollections of the kindness and friendship evinced toward me by the Comanches, especially the old chiefs, while I was with them. What their course toward me would have been had I met them "under shield" I never had an opportunity of testing; but, some way, I always thought that if I had fallen into their hands by accident they would have remembered "Wahqua."

My second term of enlistment having expired, I did not immediately return to the fort, but opened a shop in Bastrop. Captain Andrews had retired from command during my absence and Captain Eastland succeeded him. Of all the men with whom I have been associated none stood higher in my regard than Michael Andrews. In company with two brothers, Richards and Reddin, he came to the colonies at an early date and bore his full share in all the worry and danger of the long struggle with Mexicans, Indians and poverty. Though on the shady side of life, when the Cordova-Flores combination made its advent upon the scene, he went promptly to the front and remained there till the conspiracy was frustrated. Though in no sense of the word a military man, he was a successful commander. His genial, unostentatious disposition won him the good will of his men, who would have gone through fire to serve him. Instead of ordering his men to go and come, it was "Well, boys, I think we had better do" so and so; and a cheerful "All right, Captain," was the response, acted on with a will. Or, if the matter in hand seemed doubtful, there was a conference, in which every man was allowed to join; thus he maintained control over his little army. He afterward went to La-Grange, where he engaged in the hotel business, and I believe died there, never having married. His brother Richard, who was killed at the battle of Concepcion mission, left a wife, but I think no children. Reddin Andrews left several children, some of whom are to the front yet.

A little incident that occurred at the old Coleman fort after Captain Eastland took command will show the success of Captain Andrews' policy. Captain Eastland was disgusted with the want of military discipline among the men and the easy familiarity with which they treated their commander.

"If Captain Andrews can't control his men, I'll try and control mine," said he, but one morning the men all marched out on the parade, stacked arms and, turning to Captain Eastland, told him he might "go to hell and they would go home." The men had the best of the situation and the captain had no alternative but to capitulate, which he had the good sense to do gracefully and thoroughly, and thereafter had no trouble with his men. What Captain Eastland did for the country is so well known that my humble tribute can add nothing to the lustre of his name. Ever among the first to respond to the call "to arms," he fell, as brave men ever fall, with his face to the foe; one of the seventeen who drew fatal black beans at Salado.

My next public service, done in a private capacity, however, was the cutting of the first seals of office for Bastrop county.

The seals—three in number—were still doing duty in the offices of the county judge, clerk and sheriff the last I knew of them, but doubtless they have long since been cast aside. They should have been preserved, however, as interesting relics, both of the county and state, they being made of pieces broken from a six-inch shell, of which there were a number lying around town. There were two theories to account for their presence, either or both of which may have been correct. One, that Conrad Rohrer, a teamster in government employ, brought them from the Alamo as trophies of victory after its surrender to the Texans in 1835. The other—and I am inclined to think the correct version—that when Gaona's division of the Mexican army came on there in the spring of 1836 they expected to find the town fortified and came prepared to shell us out; but, finding it abandoned and being in haste to join Santa Anna, they left the shells and quite likely other heavy missiles, as the roads were very wet and boggy. Having no appliances for melting the metal, I laid the shell, which was about an inch thick, on the anvil and broke it with a sledge hammer, dressing the blocks down to their required size and shape with chisels.

As there are few now living who remember the first incumbents of the offices to which those seals were attached, I will add that they were Andrew Rabb, judge; Richard Vaughn, sheriff, and William Gorham, clerk. Some years later the district court was instituted with Judge R. Q. Mills on the bench. Having established a reputation for that kind of business, I cut several other seals and was offered a large fee to counterfeit the seal of the land office. That was not in my line, however. But the land sharks found ways and means to get on without the seal, as many an honest settler found to his cost and the disgrace of the country.

I have no knowledge of the town of Bastrop ever having been called Mina, as there was no settlement there prior to its occupation by the Anglo-Texans. It was simply the point at which the old military road leading from Bexar to Nacogdoches, crossed the Colorado and was known as the San Antonio crossing. The river and road formed the north and west boundaries of Austin's first colony. It was about 1829 that the first installment of colonists, headed by old Marty Wells and including old Billy Barton Leman and Jesse Barker, Josiah Wilbarger, Reuben Hornsby, and others went up there.

In an old book of records in the office of the county clerk of Bastrop county may be found the following entry:

Noah Smithwick presented the following account, to-wit:

1838, Bastrop County: To Noah Smithwick, debtor, to making two seals, one for the County Court and one for the Probate Court, $100.00. Signed, L. C. Cunningham, Chief Justice of the Court. Ordered paid.

James Smith, A. S. J.,
Samuel Craft, A. S. J.,
Samuel R. Miller, Clerk,
Pro tem. C. C. C. B.

CHAPTER 15

The following narrative, related by one of the few survivors of the engagement known as the Stone house fight, furnishes a striking example of the trouble that may result from the reckless deed of one unscrupulous individual.

It was, I think, late in the summer of 1837, during the temporary truce growing out of my missionary labors, that Captain Eastland, then in command at Coleman's fort, led an expedition up the Colorado river to the mouth of Pecan bayou and out on the latter stream to its source.

The precise object of the expedition, if there was any, I know not, but my impression is, that during the temporary lull in the Indian wars, the rangers at the fort became restless; and, partly to give them exercise and employment, and partly to take advantage of the cessation of hostilities to explore the unknown territory with perhaps a view to future operations against its wild inhabitants, Captain Eastland planned the jaunt. Be that as it may, he evidently had no intention of making hostile demonstrations against the Indians, and, having reached the head of the bayou, gave the order to return. A part of the company, some eighteen or twenty men, refused to obey the order, and, bent on further adventures, set out in a northerly direction, going on till they reached the rock mounds known as the stone houses, in the vicinity of which there was quite a large Indian encampment, composed of several small tribes, who for safety had formed an alliance against the more powerful tribes. Among the Indians were some Delawares, who went out to the white men's camp, and while there a lone warrior was seen approaching from the direction of the encampment.

Felix McClusky, the wild Irishman before mentioned, at once gave chase to the lone Indian. The Delawares tried to stop him, and, when he came within hailing distance, his victim made signs that he was a friendly Indian; but McClusky, heedless of signs or consequences, ran onto the savage and killed him, taking his scalp and rifling his pockets. The Delawares, thereupon, warned the men that the murdered Indian was of a friendly tribe, and his comrades would certainly avenge his death. Some of the men began to upbraid McClusky for his ruthless deed. Exhibiting a chunk of tobacco extracted from his victim's pocket, he recklessly swore that he "would kill any Injun for that much tobacco."

The Delawares made haste to withdraw themselves from the men's camp, and, true to their prediction, the little party was soon confronted by a hundred warriors clamoring for the man who had killed their comrade. McClusky wasn't hero enough to give himself up to save the lives he had imperiled, and, of course, his companions would not give him over to the hands of the fiends, who would have tortured him to death by slow degrees, so there was nothing for it but to make the best defense possible.

Intrenching themselves in a ravine, they held their assailants at bay till the Indians at length set the grass on fire and, sending some of their party around to cut off retreat, awaited the result.

The only hope of escape then lay in cutting their way through the enemy's lines. This they attempted to do, only five succeeding, two of them being wounded. But for the reckless bravado of the Irishman they might have hunted and explored the country unmolested. As is usually the case, the innocent had to suffer, McClusky being one of those two who escaped.

He was afterward killed in a drunken brawl.

As previously stated, the truce was short-lived, and the war was waged with relentless vigor. Though murders along the Colorado were less numerous in 1837–8 than those committed in other sections, a number of good men went down before the aim of the Comanches, among them Joseph Rodgers, who was run down and killed between Coleman's fort and Hornsby's station, and James Eagleston, who was shot down in his own dooryard in the town of Bastrop. The descendants of both of these men live in Bastrop county.

I have sometimes thought that there might have lurked in the minds of the Comanches some lingering respect for the treaty I was instrumental in negotiating, that accounted for the comparative exemption of the Colorado "tribe" from the fiendish work going on all around them. It may have been, however, altogether owing to less conscientious motives. Having cleaned out most of the horses in that section, they directed their expeditions further down into the interior, where there were better opportunities for booty. They made a raid into the town of Bastrop in broad daylight, running off about fifty head of horses, with which they escaped into the mountains where they were safe from pursuit.

I can not just say when it was, but I think in the winter of 1837 or 1838, that Colonel Karnes, who was stationed at San Antonio, sent in for Captain Eastland to take his men out there, as the Indians were proposing to come in for a treaty, and Colonel Karnes, suspicious that it was a ruse, wanted to be prepared for any treacherous movement. Thinking it might have a good effect on my red friends, Captain Eastland invited me to go along as spokesman. Owing to the scarcity of money, the blacksmith business was not very remunerative, and one of the rangers, Isam M. Booth, offering to give me his time if I would take his place, I once more cast my lot with the Texas rangers.

We went on out to San Antonio and struck camp, to wait for the Indians to come in. Several days elapsed and, nothing having been seen or heard of them, Captain Eastland, concluding that we were on a false scent, announced his intention of returning to Fort Coleman. On the day preceding that set for breaking camp I went into San Antonio, wearing a cloak with a gay lining in it, which so struck the fancy of a Mexican resident that he offered me a good mule for it. I accepted the offer and, returning to camp with my prize, Francisco, a Mexican boy who was with us, warned me that the animal had probably been stolen, and pretty soon there would come a claimant who would prove it away from me, that being a practice among them. Determined to outwit them for once, I sought Captain Eastland and, explaining the situation to him, asked leave to depart at once, and await the company at some point between that and home.

My request being granted, I saddled up my mule and, leaving my horse with the boys to bring on, struck out for home. At the Salado I spent the night with a couple of men who were improving a place there. The next morning I proceeded leisurely on my way, expecting the company to overtake me before night.

I kept on to the Cibolo, and still they did not come. I camped over night, and the next morning again took up the homeward route. I let my mule take his own gait, which was extremely moderate, and about sundown reached the Guadalupe. In the meantime a cold norther had come on and, there being no timber on the west bank of the river, I thought to cross over to the east side, which was heavily timbered, and make another lonely camp. The ford was an ugly one at any time, the current being very swift. Failing to observe that there had been a rise in the river, I plunged in, and almost instantly my mule was swept off its feet, and away we went down the stream. I managed to disengage myself from the saddle, dropping my gun in so doing, and losing my blankets, which I had thrown across the front of the saddle to protect my legs against the cold wind. I hung onto the bridle, and, being a good swimmer, finally succeeded in getting my mule out on the same side we went in. Having lost my gun and got my powder all wet, there was nothing with which to strike a fire. We had no matches in those days, the usual method being to take a bit of rag and rub powder into it and ram it into a gun (empty) and fire it out, the flash igniting the powdered rag. Sometimes we took out the flint from the lock of the gun, and with a steel, made for the purpose, or, in the absence of that, a knife, struck sparks into a rag or some other inflammable substance, into which powder had been poured. But my gun being gone, I was left without any of these resources, and not a dry thread on me, the wind fast approaching the freezing point, and no shelter from it. By this time it was getting dark, and I was shaking with cold.

In this extremity I bethought me of one of Davy Crockett's stories. Stripping the wet trappings from the mule, I tethered him to a bush and set to work vigorously pulling the dry sedge grass, which was everywhere waist high. I mowed the grass in great armfuls, piling it against the windward side of a clump of bushes till I had quite a respectable sized haystack. By the time this was done my blood was warmed up, and spreading my wet saddle blanket over the windward side of the heap, I wrung the water out of my clothes, crawled into my hay mow and was so warm and cozy that I soon fell asleep. When I awoke it was getting light. I pushed the grass aside and peered out. There stood the poor mule, all drawn up, shivering in the cold wind, which was sweeping, unobstructed, across the prairie. I kept my bed till the sun got up, when I crawled out. I had gone supperless to bed, and had nothing to breakfast on. I thought I might be able to recover my gun, knowing that its weight would not permit it to float. I went down to the river to look for it, and there it lay, under about six feet of water. There was nothing in the way of a drag obtainable, so I reluctantly abandoned it. With handfuls of grass I rubbed down my mule, and saddling him, took the back track, wondering whatever could be keeping the company back.

When I got back to the cabin on the Salado, where I had so lately passed the night, I was amazed to find it plundered and deserted, with horse tracks all around it. Further on the road was torn up and trampled, evidently the

result of the skirmish. Near by lay a blood-stained blanket. Unable to even conjecture what it all meant, I kept on towards San Antonio, meeting with no solution of the mystery until within a few miles of town, where I came to a Mexican rancho, and was then told that the Comanches had been on a raid, killing a Mexican vaquero and running off a drove of horses, after which they had met up with the rangers, who had started back to the Colorado. The Indians were in such numbers that, while a portion of them kept the rangers engaged, a detail got off with the horses. For some reason the rangers did not pursue them. So far from coming in for a treaty, the red devils had come in on a raid.

My hosts of the Salado, who had fled to town, were much surprised to see me, as, indeed, were all my company. The two men with whom I had stayed over night said I had been gone less than half an hour when the yelling demons charged down on their cabin from the direction in which I had gone, and, inasmuch as I was mounted on a slow steed, they were sure that I had been run down and killed, and had so reported in town.

I have often thought that within the short space of thirty-six hours I made three very narrow escapes from death in as many different forms. Had the Indians come upon me out on the open prairie mounted on a mule, they must certainly have killed me unless my identity as Wahqua had stood me a good turn. Then I had a fine chance to drown in the Guadalupe, and lastly to freeze.

So ended the second attempt at treating with the Comanches, and, fearing that there might be need of our services at home, we at once started on our return. When we got back to the Guadalupe the river had fallen so as to admit of fording. My gun was in a deep hole, however, and, on my offering a dollar for its recovery, one of the men dived down and brought it up, little the worse for its baptism. Without delay or further mishap we reached the fort, where I remained till the rangers were disbanded, some time in 1838.

Looking back through the long vista of sixty years and recalling the hard road we old pioneers had to travel, it seems almost miraculous that any are left to tell the tale. The old Tumlinson rangers were made up of citizens of Bastrop county, among them being Joseph Rodgers, who was first lieutenant; James Edmunston, Jimmie Curtice, Hugh M. Childers, John Williams, Joe Berry, Jim Hamilton, Oliver Buckman, orderly sergeant; Calvin Barker, Felix W. Goff, Ganey Crosby, familiarly known as "Choctaw Tom;" Joe Weeks and many others whose names I do not now recall. To the best of my knowledge they have all passed off the stage. Captain Tumlinson died over on the Brazos; Joseph Rodgers was killed by Indians between Coleman's fort and Hornsby's; Petty, second lieutenant, after tearing up his commission during the runaway scrape, as formerly related, disappeared from view—he had probably had enough of military glory; John Williams was killed by Indians, in Reuben Hornsby's corn field, with Howell Haggett; Joe Berry was one of the unfortunate Mier expedition, and was murdered by the Mexicans while

[147]

lying helpless in bed with a broken leg; Joe Weeks was killed in a private difficulty; James Edmunston came to California during the great gold excitement of '49 and was, up to a few years ago, living in the northern part of the state. Ganey Crosby was a nephew of Colonel Ganey of revolutionary fame, not an honor of which "Choctaw Tom" cared to boast, however, seeing that Colonel Ganey was one of the tories who gave General Marion so much to do in South Carolina. Ganey Crosby was one of the detachment left at Bastrop to guard the crossing while the families were fleeing for their lives. After we started on, it will probably be remembered, Major Williamson left us, taking with him old Jimmie Curtice and Crosby. They fell in with the army and were detailed to guard the baggage; but, knowing that a battle was imminent, they left the baggage to its fate and rushed on and participated in the glory of San Jacinto.

Nor must I pass over Conrad Rohrer, who, though not a member of any company, was always on hand for a fight. I first fell in with him at Gonzales in the fall of '35, when we were organizing for the war of independence. I have several times mentioned him in the course of these sketches, the first time when he delivered the stinging rebuke to a weak-kneed member of a squad sent to dislodge a picket force before the battle of Concepcion mission, and which is so good that I venture to repeat it.

"Boys," whispered weak knees, "if that's a big force of them they'll whop us."

"Shet up, d——n you," responded Rohrer; "don't you say they'll wip us; you're wipped already."

For reasons previously given I was not "in" at the taking of San Antonio a few weeks later, but was told that Rohrer was the man who climbed the church tower and triumphantly unfurled the Texas flag therefrom. Having a wagon and team, he was employed in moving the army supplies, and, after the occupation of San Antonio by the Texans, was sent over to Bastrop, where he was said to have taken the shells of which I have previously spoken. When Captain Tumlinson was ordered up on Brushy to build the old fort of his name, Rohrer went along to haul our supplies, and when Mrs. Hibbons came into camp after having made her escape from the Indians and besought us to rescue her child, he was on hand for the chase.

In his capacity as treasurer he followed the fortunes of the Texas army to San Jacinto, and was appointed wagon-master.

When the army was in retreat to San Jacinto, General Houston issued an order for work oxen to be taken wherever found. Rohrer—"General" Rohrer the boys called him—took a yoke of cattle belonging to an old woman—Mrs. M.—who had a farm on the Brazos. The teams were all hitched up ready to start, when up rode Madame with knife and pistol belted on.

Spurring up to Rohrer she commanded him to unhitch her oxen. Rohrer referred her to General Houston. The General being pointed out to her, the old woman rode up to him and demanded her property. Houston attempted to explain the exigencies of the case, but the Amazon swore she would have them, emphasizing her determination with oaths that took all the wind out of the General's sail, though he was accounted a proficient in the art of swearing. Throwing up his hands he exclaimed: "Take them, my dear woman, take them. For God Almighty's sake take them." Back she went to Rohrer, and, upon his refusal to unhitch the cattle, herself dismounted and released them, retiring in triumph, having vanquished both General Houston and General Rohrer, the only time either of them was ever whipped.

One night when the two armies lay on opposite sides of Buffalo bayou, Rohrer, with two or three others as daredevil as himself, swam the bayou and, surprising the pickets, fired on them, chasing them some way toward their camp and getting away with several horses. After the battle he returned to Bastrop and was shot down in Tom Moore's dooryard by an Indian in hiding in a fence corner.

Colonel Coleman's company was mostly made up of adventurers. When he built the fort a few men who had families took refuge therein and did ranging service, though not regularly enlisted; of these were Isaac Castner and ———— Wolfenberger. Thomas Blair, I think, joined the company after Captain Andrews took command. Eastland's men, like Coleman's, were a miscellaneous collection, Jim Manor being one of the few who settled in the vicinity. There was a noted individual in Coleman's company, Corporal Blish, who furnished no end of fun for the boys. He was a genuine down-east Yankee, with his peculiar twang scarcely more intelligible to us southerners than the Virginia dialect would have been in Connecticut. The corporal one day killed a fine fat raccoon while out on a hunt, and dressing it neatly hung it up outside his camp to freeze over night, thereby destroying the disagreeable flavor attached to an adult male raccoon. During the night the guard stole the coon, roasted and ate it, piling the bones up before Blish's camp.

The old fellow had stood the teasing of the boys quite patiently, but that was the last feather, and if he could have found the thief there would have been trouble. Corporal Blish was afterward killed by an angry steer, which had been lassoed and tied up. Blish unwittingly got within the length of the animal's cable and was gored before he could get out of the way.

In Eastland's company was one Roberts, a Kentucky colonel. The colonel had been engaged in the Santa Fe trade, a commerce carried on between Independence, Mo. and Santa Fe, New Mexico, dating back to 1821–22. The distance was about 800 miles, but the isolated position of Santa Fe enabled the traders to put tariff enough on their goods to make a handsome profit. As the route lay entirely through the Indian country, traders traveled in companies. In the summer of '35, Colonel Roberts, in company with several other parties, having made a successful trip, started on their homeward journey with the proceeds of their sales, all in gold and silver coin. They had gotten out about 300 miles when they discovered that they were being shadowed by Indians. Suspecting that plunder was the object of their pursuit, and that, to accomplish it without risk to themselves, the crafty redskins would attempt to stampede the horses and thus compel them to abandon their wagons, the traders directed all their energies to the safety of their teams.

They were out on the open prairie where natural protection there was none, so, selecting the best position accessible, they halted for the night, drawing their wagons round in a circle, lapping the tongues over the wheels of the forward wagons and securing them there with chains. With the darkness came the hooting, yelling savages. The white men stationed themselves around the corral formed by the wagons, and with their guns kept the assailants at a safe distance, in the meantime trying to prevent the animals from breaking out. In this way they repelled several charges. The Indians at length withdrew and the men turned their efforts toward the quieting of the rearing, snorting horses, which were just beginning to recover from their fright, when

"At once there rose so wild a yell
As all the fiends from Heaven that fell
Had pealed the banner cry of Hell."

Mingled with unearthly shrieks and yells came rasping, nerve-torturing sounds made by drawing bow-strings one across another. The horses goaded to frenzy could no longer be restrained; they leaped over the barriers and dashed away in the darkness, followed by the victorious savages, leaving the traders with their treasure-laden wagons hundreds of miles away from a human habitation. There was no hope of succor, as it was too late in the season for outbound traders and they knew there were none coming on behind, and to remain would be to die of starvation. As it was 500 miles to Independence, the nearest white settlement, there was no alternative but to turn back to the Rio Grande. This course being decided on they lost no time in getting away. In addition to their guns and the ammunition necessary to procure food along the journey, they took each a blanket, a canteen of water and what grub they could carry. Some of the men, however, could not resist the temptation to slip a few of the shining doubloons into their pockets. Their small stock of provision was soon exhausted, and they then had to depend on what they could kill. Jack rabbits being the main source of supply, such small game made heavy drafts on the ammunition; bullets and shot giving out several days before they reached a settlement. There being nothing else between them and starvation, those yellow doubloons were chopped up with butcher knives and used for shot. Gold was then worth no more than lead, nor even so much, as lead would have been easier to cut. Some time in the future those little slugs may be found and create a great mining excitement.

Arriving at Taos, stripped of everything, bare-footed and half famished, having suffered for water as well as food, their exasperation knew no bounds when they found the Indian population bedecked from head to foot with gold and silver coin, which, strung on cords, was braided into their hair, encircled their necks and arms and dangled from the fringe on their clothing.

Colonel Roberts worked his way down the Rio Grande and over into Texas, attaching himself to the ranging service to get a little stake to take him home. He bore the unmistakable stamp of a gentleman and doubtless had means, though for the time being unobtainable. He served his time out and went his way.

From Peter Wade, another of Eastland's men, I heard the full particulars of the negro insurrection in Virginia in 1833. Wade's aunt and her husband were the owners of Nat Turner, the leader, who was a negro preacher. Turner's influence with the slaves was unbounded, and his prior irreproachable conduct had also won for him the confidence of the white people, so that he enjoyed unusual liberty. But he had become imbued with the idea that he was destined like Moses, to lead his people from bondage. Having obtained access to a distillery, of which there were many in those days, Nat Turner and four associates, toned up their enthusiasm to the required pitch and started out on their mission of deliverance, Wade's uncle, aunt, and three children being the first victims. Their numbers being constantly augmented, the negroes kept up their fiendish work three days before the terror stricken whites rallied in sufficient numbers to overpower them; about fifty white people of all ages and sexes in the meantime being murdered. Some of the negroes were shot down, others captured and hung, and some who were not actually concerned in the killing, were only flogged. Nat Turner made his escape and remained at large several weeks, finally being discovered by other negroes, who, having become cowed by the punishment meted out to the murderers, hastened to report. He was speedily overtaken and soon after hung.

For our service in the ranging companies we were given 1,280 acres of land, or rather certificates for that amount, for each twelve months' service. I got three certificates for a trifle over two years' service, both the men whose terms I served out giving me the full amount. No one cared anything for land those days. I gave one of my certificates for 1,280 acres for a horse which the Indians relieved me of in less than a week. I never located any of them, nor the headright to which, under the Mexican colonization law, I was entitled.

In 1838 the land office was opened and speculators began flocking into the country, accompanied by surveyors, who at once began an aggressive movement upon the hunting grounds of the wild tribes, thereby provoking them to a more determined resistance to the encroachments of the settlers. Then, too, the Mexican government egged them on, furnishing them with arms and ammunition. It was the same old story of the troubles of the frontiersmen everywhere and destined to the same finale—the survival of the fittest.

True, the Indian mode of indiscriminate warfare was barbarous, but there were not wanting white men to follow their example. Extermination was the motto on both sides. That was President Lamar's avowed policy and Colonel

Moore carried it out when he attacked their camp over on the Red fork of the Colorado in 1843. There was a man in Bastrop county whose family had been slaughtered by the Cherokees in the United States, for which he swore eternal vengeance on Indians in toto. He came to Texas and never let an opportunity pass to get a scalp, regardless of the consequences it might entail on others. He was several times apprehended for killing friendly Indians, but could never be convicted.

After the rangers were disbanded, the settlers, left to take care of themselves, organized scouting parties to patrol the frontier, taking it by turns.

One such party was preparing to go out from Bastrop when a little Jew, Kleberg, who had lately arrived and opened a store, willing to take his share of the responsibility, asked to be allowed to accompany us. We anticipated sport in breaking him in, but we had more than we bargained for. On the first day out, Kleberg espied a polecat, ambling leisurely along, its mottled brush waving gracefully in the wind. "What a beautiful little cat," he exclaimed. "Yes," one of the boys assented, thinking only to play a joke upon the unsophisticated Israelite, "and they are easily tamed."

Before any of us could interpose, Kleberg made a dash to capture the prize, and he got it, at least the most prominent part of it. The boys roared with laughter, but they soon found the laugh wasn't all on their side, as we couldn't put the mortified victim out of camp and could hardly stay in it with him.

CHAPTER 16

In the winter of 1839 a party of Lipan Indians out on a hunt discovered an encampment of Comanches up on the San Gabriel, about fifty miles from the city of Austin. The Comanches and Lipans were inveterate enemies, so the Lipans, too weak to attack the camp alone, hastened into the settlements and gave the alarm, offering to assist in dislodging the Comanches. There were no troops in the vicinity, and knowing that if the Comanches were allowed to remain they would soon be making predatory incursions into the settlements, we at once decided to make up a party to go against them. Colonel John H. Moore being the leading spirit in the plan, was given command. Captain Eastland raised a company of thirty men at LaGrange. Bastrop raised a company of about the same number, electing me its captain. To this number was added the full fighting force of the Lipans, under command of Chief Castro, assisted by his son, Juan Castro, young Flacco and Juan Seis. When we reached the point at which the Lipans reported the camp, the Comanches had moved, leaving a trail leading up stream. We followed on up to the head of the San Gabriel, where we were overtaken by a storm of snow and sleet which was so severe that we were obliged to seek shelter. We made for a grove of postoaks on the divide between the San Gabriel and Colorado, in the shelter of which we struck camp. The storm continued with increasing cold. Some of the horses froze to death, and the Indians, loth to see so much good meat go to waste, ate the flesh. Three days and nights we remained there. In the meantime a gun which had been set up against a tree, fell down, and, being discharged by the fall, shot one of Captain Eastland's men through the body. Some of the men, discouraged by these unpropitious circumstances, wanted to turn back, but it was finally decided to move camp over to the Colorado, whither the game had been driven by the storm, and there kill wild cattle, of which there were large bands, and construct a boat of the hides in which to send the wounded man down to the settlements. The storm abated on the fourth day, but the snow had obliterated the Comanches' trail, so I took a Lipan and went on in the direction they had been heading. We kept on up the Colorado on the east side till near the mouth of the San Saba, when on ascending a rise overlooking the valley, we saw smoke rising some miles up the San Saba. The Indian said he knew it was from camp fires because it ascended in columns; if it were prairie fires it would spread out in clouds. He said it was no use to go any farther, as he knew exactly where the camp was located. It was then late in the day, but not caring to tarry, we turned back, riding on far into the night. While riding along about dark we heard a wolf howl behind us. My guide stopped short and assumed a listening attitude. In a few moments another answered, way to the right. Still the Indian listened so intently that his form seemed perfectly rigid. Then another set up a howl on our left. "Umph, lobo," said the Lipan, in a tone of relief. I can't say that I admired the music of the wolf at any time, but it certainly never had a more unmusical sound than on that occasion, and when I saw that even an Indian's ears were uncertain whether it were wolf or Comanche, I felt the cold chills creeping over me. Some distance ahead we entered a cedar brake, just in the edge of which we came upon a turkey roost. We had nothing to eat, so with the approval of my guide, I shot a turkey. Securing our prize, we hurried on, putting many miles behind us before we ventured to draw rein. Several times I suggested stopping, but the Indian said "No; there was no suitable place." Late in the night we came to a dry ravine, and the Indian said we might stop. Selecting a spot where there were no trees to reflect the light, he started a fire and prepared to roast the turkey. "You go to sleep," said he, and I was glad to obey the order, feeling perfectly safe in his care. At daybreak he roused me up to breakfast, having roasted the turkey while he kept guard. I doubt if he slept at all. A few hours' ride brought us into camp. Our men had constructed a rawhide boat and started our wounded man down the Colorado in charge of two comrades. The poor young fellow, whose name I do not now remember, died on the way down and was buried in the sand. We saddled up and started for the Comanche camp, going up within a few miles of the place, when we halted and lay on our arms, while Malcolm Hornsby, Jo Martin and two

Lipans went forward after dark to locate the exact position of the camp. On their return they reported a much larger camp than the Lipans previously reported. Disconcerted by the unexpected intelligence, Colonel Moore rather demurred to attacking, but we had come out to hunt a fight and were willing to take the responsibility. One big, rough fellow said he did not "care if there were a thousand of them, if there were horses enough to justify the fight." When within a mile of the camp we dismounted and tied our horses. We then crept upon the sleeping Indians, who were not dreaming of an attack. As soon as daylight gave us the exact situation of the camp we made a rush for it, pouring a volley right into the lodges. Taken completely by surprise the savages bounded from their lodges and scattered like partridges. Our men rushed right in among the lodges. The women and children screaming, dogs barking, men yelling and shooting, in a moment transformed the peaceful scene on which the day had but just dawned into a pandemonium. At this juncture, for some unexplainable reason, Colonel Moore ordered a retreat, which threw our men into confusion. Quick to grasp and take advantage of the situation the Indians rallied and drove us back to cover of a ravine, our only casualty being an arrow cut on the nose sustained by Captain Eastland.

The Indians then formed in line and advanced to the attack. One brave, under cover of his shield, preceded his comrades, and flourishing his bow, delivered a challenge. Jim Manor was standing beside me with his gun cocked; he took deliberate aim at the prancing heathen, and at the crack of his gun the Indian fell back, unable to rise. "By ———, I killed an Indian, didn't I?" said Jim, as if needing verification of his deed. The enemy then made a charge to rescue their companion, but our fusillade drove them back. That Indian then lay there flat on his back and shot arrows upward so that they fell point foremost among our men, till young Flacco ran out in the midst of a perfect rain of arrows and dispatched him with his lance. Flacco captured his shield, but the Comanches made such a furious charge that he retreated without getting the scalp. We drove the enemy back and Juan Seis, another Lipan, loth to leave without a scalp, offered to run out and scalp the dead brave if we would keep the Comanches from charging him, but as we could not fire on the enemy without endangering him, we wouldn't allow him to risk it. After several ineffectual attempts to dislodge us, the Comanches withdrew, and with four wounded men we retreated to a cedar brake about a mile away. The Indians came out and made some demonstrations of attack, but didn't venture within range of our rifles. They sent out a Lipan squaw, who had long been among them, with a white flag. Old Juan Seis went out to meet her. She said we had killed some of their bravest men, and asked how many of our men were killed. The wily old chief assured her that we hadn't received a scratch. Old Castro was so disgusted when Colonel Moore ordered a retreat that he withdrew his command and left. His son Juan had been detailed to run off the Comanches' horses, but only succeeded in getting a portion of them, with which they left at once, as had been previously arranged. While they were getting away with the Comanches' horses, the Comanches slipped around and got ours, so we were left afoot more than one hundred miles from home, with two disabled men to carry. Felix Taylor was shot in the knee, and Joe Martin, one of our best men, was shot in the back, paralyzing his lower limbs. He implored me to shoot him dead, which of course I would not think of. "Then," said he, "give me your pistol and I will shoot myself." I told him no, to bear up bravely and we would take him home to his family. In the shelter of a cedar brake we constructed two hand litters upon which we carried Martin and Taylor ten miles back to the river, where, fortunately, we had left our pack horses. Taylor was able to ride and we rigged a horse litter in which we carried Joe Martin home. He stood the torture of that terrible journey with heroic fortitude, never uttering a complaint. We had two doctors with us, but they were unable to find the bullet, it having lodged in his spinal column. The poor fellow lived several weeks after reaching home. So ended our disastrous expedition. I never felt sorrier for a man than I did for Colonel Lockhart, whose young daughter had been taken captive by the Comanches and who we had every reason to suppose was in the camp. When, some time afterward, she was rescued, she said she screamed as loud as she could to try to make us hear her, but there was such an uproar we failed to distinguish her cries. She said the Indians were completely routed when that ill-timed retreat was ordered. Old Castro told Colonel Moore at the time that such a thing as ordering a retreat when the enemy was routed and flying had never before been heard of. I've been something of a horse trader in my time, but that was the worst "swap" I ever made. I lost a fine horse, for those days, and when we came to divide up those we got from the Comanches, there were not enough to go around and I got none. It was generally supposed that the Lipans got away with the lion's share of the spoils.

Congress passed an act to indemnify us for the loss of our horses, the indemnity to be paid in commonwealth's paper, worth twenty-five cents on the dollar; so, for a $100 horse I got $4.00 which I didn't allow to depreciate on my hands.

The Comanches, thirsting for revenge, at once made a raid on the settlements, killing Mrs. Coleman and her son Albert and taking little five-year-old Tommy prisoner. Another badly managed pursuit resulted in the disastrous battle of Brushy, in which Rev. James Gilleland, John Walters, Jacob Burleson and Edward Blakey, four of the best men on the frontier, were killed.

Primitive as the Indians' weapons were, they gave them an advantage over the old single-barreled, muzzle-loading rifle in the matter of rapid shooting, an advantage which told heavily in a charge. An Indian could discharge a

dozen arrows while a man was loading a gun, and if they could manage to draw our fire all at once they had us at their mercy unless we had a safe retreat.

At the head of the Lipan tribe was old Chief Flacco, whose son, young Flacco, was the idol of the tribe. Brave and unswerving in his fidelity to the whites, his many services had likewise won him the friendship of all who knew him. In recognition of his service the Texas government presented him with a full colonel's uniform, including sword and plumed cocked hat and bestowed on him the title of "colonel." One of the department clerks taught him to write his name, which he persisted in doing according to the Spanish method, placing the adjective after the noun—Flacco Colonel.

When late in the summer of 1842 Somervell organized his expedition against Mexico, Young Flacco was employed to accompany the army in the capacity of scout. Taking a deaf mute Lipan, whose sense of sight was peculiarly acute, young Flacco led the van, bearing an honorable part in all the engagements along the Rio Grande, for which he and his companions were allotted a liberal share of the spoils taken, consisting mostly of guns, ammunition, horses and blankets, the things that an Indian most prizes. When the company divided at Laredo, a portion returning home, the Indians accompanied the returning party. The mute was taken sick on the Medina river and he and Flacco stopped while the white men went on. The next morning two of the white men, Tom Thernon and another, were missing and were seen in Seguin a few days later with Flacco's horses. Upon investigation the Indians were found murdered. The whites were greatly alarmed over the consequences of the dastardly outrage, knowing that, if the Lipans learned of it they would take indiscriminate revenge on the settlers. I had a gunshop in Webber's Prairie, where the friendly Indians were wont to congregate, and as they spoke very little English, using the Spanish language in their intercourse with the whites, I, having acquired a fair knowledge of the latter tongue, was often appealed to in matters of importance. Old Flacco and his wife were often at my house, bringing presents of game and little beaded moccasins for my little boy. So, when the old chief learned that the expedition had got in, and his son did not return, he became uneasy and came to me to make inquiries. I dared not tell him the truth. He then requested me to write to President Houston and General Burleson about it. In due course of time the answer came stating that young Flacco and his companion had been murdered by Mexican bandits. There was also a letter from Senor Antonio Navarro, who was a trusted friend of the Lipans, corroborating the sad tale. General Houston tendered his sympathy to the old chief and his tribe.

Armed with these documents I proceeded to the Lipan camp about thirty miles distant. It was a delicate mission, for I knew that old Flacco idolized his son, who was indeed a noble young chief. I interpreted such portions of the letters as I deemed expedient, being very careful to leave no room for doubt as

to the Mexican robber story. Having on several occasions been witness to the stoical fortitude with which an Indian accepts the inevitable, I was not prepared for the touching manifestation of human feeling that followed the reading of those letters. I had not supposed an Indian warrior would under any circumstances be guilty of such womanish weakness as to weep. I had heard the loud lamentations with which they were wont to bewail their dead, but here was a sorrow too strong to be repressed, too genuine for noisy demonstration. Tears rained down the old man's face while sobs fairly shook his frame. I felt how useless words were in such a crisis. I could only express my sympathy by the tears that welled up to my own eyes. When the first violence of the shock had spent itself, the stricken father, in broken voice, thanked me and those who had so kindly expressed their sympathy in writing. Then said he: "It has always been our custom to destroy everything belonging to the dead, but my son was the white man's friend and I want to do with his things as white men do."

"Then," said I, "keep them yourself."

"O no, no," he replied, "I don't want them where I can see them. It makes me sorry. I want to forget."

"Well, give them to his friends, then."

He then brought out the rawhide box in which young Flacco kept his uniform, only donning it on occasions of ceremony. I insisted that he should at least retain that. I never knew what disposition he made of it. A few days after he sent in four head of horses which had belonged to his son. There was a saddle horse for myself, a mare and colt for General Burleson, and a young mustang which young Flacco had caught and trained for General Houston, who wanted it to send to a friend in Tennessee. Several days later old Flacco and his wife came to see us. They had starved themselves till they were like mummies. The old man looked so broken, I tried to dissuade him from further fasting. My wife, touched by the sorrow which "makes the whole world kin," prepared dinner for them and induced them to partake of it, after which they seemed to feel better, and soon left. It was the last time I ever saw them, as the tribe shortly after left the country, going out toward the Rio Grande, and I believe are now extinct. There was but a small remnant of the band at that time, about sixty warriors, but, had they known how young Flacco died, they would have declared war to the death against the whites, and, as often has been the case, the crime of one miserable wretch would have caused the death of hundreds of innocent people.

CHAPTER 17

In the latter part of 1839 I took unto myself a helpmeet and established a home on a farm in the lower end of Webber's prairie, whither had preceded me my old time partner, "Dr." John F. Webber. He having retired from the practice of medicine, built the first house, a fort in the prairie, which bears his name. Other settlers collected around the pioneer cabin, among whom were the Dutys, the next to locate. There were five brothers of them, Joseph, the only one who had a family, William, Matthew, George and Richard.

Joseph and George Duty were among Austin's first three hundred, and located their headrights lower down on the Colorado, but, like many others, sold out to later arrivals and pushed out into the Indian country.

They, also, had built a fort into which were gathered all the families in the vicinity, the men going out in companies to work their farms and kill their meat, and incidentally Indians.

Washington Anderson was there, and with him his father, Dr. Anderson, a noted physician all through the country. There were the Hamiltons, four brothers—Alexander, William, James and John; Dan Shelf, James Dodd, the Manors, Joseph and James; Mrs. Scott and her daughter, Mrs. Hopkins and perhaps a few others.

Webber having become entangled in a low amour, the result of which was an offspring, which, though his own flesh and blood, was yet the property of another, without whose consent he could not provide for nor protect it, he faced the consequences like a man. Too conscientious to abandon his yellow offspring and its sable mother to a life of slavery, he purchased them from their owner, who, cognizant of the situation, took advantage of it to drive a sharp bargain.

Building himself a fort in the then unsettled prairie, Webber took his family home and acknowledged them before the world. There were others I wot of that were not so brave. The Webber family of course could not mingle with the white people, and, owing to the strong prejudice against free negroes, they were not allowed to mix with the slaves, even had they so desired; so they were constrained to keep to themselves. Still there wasn't a white woman in the vicinity but knew and liked Puss, as Webber's dusky helpmeet was called, and in truth they had cause to like her, for, if there was need of help, Puss was every ready to render assistance, without money and without price, as we old timers know. Webber's house was always open to any one who chose to avail himself of its hospitality, and no human being ever went away from its doors hungry if the family knew it. The destitute and afflicted many times found an asylum there. One notable instance was that of a poor orphan girl who had gone astray and had been turned out of doors by her kindred. Having nowhere to lay her head, she sought refuge with the Webbers. Too true a woman to turn the despairing sinner away, Puss took her in, comfort-

ing and caring for her in her time of sorest trial. Beneath that sable bosom, beat as true a heart as ever warmed a human body. At another time they took in a poor friendless fellow who was crippled up with rheumatism and kept him for years. By such generous acts as these, joined to the good sense they displayed in conforming their outward lives to the hard lines which the peculiar situation imposed on them, Webber and his wife merited and enjoyed the good will, and, to a certain extent the respect, of the early settlers. The ladies visited Puss sometimes, not as an equal, but because they appreciated her kindness. At such times she flew around and set out the best meal which her larder afforded; but, neither herself nor her children offered to sit down and eat with her guests, and when she returned the visit she was set down in the kitchen to eat alone. After the Indians had been driven back, so that there was comparative safety in Webber's prairie, a new lot of people came—"the better sort," as Colonel Knight styled them—and they at once set to work to drive Webber out. His children could not attend school, so he hired an Englishman to come to his house and teach them, upon which his persecutors raised a hue and cry about the effect it would have on the slave negroes, and even went so far as to threaten to mob the tutor. The cruel injustice of the thing angered me, and I told some of them that Webber went there before any of them dared to, and I, for one, proposed to stand by him.

I abhorred the situation, but I honored the man for standing by his children whatever their complexion. But the bitter prejudice, coupled with a desire to get Webber's land and improvements, became so threatening that I at length counseled him to sell out and take his family to Mexico, where there was no distinction of color. He took my advice, and I never afterward saw or heard of him.

Heroes there were then whose names and deeds history so far has failed to record, and among them Matthew Duty deserves a prominent place. I don't remember at just what date it occurred that a small party of white men, including Matthew Duty and Billy Hornsby, were surprised by a large body of Indians. All the men except Billy were well mounted, and all, with the noble exception of Matthew, ran away and left him to his fate. Not so with Matthew Duty. Dropping in behind Billy, he turned on their pursuers, presenting his gun, at which the Indians fell back, and Billy put a gap between himself and them. Wheeling his horse, Duty then ran away from the Indians, still keeping between them and Billy, and, when they began to crowd him, again turned, and, with gun presented, kept them back, till they reached Hornsby's fort in safety.

Mrs. Hornsby, Billy's mother, told me how she stood at the gate of the fort, looking on helplessly at the life and death race across the prairie, momentarily expecting to see both her son and his heroic defender killed. Matthew Duty was afterward killed in Webber's prairie by an Indian in ambush. He fell from his horse, the same one on which he saved Billy Hornsby, and the horse, being frightened thereby, broke for home, the Indians not being able to catch him. Some little time after Matthew's death, his brother Joe was out riding the same horse, when he was also ambushed, but it was after night and the bullet struck the horse, causing him to fall, when Joe bounded off and made good his escape into a thicket. The Indians would not pursue even one man into cover, nor were they rash about charging on a small party so long as they stood with guns presented. One notable instance of the kind took place over on the Yegua in 1838, where Edward Blakey and Elijah Ingram were surveying. There were several men in the party, and while eating their dinner they were charged upon by a number of Indians. All the men except Blakey and Ingram broke for their horses. The two last named grabbed their guns, and, leveling them at their companions, ordered them to stand and fight, threatening to shoot the first one who offered to mount, thus compelling them to face the foe. They stood their ground and whipped them. Edward Blakey was killed in the battle of Brushy.

One more deed of heroism I must record here lest it slip my memory, though it occurred in '46. Bartlett Simms, than whom no man in that part of the country was better known, was over in the Perdenales with three other men, one of whom was his nephew, surveying. The Indians, as previously stated, were particularly hostile to surveyors, and, watching an opportunity when the party had worked away from their horses, made a dash at them. The white men succeeded in reaching their horses, but Captain Simms' horse being frightened, jerked loose and ran; upon seeing which, his nephew, who had mounted, rushed up to his uncle, and, springing to the ground, bade him take his horse. Simms took the horse and made his escape, the only one of the party who did. Men never left home unarmed, but as a man could not carry a rifle and work—and we had few pistols in those days—it often happened that they were surprised away from their guns. Indian Jim, a friendly Tonkaway, used to tell a good story on Dan Shelf. Dan had gone down into the river bottom to get a stick of timber for an ox yoke. He looked about till he found a tree that suited him and, setting his rifle up against an adjacent tree, set to work to get out his yoke. He felled his tree and proceeded to trim it up, when, hearing himself accosted, he looked up, and saw to his horror a big Indian standing between him and his gun. I wish I could give the story in Jim's own language, accompanied by his gestures, describing how Dan trembled like a leaf: "I say, 'How do you do, sir?' He look up, see me; he shake all over; turn right white; he throw up his hands so, and say, 'Oh, Mr. Injun, don't shoot me; I've got a family!'" Dan acknowledged he was never so badly scared in his life, and it took Jim some time to reassure him. Jim was well known all through that section, and supposed Dan would recognize him after the first start, and only thought to play a little joke on him to show him how useless his rifle was when at work.

But, to return to Webber's prairie. When the mail route up to Austin was opened we were allowed an office in Webber's prairie. I was appointed post-master, with a certain percentage of all the money I took in to pay me for my trouble. That was long before the advent of postage stamps, and the charge for letters was twenty-five cents, payable at either end of the line. Letters were consequently few and far between. An occasional newspaper strayed into the office and did duty for the whole neighborhood.

Peter Carr was the first mail carrier, making weekly trips from LaGrange up to Austin on horseback with the mail, which was an imperceptible addition to the load, tied up in a buckskin wallet. Peter was very accommodating and when occasionally some one would meet him on the road and inquire: "Hello, Pete! Got anything for me?" Pete would reply: "I dunno; I can see." And down he would get, untying the mail sack and emptying the contents on the ground, where he would look it over and if there was anything for the inquirer, hand it out, free of charge. Peter's rural delivery system had been in operation some little time before it came to my knowledge. I then straight-way notified the postal department that unless they would furnish a locked pouch I would throw up my commission. I served a year or more, using my dwelling house as an office, and never got a cent either for my services or office rent. I might have eventually gotten a few worthless shinplasters, but the records of the department were lost during the archive war and my reports among them.

During the time that I was postmaster we were accorded a precinct and, notwithstanding the constitution limited the number of offices of trust or profit, one man might hold at a time to one, as neither the office of postmaster nor justice of the peace came within the scope of the provision, I was elected justice. I told my friends that I was not selfishly inclined and had no desire to monopolize the offices and therefore declined to qualify till our pedagogue took me aside and entreated me as a special favor to himself to reconsider my determination, as he was intending to get married and there was no one in the vicinity qualified to perform the ceremony. To accommodate Birt I quali-fied; my first official act being the solemnization of the marriage between himself and Miss Gilleland, a daughter of the Rev. James Gilleland, who was killed by Indians in the battle of Brushy Creek.

Birt was so near sighted that he could not distinguish one person from an-other across the room, and the bride, though quite a pretty girl, had the mis-fortune to be so lame as to necessitate the use of crutches. At the appointed time I was on hand, and, it being my first appearance in that role, I took Jim Dodd along to brace me up. Birt was stopping at Captain Grumble's, and, having only leather breeches and but one pair at that, he hired a negro to wash them after he retired on the eve of the wedding. Not being dry by morning, Birt drew them on and stood before the fire to dry them, a process which "set" them to perfection, but when he tried to sit down he couldn't make it; so he had to wet them again and sit while he dried them; consequently, when the thump of the bride's crutches on the floor of the inner room announced the approach of the bridal party, the first object that met the expectant eyes turned to the door, was the knees of the bridegroom's pantaloons performing the part of ushers as it were. Captain Grumble said he didn't "see how in thunder he ever got out of them."

Dodd, in reporting the wedding to my wife, characterized it as the marriage of the halt and blind. School teachers those times were not to be envied. There was no public school fund to draw upon and no private fund, either, to speak of, except such surplus produce as farmers happened to have. Our first school was taught by Captain Beach, in a log cabin having nether floor nor window, or even a door. A couple of the lower logs being left uncut in the doorway, over which the little tots had to be lifted, prevented the ingress of the pigs. When Beach's term expired, he was paid off in corn, for which there was no sale nearer than Austin; so he borrowed a team and hauled it to market.

There were no school houses or churches. The schools were kept in any vacant cabin, and when a preacher happened along he was invited to hold forth in some dwelling.

Some time after Birt's wedding Phillip Golding requested my services to unite him to the Widow Baker, relict of Rodney Baker, who had fallen a victim to the Comanches. After the wedding was over Phillip took me aside and asked what my fee was. "Nothing," I told him.

"Well, now," said he, "if I had known that I might have been married some time ago. I've been working several weeks to get five dollars with which to pay you."

The bride had several small children and no means to take care of them with. Said I: "All I charge you is to take care of that woman and be a father to those little helpless children. If you do that you will have need of all your money."

To the best of my knowledge he faithfully discharged the debt. Two other couples, I believe, completed my official labors in the matrimonial line. They were Elias Marshall and his brother Joe, they having stolen their brides—the two Graham girls—down at Washington. Young people didn't hesitate about marrying on the score of endowments or incomes then. Any young man who was willing to work could get himself enough good land to raise bread on, and with a cow or two and a few pigs and chickens he was prepared to maintain a family. He could cut down trees and build himself a house. If he was vain it would be a double cabin with either a wide passage between or a big double chimney, and by and by, when there was need of it, a smoke house. Girls all expected to be married some time, and early began to spin and weave the household linen, which was their only dower, so that they usually had on hand a stock sufficient to last many years.

On the bench I was a shining success, not one of my decisions ever being excepted to. People were all poor and struggling for a foothold in the country and I disliked to see them wrangling and wasting their slender substance in suits at law, so my usual plan was to send out my constable, Jimmie Snead, and have the contending parties brought before me, when I would counsel them to talk their difficulties over between themselves and try to arrive at a satisfactory settlement, a plan which was generally agreed to, thereby throwing the burden of costs on the judge and constable.

The most perplexing case I ever had to deal with was one in which I really had no jurisdiction. Three worthless scamps made a raid on the Lipan Indians and stole a number of their best horses. The Indians missed them almost immediately, and getting track of them, came to me to assist them in their recovery. I took the responsibility of sending two white men, Captain Beach and Andy Cryor, along with Chief Castro and a posse of Indians. They overtook the thieves down near LaGrange. The ringleaders decamped, leaving a half-witted fellow to bear the consequences. The captive was brought back to me. In a quandary as to what to do with him, I turned to old Castro.

"What shall I do with him?" I asked. The old chief looked contemptuously at the poor trembling wretch, who frightened out of what little wit he ever possessed, was literally crying.

"Oh," said he, "turn him loose." I gave the young man some wholesome advice and let him go. Old Castro gave each of his white assistants a pony to compensate them for their services, and I got nothing. I have often contrasted the conduct of old Castro on that occasion with that of white men under similar circumstances. When an Indian stole a white man's horse, hanging was the penalty if he could be caught.

When my time expired my constituents were anxious to again invest me with the judicial ermine; but as I had never collected a dollar from the office, I told them I thought it should go round, and when it came my turn again I would take it. Peter Carr was the next incumbent. I was also elected lieutenant-colonel of militia when it was organized, and so held three offices at one time, but as there wasn't a cent profit in any of them, and the trust only nominal, any man could safely assume as many offices as he chose. The fees were small at best, and when paid in commonwealth paper would not keep a man in tobacco. Offices went begging. At one time there was no district attorney for Travis County, and the judge having to appoint one, the only lawyer in the county who was patriotic enough to accept it was Alex. Chalmers, a youth about eighteen who had never been admitted to the bar. But Alex. took hold and managed the business so successfully that he thus laid the foundation for a good practice.

Coin there was absolutely none, and the constantly downward tendency of the commonwealth paper kept it moving lively, something like the old play, "If Jack dies in my hand, packsaddle me." I received a hatful of new, crisp, one-dollar bills in payment for a horse lost in the San Saba Indian fight, which I immediately turned over to a creditor, without ever having folded them. People would almost rather have anything else than the commonwealth paper. Under those circumstances we established a currency of our own, a kind of banking system as it were, which though unauthorized by law, met the local requirements. Horses were generally considered legal tender; but, owing to the constant drain on the public treasury by the horse-loving Indian, that kind of currency became scarce, so we settled on the cow as the least liable to fluctuation. Mrs. H., a widow living near me, having need of merchandise, for which the cash was not on hand, offered a cow and calf in lieu thereof, a cow and calf being rated at ten dollars. The tender was accepted, Mrs. H. reserving the use of the cow during the milking season. The bill of sale being made out, the merchant paid off a debt with it and the creditor likewise passed it on. That bit of paper passed from hand to hand, always with the original reservation, till it paid about one hundred dollars; when the widow made a deal and bought the cow back again before it went dry. That was a fair illustration of the potency of confidence. We all felt satisfied that the cow was safe in the widow's keeping and would be forthcoming on demand, the only risk being the possible death of the cow.

And that reminds me of an incident arising out of a similar contingency. A couple of well known citizens of Bastrop County, in squaring up their accounts found a difference of five dollars, which they agreed should be liquidated by the payment of a yearling. There was no bodily transfer made at the time, and the two men meeting again, one said to the other, "Jake, that yearling of yours died." "What yearling?" inquired the other. "Why, that yearling you was to have from me." Thereupon a spirited controversy arose which came near ending in a lawsuit. The bill of sale called for a yearling, and as it specified no particular animal, though the vendor doubtless had such a one in mind, the holder of the bill claimed face value and got it, the aggrieved party taking care that the goods were delivered and receipted for, a safe course in every business transaction.

CHAPTER 18

It was, I think, in 1840, that the little village of Webberville was started by the opening of a store, of which Jo Manor and Frank Nash were the proprietors. After a time the "grocery" was added, and the place became notorious. Parkerson called the place "Hell's Half Acre," a name which seemed so appropriate that it came to be generally adopted, being shortened by decapitation to "Half Acre."

In 1839 a colony of Mormons, headed by Elder Lyman Wright, made their advent into Texas, pitching their tents for a brief time in Webber's prairie. They were a novelty in the religious world, and, curious to know something of their peculiar views, I permitted the elder to preach in my house. Preaching of any kind was so rare that the neighbors all gathered in and listened with respectful attention while the elder expounded the doctrine of the Latter Day Saints, being careful to leave out its more objectionable features. But amongst most people the idea obtained that they were a lawless band, and the subject of rising up and driving them from the country was strongly advocated. They were in sufficient numbers to stand off the Indians, and, it being their policy to isolate their communities which relegated them to the out-skirts of civilization, I was willing to utilize anything that formed a barrier against the savages. I therefore counseled suspension of hostilities till some overt act called for their expulsion.

The company included artisans of all trades. They took the contract for the first jail in Austin, and, establishing their village about six miles above Austin, at the falls of the Colorado, site of present dam, built the first mill in the country. Up to that time we were under the necessity of grinding our corn on steel mills run by hand—a tedious and wearying process, so that in the building of the mill the Mormons became public benefactors, and it was a great catastrophe to the country when a rise in the river swept their mill away. They gathered up the machinery, but, discouraged with the prospect, began to look about for a better location. Parson Dancer then bought the plant and set it up in the same place, building a fender on the crest of the falls of logs bolted to the solid rock, against which were piled stones and earth, presenting a formidable barrier to the river. But the falls being at the lower end of a narrow gorge, the compressed volume of water rose higher and higher, till it broke over the fender, and pouring a flood down directly on top of the mill, quickly demolished it. When the flood subsided Parson Dancer got out his machinery and prepared to set it up again. He went around among the citizens soliciting aid to rebuild the mill and also to raise his fender higher. Feeling the necessity of a mill, the people turned in and helped, raising the fender clear above the high water mark. But the Colorado was not a stream to be defied by man, so it gathered its strength and swept down against the imposing structure which was interposed between it and its prey, sweeping it from its foundation and burying the mill under the debris. With indomitable courage, Dancer proposed to dig out his mill and set it up again, arguing that, in watching the course of the flood, he saw where he had erred in his former plans, and felt sure he could make it secure next time, but the people were not so sanguine of the success of the scheme and refused to lend assistance.

The next mill was built at Georgetown by George Glasscock, who put up the first bolting works in that part of the country, and, I think, in the country at large. After people began to raise cotton and build gins there were corn crackers attached to the gins, which was a vast improvement on the old crank handmill. Captain Jake Harrell said that after a man had hauled water and ground his bread on a steel mill or beat it in a mortar for a year he was unfitted for any business requiring energy and perseverance. Said he: "I got so that I knew to a grain how much corn it would take for a meal and I couldn't turn another lick till driven to it by the necessity of bread for the next meal."

A hard road we old Texans had to travel; particularly the prairie folks, where the underground streams lay so far down under the blue clay that no one ever succeeded in digging through it, and boring for water had not been thought of. We had either to build on the lowlands along the rivers and take chances on overflows and ague or haul our water in barrels.

But those old mills and mortars were a kind of connecting link; a touchstone as it were, to test a man's willingness to earn his bread. When you rode up to a cabin and heard the old mill grinding away or the pounding of the mortar, if you were willing to earn the welcome that was sure to be extended to you, you recognized your opportunity. To your "hello," no matter how much of a stranger you were, the miller stopped his work long enough to reply, "Light, stranger; light and stake out your hoss." That being attended to, you then walked over to the mill or mortar and said to the operator: "Let me spell you awhile," an offer which was gratefully accepted. Then if you were ambitious to still further ingratiate yourself, you would be up betimes in the morning and bag a wild turkey or perhaps a deer to replenish the stock of provisions you were helping to diminish. Corn was generally plenty, and so long as you were willing to assist in converting it into bread you were welcome to remain. Thus every family had its retinue of retainers if it could boast of no other evidence of aristocracy, and, in fact, it was necessary to keep up the retinue to guard against the Indians. And, by the way, those same Indians were an important factor in the solution of the social problem. But for the ever present danger which kept the white people "rounded up," herded together as it were, love of dominion would, like with the patriarchs of old, have isolated the families, precluding the possibility of schools or any other social organization.

Though socially inclined and hospitable to the last degree, most of them were somewhat averse to having any bounds set to their hunting grounds, like old Billy Barton, who gave name to Barton's Spring, near Austin. The old man was one of the earliest settlers on the Colorado, making his first location on the river near the present town of LaGrange, in the richest agricultural district of the state. When other settlers began to take up claims in the vicinity of eight or ten miles of him he became restive and said "they were beginning to crowd" him, so he pulled out for the upper Colorado, settling at the spring where for several years he maintained his supremacy as "monarch of all he surveyed." He had several sons and the usual number of retainers. His nearest neighbor was at least ten miles distant and Bastrop the nearest trading point. The old man, at one time, sent his sons down to Bastrop with ox teams for supplies. The roads were wet and heavy, impeding the progress of the teams, delaying the boys beyond the usual time consumed in the trip, at which Uncle Billy became uneasy, and as it grew toward night and still the boys failed to arrive, he ascended a hill overlooking the road near his home to take a look for them. Instead of his sons he was startled to see several Indians at the foot of the hill. Uttering a yell, they made a dash for him. He fired one shot at them and then broke for home. Like all frontiersmen, he kept a number of savage dogs, and hearing the yells and shots, they ran to meet the old man, whose age had stiffened his limbs and shortened his wind. He hissed the dogs on his pursuers without slackening his speed, and, the Indians being unable to pass the barrier thus opposed to them, he succeeded in keeping out of their clutches till some of the men came to the rescue. In recounting the adventure Uncle Billy said:

"When I saw the Injuns I fired at them and then just cut loose and run and they after me, but I showed 'em that they couldn't run for shucks."

Our common danger was a strong tie to bind us together. No matter what our personal feelings were, when, in response to the sound of galloping hoofs, in the middle of the night, which we well knew heralded a tale of blood, we started from our beds and were at the door in anticipation of the "hello" which prefaced the harrowing story of a neighbor slain and his family either sharing his fate, or worse still, carried away into horrible captivity, we hastily saddled our horses, if the Indians had not been ahead of us, and left our wives and children, to avenge the atrocious deed. Gathering at the scene of the outrage, we stayed not to gaze on the murdered and mutilated forms or the pile of smoking ruins which marked the site of the late home of the dead and captive family, but taking up the trail followed on with what speed we might, only hoping to be allowed to overtake and inflict a deadly blow upon the foe, though we well knew it would call for retaliation from the savages, and we knew not where their fiendish work might next be directed. Again and again we pursued them without success; they neither staying to eat or sleep until safe beyond pursuit.

I think the last victims in Webber's prairie were Mrs. Coleman and her son in '39, but the war raged around Austin clear on up to the time that Uncle Sam took us under his protecting care and stretched a chain of forts across the frontier, when settlers gathered round them, and the Indians had prey nearer home. But they kept up their thieving excursions till there were few horses left. Every device to outwit them proved futile; if they could not get away with a horse they would kill or disable it. We built strong log stables with stout doors, which we fastened on the inside, going out at the top of the building. Still they would get the horses or kill them. John Hamilton and Milton Hicks each had a fine horse killed in the stable by being shot through the cracks with arrows.

My old brother-in-law, Bobby Mitchell, had lost several horses. At last he got hold of a pair of puzzle hopples. He took them home and put them on his horse and turned him out to graze. He went to bed feeling quite happy over the way he had got the better of the Indians. Next morning he went out to look for "Old Paint," and found him lying dead minus his forefeet. Looking around he perceived the missing feet, still hoppled together, hanging on a limb. Wain Barton, a son of old Billy Barton, a waggish fellow with a strong sense of humor, dramatized the performance, and whenever he got the old man in a crowd he rehearsed it. Old Bobby swore he would rather have "Old Paint" lying there dead than that the Indians should have him.

Of course it was aggravating to have one's horse stolen right from under his nose, but the situation was often so ludicrous as to provoke a laugh. The Indians always chose a dark night, a rainy one preferred, for stealing. Their keen sense of sight and hearing, aided by the darkness, gave them a big advantage in their pursuits. I can't remember the names of all the parties who figured in these stories, but can vouch for the truth of the stories. There was one to the effect that when the first colonists went up to Bastrop, Martin Wells was the leader, he having had experience with Indians tactics during the Creek war. One evening some of the boys reported having seen Indians skulking around; they were not particularly hostile at that time, so old Marty at once surmised that they were bent on mischief. "Boys," said he, "they are after our horses, but we'll fool them this time; we'll go and stake out our horses, and then take our guns and watch them, and when the Indians come up to steal them we'll shoot the rascals." So they took out their horses and staked them and went back to get their supper before returning to take up the watch. But the Indians didn't waste any time, and when the guard stole softly back to lie in wait for them, they were gone, and the horses likewise. The situation was so ludicrous that some of the boys burst out laughing. The old man didn't appreciate the joke. Said he, "Boys, I tell you it's no laughing matter." The phrase became idiomatic. Another time a party of men were camped out, and suspecting the presence of Indians, took various precautions to guard their horses. One fellow, who had an extra good animal, determined to hold his horse at all hazards; so tying his rope around the horse's neck, he sat himself down against a tree, with the rope in his hand. Everything was still, and the horse having fed off the grass within the scope of his cable, became still, the owner dropping into a gentle doze, from which he awakened by a cold hand suddenly coming into contact with his own. The owner of the hand, as much surprised, apparently, as himself, started back. Springing to his feet the owner of the horse let fall the rope, upon which the Indian seized it and got away with the horse. The night was so dark that the savage who had found the horse and was running his hand along the rope, to find where it was fastened, did not perceive the white man till their hands came in contact, but, though startled for the moment, he didn't lose his head. Another man, under similar circumstances, waked up to find a fragment of rope dangling from his hand, the Indian having cut it off after getting near enough to see the holder.

Again, a couple of men put their horses in a stable, the door to which was fastened on the inside by a stout wooden pin, which one of the men drove in with a maul, the men themselves going into camp in the hay loft. Not a sound disturbed them during the night, but when morning dawned the stable door was open and the horses gone. The Indians, by some means, found how the door was fastened, and by steady perseverance succeeded in working the pin out. It perhaps took them an hour, but they had plenty of time.

My stock of horses had been depleted till I had none left except a blind mare and a colt, the latter a fine little fellow, of which I was very proud. That being the year of a brilliant comet, I called my colt Comet. The mare being stone blind I had no apprehension of their being stolen, so I let them run loose, they seldom being out of sight of the house. But there came a morning when the blaze of the Comet failed to catch my eye when I sallied forth in search of it. Looking about I found moccasin tracks and at once divined that the horses were stolen. When I found by the trail that there were only two Indians, I thought I could manage them, so I took my rifle and struck out on the trail, to which the colt's tracks gave me the clue. Crossing Coleman's creek I found where the mare had apparently stumbled in going up the bank and fallen. Coming to a clump of cedars a short distance beyond the creek and not daring to venture into it, I skirted around and picked up the trail on the further side, where the Indians, seemingly disgusted with the smallness of the haul, turned back toward the prairie. I kept right along the trail, and on gaining the top of the rise above "Half Acre," discovered the missing animals feeding. I looked to the priming of my gun, and then scanning the vicinity without perceiving any sign of Indians, went to the mare, near by which on a tree I found a piece of dried bear meat, of which I took possession. It was then quite late in the afternoon and I had left home without eating any breakfast, but I had recovered my horses and felt in a good humor with the world. I went to the village, where I recounted the adventure, exhibiting the bear meat as a witness thereto. The boys swore that when the Indians found that the horses were mine they brought them back and left the meat as a gift of atonement.

The sequel, however, which came a few days later, developed the fact that they only abandoned the mare and colt to get a bigger haul, which they made in Well's prairie, and coming on back again, picked up the mare and colt, which they failed to return. I was mad to recklessness. Taking my rifle on my shoulder and my saddle on my back, I walked four miles to Colonel Jones' to borrow a horse to pursue the marauders. With others who had suffered by the raid we followed on up to Hoover's bend on the Colorado, ten miles above Burnet, where upon breaking camp, they scattered in every direction; but here my Comanche lore came to direct the search. Going to the ashes where the camp fire had been, I found a twig stuck in the ground with a small branch pointing northward, it having been so placed to guide stragglers.

Taking the course indicated, we soon had the satisfaction of seeing their trail increasing, and presently some one called out: "Here's the Comet's track." Guided by the Comet, we kept on to the Leon river, where were encamped the Lipan and Tonkawas, friendly tribes. They were in a state of commotion over the loss of their horses, the Keechis, who were the marauders in this instance, having taken them as they passed. We followed them twenty days but never came up with them.

Of the many different tribes inhabiting Texas prior to its occupation by the Anglo-Saxon only the Karankawas and Tonkawas were known to be cannibals. The Kronks as the former were called, inhabiting the region along the gulf, becoming hemmed in by the whites and their numbers constantly diminishing, were obliged to maintain a semblance of docility; but their unnatural savagery asserted itself whenever an opportunity offered and a ghoulish feast made up for the enforced abstinence.

The Tonkawas, on the other hand, had uniformly manifested a friendly disposition toward the whites, assisting them in their warfare against the hostile tribes, gathering in the scalps and devouring the flesh of the enemy killed in battle, celebrating the victory with a feast and scalp dance, to which the scalp dance given by the Sioux at the Columbian exposition probably bore about the same resemblance that a sham battle does to a real one.

The only one I ever witnessed was in Webber's prairie, the occasion being the killing of a Comanche, one of a party that had been on a horse stealing trip down into Bastrop. They were hotly pursued, and, reasoning about horses as the Chinaman does about boots—that the biggest must naturally be the best—they mounted a warrior on Manlove's big horse, which was part of the booty, and left him behind as rear guard, while the balance hurried the stolen horses away. The Tonkawas joined in the pursuit and when the pursuers came in sight of the lone rear guardsman three of the most expert Tonks were mounted on the three fleetest horses and sent to dispatch him. This they soon accomplished, his steed being a slow one. After killing and scalping him they refused to continue the chase, saying they must return home to celebrate the event, which they accordingly did by a feast and scalp dance. Having fleeced off the flesh of the dead Comanche, they borrowed a big wash kettle from Puss Webber, into which they put the Comanche meat, together with a lot of corn and potatoes—the most revolting mess my eyes ever rested on. When the stew was sufficiently cooked and cooled to allow of its being ladled out with the hands the whole tribe gathered round, dipping it up with their hands and eating it as greedily as hogs. Having gorged themselves on this delectable feast they lay down and slept till night, when the entertainment was concluded with the scalp dance.

Gotten up in all the hideousness of war paint and best breech-clouts, the warriors gathered round in a ring, each one armed with some ear-torturing instrument, which they operated in unison with a drum made of dried deer

skin stretched tightly over a hoop, at the same time keeping up a monotonous "Ha, ah, ha!" raising and lowering their bodies in time that would have delighted a French dancing master, every muscle seeming to twitch in harmony. Meanwhile some old hag of a squaw would present to each in turn an arm or leg of the dead foe, which they would bite at viciously, catching it in their teeth and shaking it like savage dogs. And high over all waved from the point of a lance the scalp, dressed and painted, held aloft by a patriotic squaw. The orgies were kept up till the performers were forced to desist from sheer exhaustion.

At length one of the tribe died. After making darkness hideous for two nights with the most outrageous shrieks and yells that ever tortured civilized ears,* they buried the departed brave and immediately pulled up stakes and moved away. Just before the funeral took place, while the dead warrior lay in state wrapped in his best buffalo robe, a young squaw entered the wigwam with a pair of nice, new beaded moccasins, with which she was in the act of clothing the feet of the corpse, when an old squaw who stood near snatched them from her and with a dexterity which would have done credit to a professional juggler slipped them under her shawl, substituting an old pair and wrapping the feet up in the robe. When time for the funeral arrived the white men present were requested to retire, which they did for the space of half an hour, when they returned to find every vestige of the camp gone, nor could the most diligent search discover the place of interment; there was not a clod of new earth to designate the spot, not a blade of grass that had seemingly been disturbed, so careful were the Indians to obliterate every trace.

The friendly relations between the whites and Tonkawas was never seriously disturbed, the only cause of dissension being the pecan crop, from which the Indians derived quite a revenue, but with reckless prodigality they persisted in killing the goose that laid the golden egg, in chopping off the limbs of the trees to facilitate the gathering. This the owners of the land on which the trees grew objected to. The objection not being regarded, it was found necessary to sustain it with a shot gun in one or two instances, a proceeding that might have been productive of serious consequences had not the old chief, Placido, stood in the breach. It was old Placido's proudest boast that he had "never shed a white man's blood."

Another source of income after settlers became more numerous was game which, frightened away from its old feeding ground, was less easily obtained than formerly. Venison was the meat most frequently for sale. A lady who was in the habit of buying game once asked the vendor why he didn't bring in turkeys, they being quite numerous.

*An Indian funeral is very suggestive of the demonstrations made by cattle over the blood of their kind.

"Oh," said he, "turkey too hard to kill. Injun crawl along in the grass, deer; he say 'Maybe so, Injun; maybe so, stump,' and then he go on eat. Injun crawl a little closer and shoot him. Turkey look, 'Injun, by God,' and he duck his head and run." That was a fair illustration of the difference between the deer and the turkey. I have seen an Indian crawling upon deer, holding his head just far enough above the grass to watch the motions of the game, and whenever the deer threw up its head, instead of ducking his own, the Indian would remain perfectly still, while the quarry gazed suspiciously at him for a few minutes until apparently reassured, and then put down its head and went on feeding; but let a turkey catch sight of a suspicious object he didn't wait to investigate it; it was "Injun, by God," and he was off.

The Tonks took much interest in the social affairs of their white neighbors, attending every gathering that came to their knowledge, without waiting for an invitation. On one of the rare occasions that brought the people together for preaching, a lot of Indians assembled around the door, watching and listening as intently as if fully understanding all that was being said. At last a squaw, weary of holding a chubby baby boy in her arms, stood him up in the door where his highly original costume, consisting of a tiny bow of pink ribbon in lieu of the traditional fig leaf, attracted much attention.

A laughable little comedy enacted by a Tonkawa buck and his squaw at Half Acre affords a good example of the lofty forbearance of the Indian lord of creation toward the weaker vessel.

A lot of Indians were in and around the store when one of the squaws becoming irritated, presumably over the propensity of her lord for gambling off everything he could get his hands on, proceeded to give him a genuine tongue lashing, to judge by the volume and intensity of it. The buck only laughed at first, but becoming weary of the harangue, lit out at the door and started on a dead run. His long queue floating back was grasped by the squaw and away they went, followed by the applause of the spectators.

I don't know what eventually became of the Tonkawas. My impression is, however, that they went to Mexico to avoid the humiliation of being put on a reservation and made to work.

CHAPTER 19

In the spring of 1840 a third attempt to treat with the Comanches resulted in the Council House fight, the first of a series of bloody engagements with which all old Texans are familiar, but of which, for the benefit of the younger generation, a large majority of whom are probably, like those of other sections, averse to reading historical works, I beg leave to here insert a brief sketch.

Having signified their willingness to make a treaty to General McLeod, who was in command at San Antonio, they were informed by that gentleman that in order to secure a hearing they must bring in all their white prisoners. This they promised to do, but when they came in, brought only one, Miss Lockhart, she informing the commissioners that there were twelve others at their camp sixty miles away.

General McLeod in anticipation of trouble had summoned to his aid another company of militia, and it was well he did so, for about thirty warriors accompanied the twelve chiefs who composed the embassy. Therefore, when the chiefs assembled in the council chamber without the other captives, they were informed that they would be held as hostages for their safe delivery. At this the twelve chiefs, headed by my old friend Muguara, true to their character, sprang to arms, preferring certain death to the disgrace of captivity under any circumstances, and not till the last warrior—together with three women and two children—was killed, did the fight cease. Seven white men were killed and eight wounded. Among the killed were Judges Thompson and Hood and Lieutenant Dunnington.

Twenty-seven women and children were held prisoners while a squaw was dispatched to the Comanche camp with a demand for the white prisoners in exchange. Several captives were then brought in and the Indians released. Deeply exasperated at what they deemed an act of treachery, the Comanches returned to their distant home to put their women and children out of harm's way and collect the various branches of the tribe to avenge their fallen comrades. Having perfected their scheme, they a few months later swooped down on Victoria and Linnville, plundering and burning the latter place, killing twenty persons and taking a number of prisoners, together with about two thousand horses and mules.

Apparently satisfied with the result of their raid, they were returning home in triumph when they were intercepted at Plum Creek by two hundred volunteers, conspicuous among whom were old Chief Placido and his little band of Tonkawas. Though the Comanches outnumbered their adversaries more than three to one, they were completely routed, leaving about eighty dead, while there was not a single loss of life on the Texan's side, and only a few wounded, all of whom recovered.

Hoping to put a lasting quietus on the tribe, President Lamar determined to follow up the victory at Plum creek by dispatching Colonel Moore with one hundred men, including twelve Lipan Indians, to find and rout them from their lair, which was located on the Red fork of the Colorado.

The expedition was entirely successful, the camp being burned and the occupants indiscriminately slaughtered, only thirty-four women and children being spared, and they were carried into the settlements and made servants of. It was but the counterpart of the Indians' raid upon Victoria and Linnville, and yet what a different aspect it assumed when the parties changed places. But, in spite of the heavy losses sustained by the Comanches in the three engagements narrated above, "enough for vengeance still remained," as the many ghastly deeds committed in the vicinity of Austin in the four succeeding years bore testimony. They, together with the threatening attitude of Mexico, constituted strong arguments in support of President Houston's claim that the exposed situation of Austin rendered it unsuitable for the seat of government. With hostile savages constantly lurking around (as their ever present moccasin tracks attested) and liable at any time to fire the town, it did seem an insecure place in which to store the archives of the republic. Still the capitol was maintained there till the occupation of San Antonio by the Mexican army rendered the position untenable, in the president's opinion, though the removal thence back to Houston made Gen. Houston many bitter and lifelong enemies. He was assailed through the newspapers; every incident of his life, including the sad domestic drama which darkened his early days and well nigh wrecked a noble life, being mercilessly dragged to the light and perverted to heap ignominy upon him. One of these vilifiers, presuming on the personal enmity known to exist between General Houston and Colonel Neill, reported the latter as saying that "when Houston was wounded at the battle of the Horseshoe, he bleated like a calf; and when he received a scratch at the battle of San Jacinto, he shouted 'Retreat, your general is wounded!'" This was more than Colonel Neill could stand. He came out in a communication to a conservative journal denouncing the story as a lie. Said he: "No personal quarrel, however bitter, could influence me to traduce General Houston's character as a soldier. At the battle of Horseshoe Bend he was the first man to mount the breastworks, and, even when wounded, continued to fight till several additional wounds completely disabled him. And a petty 'scratch' it was he got at San Jacinto, his ankle being shattered so that twenty pieces of bone were taken out."

Those were dark days for the Lone Star republic—her treasury bankrupt; without credit at home or abroad; racked by internal feuds and beset by cruel and savage foes without; and the little army, which had been raised and equipped, sent to its death in Mexico, while our frontier was without protection.

In these desperate straits France consented to come to the rescue with a loan, to secure which the republic was to give her a lien on the public domain, which would virtually have made Texas a vassal of France.

From this humiliating condition the country was saved by a providential interposition in the character of a personal quarrel between the French representative at the capital and one Bullock, a pugnacious hotel keeper. The facts in the case were substantially these.

M. de Saligny, the French charge d'affaires, kept a pair of fine horses, which he fed on corn, a proceeding which did not long escape the attention of a drove of pigs belonging to Bullock. Having the freedom of the city, the pigs soon became regular visitors at monsieur's stables, ostensibly to pick up the

[185]

grains of corn scattered on the floor; but, hog like, they were not content with the meager share that thus fell to their portion, and, climbing into the feed boxes, they helped themselves. Becoming exasperated at the troublesome visitors, the hostler finally pitchforked one of them and threw it over the fence. Old Bullock wasn't a man to be trifled with, so he thrashed the hostler, at which De Saligny swore out a complaint against Bullock, which so incensed the latter that when Saligny went over to pay a visit to the United States representative, the Hon. George Flood, who was domiciled at Bullock's hotel, the landlord, ignoring his high official position, promptly ordered him off the premises. The minister applied to the government to redress his wrongs, and, failing to get satisfaction, demanded his passports and returned to France, where his unfavorable report put an end to the pending negotiations.

Thus the amicable relations between the sister republics were disturbed, and a great international treaty which we had sent envoys across the ocean to secure was frustrated by so insignificant a creature as a pig. What M. de Saligny doubtless intended as an injury, proved a fortunate deliverance for Texas. We were poor, but still freemen.

Such was the condition of the country when news of the occupation of San Antonio by General Woll came as a climax to our numerous troubles. Prompt to meet the new danger which confronted us, men hastened to the front to repel the invader. But news traveled slowly, and by the time the Colorado contingent reached Seguin, Dawson and his men had been annihilated and the Mexicans were on the retreat, with Captain Caldwell in close pursuit. I had found out by this time that a man with a family was less eager to get into a fight than were those who were alone in the world; at least that was my experience, and, there seeming to be no further need of our services, Jonathan Burleson, Hutchinson Reed, David Burnett, Jacob Standifer and myself concluded to return home, the rest of the party going on.

The night we stayed at Seguin, Sam Craft's mare disappeared. The next morning our little party, all unsuspicious of danger, started for home. Arriving at the San Marcos, we camped for the night and were sitting down eating our supper when we were startled by the clatter of hoofs and were a moment later apprised of the near presence of a foe when Craft's missing mare ran up to our horses.

We knew at once that she had escaped from the Indians who were doubtless camping on our trail, waiting for us to go to sleep, when they would have fallen upon us. It was getting too dark to see any distance, so we concluded to get away from there as fast as possible. My horse was a poor one, so I caught Craft's mare and appropriated her. The weather was threatening and, the sky becoming heavily overcast, we were soon enveloped in an inky darkness which we trusted would conceal our movements from the savages until we could get a good start on them. By and by the darkness was relieved by occasional flashes of distant lightning, coming nearer, till low, rumbling thunder announced an approaching storm. We rode on at a rapid gait and, on the divide between the San Marcos and Plum creek, we met the full force of the storm, accompanied by the most imposing display of fireworks I ever beheld. There was one continuous flash of lightning darting its tongues of lurid flame so near us that some one suggested we had better throw away our guns. I said "No; hang onto the guns at all hazards and keep them dry if possible; we are liable to have use for them at any time." The crashes of thunder were deafening; the air was so charged with electricity that we could smell the brimstone. Our horses became confused and frightened, as when in the midst of fire, and refused to budge. The rain came down in torrents; but, it was not cold, and we comforted ourselves with the thought that if the Indians were in pursuit their horses were doubtlessly as completely paralyzed as our own. The violence of the storm soon passed, and we resumed our journey at as brisk a pace as the condition of the ground would permit. Late in the night we reached Plum creek, thankful that we had so far escaped. Our horses were considerably jaded and, after crossing the creek, we struck down stream about half a mile, where we turned into the bottom and, dismounting, sat on the wet ground and held our horses till morning, when, cautiously reconnoitering and finding the coast clear, we started back to the road. Soon we had ample evidence that the red devils had been hot on our trail in the large number of tracks they left, where they had apparently lost our trail and circled round in search of us; and had they pursued their search but a little further they would have found us. The rain had saved us by obliterating our tracks; but for that and the warning given by Craft's stolen mare the Indians would have had five more scalps to atone for comrades slain. Satisfying ourselves that they had not gone on in our direction, we breathed free again and felt our scalps to make sure they were in their natural places. Our pursuers had evidently abandoned the hunt.

The story of the Dawson massacre has been too often told in print to require a repetition here. There was, however, one pathetic incident connected with it that I do not remember to have seen, and yet it should not be allowed to disappear from view. Old Zedic Woods, as he was familiarly called, was then living at LaGrange. He had fought with General Jackson at New Orleans and with the Texas army in the war for independence, and was getting well along in years when the Mexican invasion rallied young and old once more to do battle. Although his form had lost its vigor and his eye its keenness, his martial spirit was undaunted and he was among the first to respond to Captain Dawson's call for volunteers. His family and friends tried to dissuade him from going, on account of his age.

"O, no!" said he, "I fought with General Jackson at New Orleans and with General Houston at San Jacinto, and I must give them one more chance at Old Zedic."

The old man and three sons joined the company. The father and two sons,

Montroville and Norman, were killed, and Gonzalvo, the youngest, made his escape almost miraculously. As I was not there, I can only "tell the tale as 'twas told to me," but the story current at the time was that Gonzalvo's horse having been shot, a Mexican rushed upon him with a lance. Catching the lance, which was attached to the Mexican's wrist, he jerked his assailant to the ground, and himself mounting the Mexican's horse, dashed among the soldiers, yelling as loudly as any of them; and, having on a Spanish sombrero, he escaped detection amidst the confusion, and thus succeeded in getting through the Mexican line, and, once clear, having a good horse under him, he made good his escape.

Plum creek seemed to be a kind of haunted stream for me. It was at Plum creek where Early was murdered, and his horse, which brought me under suspicion of having committed the deed, was caught among a drove of mustangs, a full account of which is given elsewhere.

Some time after our narrow escape from the Indians at that ill-omened stream, I made arrangements with some parties from Bastrop to go out on the San Marcos and buy land, it being our intention to build a mill there. Mills had been a hobby of mine from the time I could remember. I started out from Webber's prairie alone, expecting to fall in with the balance of the party at Cedar creek. I was too late, however, and, thinking I might overtake them, I kept on to Plum creek, where night overtook me and I concluded to camp. The Indians, though still hostile, were confining their operations principally to prowling around the frontier settlements in small parties, but I took the precaution to turn off the road after crossing the creek, going some little distance up the stream. Feeling little apprehension of danger, I unsaddled my horse and staked him out, and, spreading down my blankets, lay down and was just beginning to doze when I heard an owl hoot a little way below, answered at a short interval by one above, and then another in another direction. I didn't wait to see whether it was owls or Indians, but just saddled my horse and struck out at a lively canter, nor drew rein till I reached the San Marcos, where I found my friends. Our land speculation fell through for want of title by the party holding it. I bargained for a hundred acres, including the site where General Burleson and Firebaugh afterward built a mill, for which I was to pay two dollars an acre, only one-half of it being cash; the other half was represented by a horse. I would like to know what the land is worth at present. There was not then a single settler on the old San Antonio road between Cedar creek and San Antonio.

As the Indian incursions gradually ceased settlers began to move out, but I was never out that way after it became settled. I may be somewhat at fault in locating some of the scenes and incidents in these sketches. Your newfangled maps, all bisected with railroads, throw me off my bearings. If I could get hold of one of those old Texas almanac maps, issued away back before the war, showing the wagon roads and crossings, I would know exactly where I was "at."

And speaking of "crossings" reminds me of a laughable story Jake Harrell used to tell on one of the old pioneers. The old man was one of a party of explorers that went out to look at the country along Onion creek. On his return his friends all gathered in to hear his report, which I give verbatim, as nearly as I can make the English alphabet answer to it.

Said he: "Low down on Ingern creek, down about the Sasser crossin', there's as fine sile as ever was seen on the face of the yearth, but high up on Ingern it's a nasty, rocky country, just precept upon precept."

Saucer crossing got its name from a saucer containing bee bait, which had been set on a stump at the crossing by some early explorer and left there. It is on the road leading from Austin to San Antonio, and may be known by that name still for aught I know. The first settler there was one of old Joe Burleson's sons, known as "Hopping" John on account of a lameness. Others of the early settlers on Onion creek were the Soul and Baker families.

Just above the mouth of the creek on the west side of the Colorado was located old Bobby Mitchell, who, having been the first settler, gave name to the locality, which was designated Mitchell's Bend. Uncle Bobby had his own troubles. He had an old trusted horse, John, which had long eluded the Indians, but one day old John made the acquaintance of a band of mustangs, and, being of a sociable disposition, concluded to take up his abode with them. The old man went out to hunt up John and found him, but the mustangs sped away like the wind, leaving old John far in the rear. Mitchell was riding a very good horse and gave chase. He swore he wanted to kill old John when he kicked up his heels and rushed away as wild as any of the band. His old joints were too stiff to keep pace with them, though he did his level best, and "fairly grunted" in his efforts to get away from his pursuer. Mitchell was very solicitous for the welfare of his animals, and would not see any of them hurt if he could help it. On one occasion he was out looking after his hogs, when his dogs, which always accompanied him, treed a panther. He shot the panther, wounding it, when it sprang upon the two dogs, which were unable to handle it. There was no time to load his gun; the enraged panther seized one of the dogs, and, lying on its back, proceeded to tear its victim with its hind feet. Mitchell jumped upon the panther's tail, thus holding its claws back till the dogs dispatched it.

Just across the river from Mitchell's Bend was Reuben Hornsby's place, which was the first settlement made above Bastrop. The family, consisting of Reuben, senior, and wife, Aunt Sallie; their six sons: William, Malcom, Reuben, Joseph, Daniel and Thomas, and one daughter. With them came Smith Hornsby, a brother of the elder Reuben. He was accidentally killed by one of his own party in an Indian fight. The Hornsbys built themselves a strong fort, which was several times attacked, but never carried. When there were no men on hand to defend it, Aunt Sallie was equal to the task. A party of Indians once made a demonstration of attack when all the men happened to be away. There were several families stopping in the fort, and Aunt Sallie mustered the women and, commanding them to don male attire, armed them with broom sticks and sallied forth. The Indians, surprised to find the place so well garrisoned, took to their heels, leaving Aunt Sallie and her broom-stick brigade in undisputed possession. To Reuben and Sallie Hornsby and their bold and hardy sons the country owes a debt which it can never repay. Pitching their camp in the very gateway of the Indian country, they not only maintained their position, but opened their doors to all who chose to avail themselves of their hospitality. Thither in times of peril other families re-paired for safety, and, if they needed it, more substantial aid was generously given.

There was another brother of the old man's, Thomas, who came on later. He was a good natured, simple soul; but, not having had the advantages of education to aid a naturally studious mind, he evolved some amusing ideas. He and I were out in camp together, when he fell to talking about the mo-tions of the earth, while we sat around the camp fire after supper.

"Talk about the earth turning over every twenty-four hours," said he, "why, I can convince any man on earth that's got a particle of sense in five minutes that that's all nonsense."

Surprised and curious to hear his formula, I replied:

"If you can do that, Uncle Tommy, your fortune's made."

He got up and cut three stakes, then, pointing to the polar star, he said:

"That's the north star, ain't it?" I agreed that it was. He then set his three stakes in a line with the star.

"There now; you may get up at any time of the night and look at those stakes and you'll find them still in line. That ought to convince anybody that the earth doesn't move."

I knew it was useless to argue the question, so I acknowledged that the proof was convincing.

One other short story I wish to add to the long chapter of Indian outrages, and then we will pass on to another phase of the troubles of the settlers.

It was in 1840 that a little party of men went out to Brushy to kill buffalo. Claiborne Orsburn, a lad of 18, was left to bring up the pack animals while the men killed the game. There were a couple of Indians on the watch and, as soon as the men became engaged with the buffalo, they ran upon Claiborne, shooting his horse and then clubbing him over the head with a gun. Hearing the shots, the other members of the party hurried back to the rescue. Orsburn was stunned by the blow and his assailants, supposing him dead, scalped him. The flow of blood restored him to consciousness; but, hearing the Indi-ans talking, he lay perfectly still for a few moments. He said they seemed to

be disputing about the possession of the scalp, and, there being a double crown curl on his head, were apparently discussing the propriety of availing themselves of the remaining one to settle the dispute. Claiborne didn't relish that; so, taking advantage of their momentary distraction, he sprang to his feet, and, at the same instant perceiving Alec Hamilton galloping to his relief, ran to meet him. The Indians made off and, meeting Hamilton, Orsburn's first words were:

"They've cut my head; have they scalped me?"

His companions bound up his head with wet handkerchiefs and brought him to my house, where my wife dressed the wound, which was small, and soon healed over. Claiborne lived to a good old age, raising a large family; dying at his home in Bastrop County, March 6th, 1899.

CHAPTER 20

Though there had not been a tree felled anywhere in the vicinity of the city of Austin prior to the location of the capital there, as soon as the seat of government was established in the new log cabins provided for its reception, people began to gather about it; by far the larger portion outside of official circles being lawyers and gamblers.

The wholesale issue of bogus land certificates, together with numerous other irregularities in the land business of the colonial period were a prolific source of litigation, offering a fertile field for legal talent; and thither, accordingly, came lawyers of all grades, including some of the best in the United States. Among the latter, none ranked higher than William H. Jack, or, as he was commonly called, Bill Jack, and the latter name seems the more appropriate as it is suggestive of strength, which was characteristic of the man. With him were associated his two brothers, Patrick and Spencer, all lawyers, natives of Alabama. Barrie Gillespie, also of Alabama, was early in the field, as were Judge Webb, Judge Lee, Sneed and Oldham, George W. Paschal, and, a little later, A. J. Hamilton, William P. Duval (ex-governor of Florida), John Hancock, and perhaps others.

Captain Jacob Harrell, at the lower end of Congress avenue, and Bullock, further up, dispensed the hospitality of the city to the stranger within the gates. The first two men to venture into the mercantile line were Martin Moore and Blessin, both Irish. Michael Ziller started it with a junk shop, gradually enlarging his business until it became too large for the modest quarters in which he began. The indefatigable Ziller then set to work, and, with only such assistance as was absolutely necessary, himself quarried, hauled and prepared stone, with which he erected the first stone building in the city.

Lamar Moore put up the first brick building, on the corner of Congress avenue and Pecan street, in which he carried on a general merchandise business until his death. Dietrich & Horst opened the first meat market; Dietrich subsequently retiring to open a dry goods store with George Hancock.

Austin was an exceedingly healthy location, hence poor pickings for medicos, the fraternity being represented by Drs. Cook, Johnson and Chalmers, with old Dr. Anderson of Webber's Prairie to fall back on in critical cases. Nor must "Old King Cole, the jolly old soul," be omitted. Being flat broke and afflicted with an ulcer on his leg when he struck Austin, a friend set him up in the whisky business with a half barrel for a starter. His kindly disposition soon won him friends and his business thrived apace, enabling him to open the first decent saloon in town. The militiamen made Cole's place their favorite resort and often made the walls ring with the song, "Old King Cole is a Jolly Old Soul." Being also headquarters for the gentlemen of the green cloth, who are notoriously generous while luck runs in their favor, it came to be the regular thing for all schemes of a benevolent nature to be carried first to Cole, who unhesitatingly took charge of them and, heading the list with a generous donation, laid for the sports and, whenever one made a winning, struck him for a subscription, which was collected on the spot. Having acquired a comfortable fortune, he sold out his business and, turning country gentleman, procured a piece of land above the city on the Colorado, where he established himself in a bachelor's hall and was still there the last I knew of him.

Another noted character associated with the republic was Thomas William Ward, otherwise known as Peg Leg Ward, he having given his right leg for the freedom of Texas in the taking of San Antonio in 1835. In consideration of his patriotism he was made commissioner of the land office. Later, while engaged in firing a salute on some state occasion, the cannon was prematurely discharged, depriving the luckless Ward of his right arm and right eye. He then set to and learned to write with his left hand and by the time he recovered sufficiently to resume his official duties could write a respectable hand. People honored him for his indomitable courage as well as his patriotism, and he was allowed to continue in office. John Nolan, a brother Irishman, of whom I shall have occasion to speak again, was rather jealous of Ward's popularity. "Yes," said he, "he is a great man now, but when I knew him in New Orleans he was shovin' a jack plane while I was a gintleman marchant."

It often happened that legal acumen cut a small figure in the decision of cases. John Anderson, a son of Dr. Anderson, was reading law in the office of Barrie Gillespie. He said they once had a client in a dispute over a land title. Gillespie took the client aside and asked: "What can you prove?"

"By ———, sir, that's not the question; what do you want proved? My witnesses are here," was the reply. The lawyers for the other side, being made

aware of the state of the case, advised their client to compromise, a piece of advice he accepted, thereby saving himself a goodly sum in the way of costs.

Old Ziller had some very practical views on the dispensation of justice. He, with characteristic generosity, had taken in a destitute fellow countryman and was rewarded for his kindness by being robbed by his protege. I give the story in his own words.

"I go way and leave him to keep my store. When I come back all my money and some my goods gone. I go to Judge Johnson and tell him I want one paper for catch ze d——d scoundrel. Ze judge make out ze paper and I say, 'Where is ze constabler?' He say, 'I make you ze constabler, Captain Ziller.' I take ze paper and go after ze tief. I catch him at Walnut Creek. I get all my goods and zen I tie him to a tree and give him one d——d good whipping. I turn him loose and go home. I go see Judge Johnson. He say, 'W'at you do mit him?' 'I tie him to one tree and give him one d——d good whipping,' I say. 'O, well,' he say, 'You make one very good constabler, Captain Ziller.'"

In those days and for many long years thereafter goods for all the upper Colorado were brought from Houston by ox-teams; slow transports under the most favorable circumstances, and when the rain transformed the black soil into vast beds of wax, they were sometimes several weeks on the trip. Old Ziller had sent by the Thompson boys, who were regular teamsters, for a barrel of whisky. The rain retarded their progress, the whisky in the meantime getting rather "wet." Ziller was wrathy when he discovered the damage to his goods, giving vent to his feelings in the following language: "G————n dem Thompson boy; he pull all ze whisky out of my barrel and fill him wis water."

A genial, entertaining old fellow was William P. Duval, ex-governor of Florida. Possessed of an inexhaustible store of anecdotes, gathered from the varied experience of a long life, with the characteristic genius of the French-man for story telling, his appearance in public was a signal for all the lovers of good stories to assemble around him. In recounting his experience in Florida during the four years in which he was the head of the territorial government, he averred that, "if he went to hell when he died and the authorities who presided over that institution did not give him credit for those four years, he should always think they did him an injustice."

The gubernatorial mansion was a pine log cabin located on a low sandy flat, destitute of vegetation. The air was alive with mosquitoes, and the sun, beating down with almost tropical fierceness upon the thin pine board roof, gave to the situation an atmosphere as nearly resembling that ascribed to the infernal regions as anything he could imagine. Thomas H. Duval, his son, was our third district judge, Mills and Baylor having preceded him.

It was about 1840 or 1841 that T. J. Chambers laid claim to four leagues of land on the west side of the Colorado opposite Bastrop, on which my mother-in-law, the Widow Blakey, the Hemphills, old Colonel Knight and a number of others had located headrights. Chambers was appointed judge by the Mexican government and he advanced a modest claim for forty leagues of land in compensation for his services, though he never held a term of court. His claim may have been just, that is to say legal, for anything the trial of the case developed to the contrary, but there certainly was an element of injustice, especially in the case of Mrs. Blakey, who had given two sons to die in the defense of the country and then was threatened with the loss of her home.

Having then no son old enough to attend to her business, Mother Blakey made me her agent. I went around to the other interested parties and proposed to them to all go in together and fight the claim before the courts. This they agreed to do. Without loss of time I retained Bill Jack and Judge Webb to conduct the defense, but when I called on the balance of the defendants for their share of the retainer's fee they hung back, saying that one case would decide all. Disgusted with the desertion of our natural allies, I went to Mrs. Blakey and, acquainting her with the situation, advised her to compromise with Chambers. Being empowered to act according to my judgment, I went to Chambers and, stating the case, asked what terms he would make. Chambers was gentlemanly and affable and a likeable fellow, withal. Said he: "I have no wish to rob the widow and orphan; but, if I relinquish my claim in her instance, it will weaken it in the others. If Mrs. Blakey will accept a deed to half her headright—4,400 acres—she can then raise her certificate and relocate the whole amount." To this we assented, and the family thus saved their homestead. When the other parties heard of the compromise they came post haste to know why we didn't go on with the suit. I told them to go ahead and get all their claim if they could, we would take what we could make sure of. They went on and lost the case and had to buy their land from Chambers. They made a big mistake in not standing by us, as it would have been hard to find a jury to dispossess Mrs. Blakey, whom everyone knew; at least from character. Lemuel, her second son, was one of the seven heroes whose ashes are mingled with the historic dust of San Jacinto, and her eldest son, Edward, lost his life in the battle with the Indians at Brushy.

As to the rights of T. J. Chambers, he could at least advance the claim of being one among the first Americans to pitch his tent in the wilderness, and, having been appointed surveyor-general for the colonies, it was quite reasonable to suppose that he would select the most desirable locations obtainable on which to lay his certificates. But there were those who came to the state after its annexation and bought up or manufactured old Spanish grants, and, with witnesses made to order, robbed the old pioneers of their hard earned homes. Judge Lucket, who lived below Austin, once asked me: "Do you know where that old Spanish mission on the San Gabriel is?" I told him I did. Said he: "Colonel Snively will give any man a league of land to show him that old mission." I began to smell a rat. "And what does he want to find it for?" I asked. "Why, he has a grant for thirty leagues of land cornering on that old mission." The situation flashed over me like fire. I was at that time located on Brushy creek, some ten miles above its confluence with the San Gabriel at which point were the remains of an ancient mission built by the old Spanish missionaries away back in the seventeenth century. There was nothing left of it but a kind of mound, preserving the size and shape of the building, which, being of adobe, had succumbed to the influence of the rain, or perhaps an inundation, so long ago that goodly sized trees had grown up from the ruins.

Without stopping to inquire how the grant was to be run, I thought of the numbers of families who had by the time settled in that section and hewed themselves homes out of the wilderness. Said I, "I can show Colonel Snively the old mission, but if he comes fooling around out there with his thirty-league grant we'll establish a permanent corner for him on some convenient tree." The community indorsed my sentiments and that was the last I ever heard from Colonel Snively's thirty-league grant.

There was still another class of land sharks who victimized those who through ignorance of the law had not exactly complied with its requirements. These lynx-eyed land grabbers had their emissaries in the land office and whenever a flaw was discovered in a settler's title they had certificates ready to file on the land, thus compelling the settler to buy the land from them or lose his improvements. And often there was no flaw, but these unscrupulous villains would persuade the holder that there was, offering to make the settler a deed to the land if he would lift his certificate and transfer it to them. By this means they came into possession of many genuine certificates in exchange for lands to which they had no title whatever. As almost all public service was at first paid in land warrants, there were, of course, thousands of them in circulation, and whenever one was located on land claimed by another the locator had the privilege of "lifting" his certificate and laying it elsewhere, a process which of itself was productive of much confusion. The honest settlers at last reached the limit of endurance and began to talk shotgun and hemp. A noted land pirate, who operated all over the state, discovered a flaw in the title by which the settlers along Oatmeal creek held their land and promptly notified them of the fact; also that he had located the land. The settlers held a meeting and passed a resolution breathing strongly of powder, I being present though not an interested party. I shortly afterward met the would-be locator of the disputed territory and told him of the talk I had heard. "Why," said he, "do you think they'd kill a fellow?" "I know they would," I replied. "Old J. J., the leader of the crowd, has already killed one man and would shoot you as soon as he would a wolf that came prowling around his premises." The legislature meanwhile being appealed to, confirmed the original title and the settlers were left in peaceable possession of their homes.

I see that those old grants still crop out from time to time and will probably continue to do so for years to come.

But, to return to Austin. When the first issue of treasury notes came to take the place of the land scrip and military scrip the sporting fraternity hailed the change with delight; but, when, under the endless chain system, of the workings of which we have had a view quite recently in the United States, the treasury notes ran down till it took a mountain of them to represent a small stake, the gamblers grew discontented. Their distress was relieved when the exchequer bills replaced the dishonored redbacks, as the treasury notes were called. But again the currency depreciated till a small jack-pot could not accommodate the bulk of paper. Then they began to talk about the advisability of "a new ish," and, that hope of relief failing, some of them went off and joined the army. Sowell tells of one who drew a black bean and went to his death with a smile. I have heard the story often.

Preachers were a little slow in getting around to look after the lost sheep, and in truth met with little encouragement when they did come. The Methodists held one camp meeting in Webber's prairie during my residence there, but the constant dread of Indians made outdoor gatherings rather poorly attended. Parson Whipple came to the country as early as 1838 and was for forty years the leading preacher in western Texas. Then there were two of the Dancers who preached, and Parson Haynie, father of Dr. Haynie, who lived with his son-in-law, John Caldwell, in Caldwell's prairie. Parson Haynie did not preach much; but, whenever there was need of revenue to carry on the crusade against Satan, he took hold, and few could equal him when it came to raising the wind.

John Caldwell came to Texas in 1830, going at once to Bastrop County, where he located the land upon which he spent the greater portion of his life. A lawyer by profession, highly educated, and very intelligent, he necessarily found his surroundings very uncongenial and was often attacked by hypochondria, under the influence of which he would persuade himself that death was near. Having occasion to go to his house one day, Mrs. Caldwell met me at the gate. Said she: "I am very glad you came; Mr. Caldwell has one of his blue spells on and if anybody can rouse him you can."

I took my cue and upon entering the room took a seat beside his bed and, without any comment upon his situation, plunged at once into the all-absorbing topic of the removal of the seat of government back to Houston, taking pains to be a little aggressive in my endorsement of the president's course. Caldwell was one of his bitterest opponents and he couldn't stand it long. At first his voice was so weak as to be almost inaudible, but it soon began to strengthen, and directly he raised himself in bed. I kept up my hot applications and soon had him out of bed and dressed and by the time I was ready to go he was entirely recovered.

"Now," said Mrs. Caldwell, "when Mr. Caldwell gets sick again I'll know what doctor to send for."

That might have been termed a "faith cure" and might have given me prestige in some circles.

John Caldwell represented Bastrop County in the Texas congress and subsequently in the state legislature. It was mainly through his efforts that the settlers on Oatmeal creek, before spoken of, were confirmed in their claim to the land they had settled on and improved.

CHAPTER 21

The Santa Fe expedition, a piece of folly to which the Texas congress refused its sanction, though the president gave it his approval, took away many good men who were destined never to return; and those who did survive to tell the tale, suffered untold hardships during their enforced sojourn in Mexican prisons, together with their countrymen who were taken at Bexar when General Woll made his descent on that town, taking the court, which happened to be in session, prisoners, and the survivors of the miserable Somervell expedition, which cost the struggling republic so many of its bravest and best men.

Being personally acquainted with many of the men in all the above named parties, many of the stories incident to their wretched life in the fortress of Perote recur to mind which may be of interest to my readers.

Sam Norval, than whom no man was better known about Austin, was one of the Bexar prisoners, and as they were not taken in arms, they were less harshly dealt with than those of the other parties, many immunities being offered them on condition that they embrace the Roman Catholic religion. Sam had no taste for prison life and was not disposed to allow a small matter like religion to stand in the way of liberty. He accepted the good offices of the padre, who took a lively interest in the spiritual welfare of the prisoners, as did some of the officers, and became so exemplary a proselyte that the proud missionary took him under his protection, sharing his quarters and clothes with him. The good father was a bit worldly withal, and loved to while away the time over the cockpit, himself being the possessor of several fine birds. Sam Norval had spent many years in New Orleans, where cock fighting was also a popular amusement, and was therefore able to give the padre many valuable hints, which tended to greatly enhance his zeal in behalf of his convert. Among other marks of the high estimation in which he was held by the father, Sam used to exhibit a fine cloak, such as is worn by the priesthood, and when enveloped in its folds declared himself "clothed in righteousness." The priest was derelict in his duty as a spiritual ministrant in that case. He should have put Sam to death while under conversion, for on his final release he apostatized, declaring that he had merely wrapped his Catholicism in the padre's cloak and laid it by for a future emergency.

John Taney, on the contrary, who had been raised a Catholic, stubbornly refused to give any intimation of the fact; so intense was his hatred toward his captors, that he would rather suffer all the horrors of the loathsome prison than gratify them by acknowledging his connection with their church.

The Mexicans firmly believing that those only who were within the pale of the Roman Catholic church were Christians, and in some instances solicitous for the future welfare of their charges, attempted to lead them to the light. An officer one day attempted to do a little missionary work on his own account, the object of his solicitude being the aforesaid Taney.

"Do you know who Jesus Christ is?" asked the evangelist.

"Oh, yes," Taney replied. "He was a good, kind old man who traveled over the country doing good everywhere. He came into Mexico and the Mexicans caught him and killed him."

"Carrajo!" ejaculated the infuriated catechiser, and, turning on his heel, left the "brute" to his fate. The Mexicans applied the term "brute" to all non-Catholics. I recall a laughable incident that occurred away back in the colonial days at San Felipe. A Mexican official came out on some business, having with him as interpreter a Mexican who had spent most of his life in Texas, and, having been a good deal among the Americans, had adopted their ways and was proud to class himself as an Americano. Some one asked him if he was a Christian.

"Oh, no!" said he, "me one brute, same like Mericans."

Felix McClusky, whose name has frequently occurred in these pages, voiced the sentiments of the Texans as to the Christianity of the Mexicans in an "aside" at San Antonio. A number of Mexican women visited our camp, and, not dreaming that their conversation was falling on understanding ears, were discussing the personnel of the Texans.

"A fine looking lot of men," was their verdict, and "what a pity it is they are not Christians like us!"

McClusky had mustered enough Spanish to catch the last sentence, and eyeing the group contemptuously, he snarled out:

"Ye—es, now, you're a d—d pretty lookin' set of Christians, now, ain't you?"

To this we all responded "Amen!" And yet many of those women were possessed of true Christian principles, as many a hapless prisoner testified.

But to return to the unfortunates imprisoned in the castle of Perote. The Mexicans did not believe in keeping a lot of idlers, even though they were captives, so they were put to work on the public highways. The first plan adopted was to make them up into pack trains, each man having a bag containing a bushel of sand slung over his shoulders, the sand being obtained at the river, and used to repair the roads leading into the city. Not relishing the job, some of the party devised a plan whereby the load might be considerably lightened. Slyly collecting scraps of hoop iron, they employed their leisure time in breaking it into small bits, which they could conceal in the palm of the hand, whetting the edge on the stone walls of the prison. Thus armed, they started out almost gaily for the next day's work. They were loaded up at the river and started citywards. On pretense of easing their burdens, they put their hands underneath the sand bags and with the improvised knives cut holes in the bags, so that little streams of sand began to trickle down, constantly diminishing the load until some of the bags contained less than a quart by the time the town was reached. The officers in charge of the gang eyed the perforated bags suspiciously and instituted a search for the instruments employed to do the mischief. Failing to find anything suspicious, they procured new bags and again went for the sand. But the bags continued to spring leaks, giving the road over which they passed a beautiful coat of sand, but there was none left in the bags by the time they reached their destination. The supply of bags and also the patience of the guards becoming exhausted, they devised another plan to utilize the physical powers of the "brutes." They rigged up rawhide harness, composed of breast and shoulder straps, with which they invested the prisoners, and, coupling them together in long strings, hitched them to wagons and set out for the mountains to bring in stone for paving the streets. There was no chance to shirk then, as they were accompanied by drivers, who treated them exactly as they did mules, except that the "teams" were made to load and unload the stone. Long suffering, with scarcely a hope of relief, had made them reckless, and they desperately resolved to put an end to the stone hauling, for one day at least, even at the risk of more serious consequences. During the night they arranged their plans. They were driven as usual to the mountains on the following morning, loading up the wagon and starting on the return with remarkable docility. Everything went so smoothly that the guards began to congratulate themselves on having at last found a means of subduing the lively Texans. It was but the calm before the storm. Arriving at the top of a long incline, they were allowed to stop and take breath. When the word was given to start again it was obeyed with an alacrity that astonished the natives. John Taney and his mate were working in the lead. Taney gave a loud snort, and simultaneously the whole team kicked up their heels and started on a mad race down the hill; running over stones in the road, the stones in the wagon were thrown this way and that, making it warm in the vicinity of the road; but on they went, knocking down and running over several of the guards who attempted to stop them, and at length in true runaway style swerving from the road crashed the wagon against a tree, utterly demolishing it.

For this escapade some of them came near suffering serious consequences, but as none of the Mexicans run over were killed, they were not put to death and there was little more in the way of punishment, short of death, than that which they had already endured.

John Taney was one of the number who made their escape from Hacienda del Salado, and being recaptured, had to draw a bean for life or death. Noticing that the black beans, several of which had been drawn before, were rather smaller than the white ones, he plunged his hand into the bowl, and feeling for the largest bean in the lot, drew a lucky white one. He was one of the eight who tunneled under the prison walls at Perote, and was again retaken. The prison was floored with large flat stones laid in cement; the prisoners managed to remove one of these stones and with only bits of iron and the horn spoons given them to eat with they excavated a tunnel, concealing the dirt under their pallets. Taney who was the leading spirit in the enterprise was nicknamed "the Gopher" on account of the dexterity with which he spooned out the dirt. When all was in readiness they filed off their irons and got out, but were not enabled to get away. They several times cut off their irons and hid them under a stone which they had loosened, concealing them so successfully that the Mexicans never found them during their stay.

They had again completed a tunnel, but upon learning through the United States minister that there was a prospect of their early release they abandoned the attempt to escape. After their release the officer in charge of the prison asked as a special favor that they tell where the missing irons were stored, but even this small favor they stubbornly refused to grant, averring that "they would be used on some other poor fellows." Taney said that he often wished he were some good man's dog, so that he might at lest get enough to eat. He was a great whistler and in the absence of any other music he whistled a quickstep to which the company marched to their fatal encounter with Ampudia's army at Mier. I don't know what tune it was Taney whistled and there is probably no one left who heard it. When the Bexar prisoners were released, Taney, with several others, presented themselves among them. The commanding officer suspected them, and halting them, asked them if they were the Bexar prisoners. At this the man to whom the question was addressed turned hesitatingly to his companions and said: "Shall I say yes or no?" The commandant caught the word "no," and at once halted them till the case could be investigated, a proceeding which proved fatal to their hopes of freedom. At length, as much to the relief of the guards, whom they had taxed their ingenuity to annoy as much as possible, as to themselves, the last of the prisoners were set at liberty and allowed to depart for Texas, leaving behind them the bones of many of their comrades, some of whom had fallen in battle, the seventeen who drew the fatal black beans and many who had died of disease and harsh treatment while confined in the foul dungeons of Perote and other prisons.

While the disastrous expeditions just mentioned were meeting their fate on the western border and the extreme eastern section was being made a bloody battle ground between the Regulators and Moderators, jealousy and ambition among the leading men congregated around the capitol was crystallizing into bitter partisanship which was now and then stimulated by bloodshed. Attempted canings were resented with bullets, several prominent men thus losing their lives, their adherents, in some instances, taking up the quarrel, till at last the system of vendetta culminated in the most villainous and cowardly murder that ever disgraced a city.

Of the many promising young men who came to help the Texans in their struggle for independence, none were more highly esteemed than Mark B. Lewis. I cannot give his nativity further than that he was an American; but he was one of the many who came out during the revolution of Texas. I met him first at Victoria in the summer of '36, his company arriving after the battle of San Jacinto.

When the regular army was organized Lewis was made captain of a company, and in that capacity was assigned to duty at Austin. He commanded the company that rescued the archives, which were being surreptitiously removed from the capitol.

Brave and honorable, Captain Lewis was deservedly popular, thereby incurring the enmity of a certain lawyer whose inordinate vanity and ambition could ill brook the favors lavished on one whom he chose to consider his rival. Burning with envy and hatred, this lawyer plotted to work Lewis' destruction, employing for his instrument a big Irish bully who took occasion to provoke a quarrel with Captain Lewis, and meeting him on the street shot at him. Lewis being untouched, was passing on, when his assailant taunted him with being afraid to return the shot, upon which Lewis turned about and shot the Irishman dead.

Captain Lewis gave himself up to the sheriff, who locked him up for the night, and the next day started his prisoner to the justices' office for a preliminary examination. The sheriff was, unfortunately, a satellite of the instigator of the trouble, and when at a crossing the same principal and a nephew of the dead Irishman stepped out from behind a building and called to him to "stand out of the way," he obeyed with an alacrity that was strongly suggestive of a preconcerted arrangement. Seeing the two men step out with leveled guns, Lewis called to them:

"Gentlemen, there are two of you against one, and I am unarmed; give me a chance to defend myself." The only reply to this appeal to honor was another warning to the sheriff to clear the way. Lewis then turned to the sheriff and appealed to him for protection, but that worthy only shoved his prisoner away from him so as to give the murderous cowards a good chance at him. Seeing there was no other chance, Lewis broke to run, when the wretch who had engineered the whole miserable business fired and killed him. This dastardly deed roused the indignation of the people and had lynching been in

vogue at that time there would have been short shift for both the man who fired the fatal shot and the recreant officer who refused to protect a defenseless prisoner in his charge. The law was allowed to take its course, however, and the murderer arrested and sent to Bastrop for safe-keeping. The jail was only a log house and the jailer being a friend of the prisoner allowed a log to be pried out and the murderer escaping made for Mexico, whither his wife and children followed him, he dying there a few years later.

The sheriff was a young man, highly esteemed, but that one act of his blasted his prospects in that part of the country. He strenuously denied any complicity in the murder of Mark B. Lewis, but no one believed him, and he found the atmosphere so uncongenial thereafter that he sought fresh fields, as did the nephew of the man whom Lewis killed.

And, speaking of the rescue of the archives, I have recently been interrogated by letter regarding the meeting that was held in Austin to take action upon the removal, my interrogator disclaiming that there was anything "revolutionary" in the sentiments expressed thereat. As I was not present I am unable to assert anything to the contrary, but this much I am positively certain about, that as a result of that meeting there were printed circulars sent out, conspicuously headed "Nullification on Our Own Hook." I was at the time lieutenant-colonel of the militia, and as such was waited upon by Colonel Jones, who insisted on my taking a hand in the business; but, nullification and revolution being synonymous terms in my vocabulary, I declined to mix myself up with it, thereby incurring the ill-will of many of my acquaintances to the extent that when I was again put forward as a candidate for office they opposed me on the ground that I was a "Houston man," a charge which I was proud to substantiate then and always.

There is one other noted episode that occurred about that time, about which much has been written, and yet the truth has not all been told, viz., the expulsion of the Cherokees, a very interesting article on which I noted in the Quarterly of the Texas Historical Association, written by John H. Reagan, in which the writer confirms my own impression of that affair. There were doubtless some bad men among the Cherokees, but there were worse ones among their white neighbors, who coveted the Cherokees' land, stock and improvements and spared no pains to place the Indians in the position of aggressors, when they had really exercised remarkable forbearance under the trying situation in which they were placed.

General Burleson, as all his friends knew, was in no wise partial to the Cherokees, but he had a strong sense of justice, and he himself told me that it made him furious to see those white reprobates, who were doubtless to a great extent, responsible for the trouble following in the wake of the military appointed to dispossess the Indians, and locating their lands as fast as the rightful owners were driven off. Another most revolting story, too, I heard of the mutilation of the body of Chief Bowls, one ghoulish wretch cutting strips of skin from the brave old chief's back, avowing his intention of making bridle reins thereof. Poor Lo, like Sambo, he "had no rights that a white man was bound to respect." Their traditional theory that it would be death to the red men to try to live like their white brethren doesn't seem to have stood the test of experiment, as demonstrated by the census of the Indian territory, which surprises me, as I had shared the opinion of the Indians.

Gradually the irresistible Texans drove the natives back till at the time of the annexation, hostilities along the Colorado had ceased, the savages having transferred their operations to the southwest. The last murder by Indians in the vicinity of Austin was in June, 1845, when Daniel Hornsby and William Adkinson were killed while fishing on the Colorado below Austin. With the removal of the capital back to Washington many of the inhabitants flitted away, and perhaps that state of affairs encouraged the Comanches to hope that the obnoxious pale face had begun a retrograde movement; or it might be that the lonely deserted look of the deserted cabins inspired them with a superstitious dread of the place—certain it is that had they been so disposed, they might have burned a large portion of the town.

Though President Houston by a vigorous application of the pruning knife, both to the number of offices and the salaries attached thereto, had succeeded in reducing the expenses of the government within the limits of its resources, and by his pacific Indian policy secured a cessation of hostilities from most of the native Indians, yet the condition of the country was so unsatisfactory that many of the inhabitants looked to annexation as the only hope of peace and prosperity. The last presidential contest being along that line, and though General Burleson, who led the annexation party, was defeated by the opposition candidate, Anson Jones, the sentiment in favor of annexation grew so rapidly that the first year of his administration saw the Lone Star absorbed into the glorious constellation established by the fathers of its citizens, and with few dissenting voices. After all those years of trial and sore distress, being as it were a kind of football for the greater powers on both sides of the Atlantic, it did seem good to see the old stars and stripes again floating over us, giving assurance of strength and protection, saying to the nations of the world, "Hands off," an injunction which only poor old Mexico refused to obey till General Scott taught her the lesson that more enlightened nations had already learned.

CHAPTER 22

District court was in session in Bastrop when the news came that the bill for the annexation of Texas had passed the United States congress and received the approval of President Polk. Judge Robert E. B. Baylor, who was presiding, in announcing the glad tidings, quoted Chief Justice Marshall as saying that "No man should be considered drunk on Independence day, so long as he could pronounce the word 'Epsom,'" and added that in his opinion the same rule should apply to that occasion; and he therefore adjourned court till 10 o'clock the next morning, that we might celebrate, and celebrate we did with a will.

In the absence of cannon we brought out all the anvils the town could muster, and taking up a collection to pay for powder proceeded to get all the noise possible out of them. Had there been any Indians anywhere in hearing they would probably have gotten away from that vicinity in short order. We felt something like the children of Israel probably did, when Jehovah flung the Red sea betwixt them and their foes. Judge Baylor, Baptist preacher though he was, made a full hand with the boys.

My recollection of the details is not quite clear, therefore I will not undertake to say whether we stopped at Epsom or not, but we were all on hand at ten next morning.

Honest, earnest Robert E. B. Baylor! Of him might well be said, as Daniel Webster said of John Jay: "The spotless ermine of the judicial robe, when it fell on his shoulders, touched nothing not as spotless as itself." Whether as lawyer, preacher or judge, the same humanity and sense of justice guided his course, and never did a breath of reproach tarnish the name which was bestowed upon one of the oldest institutions of learning in the state, first located at Independence and later removed to Waco, where it still seems to flourish.

The first and most difficult step in our route toward statehood had been achieved, but the end was still a long way off. President Polk signed the bill on March 1, 1845. On the 5th of May following, President Jones called a convention to meet in Austin on the 4th of July to consider the proposition, which was submitted to the people on October 13, and being almost unanimously indorsed, then went back to the United States congress for final action, receiving the approval of President Polk on the 29th of December. The state constitution had been promulgated, the first governor elected and it was only needed to set the new machinery in motion, to touch the button, as it were. The first legislature met on the 16th of February, 1846, and three days later the curtain fell on the last, and in many respects, the most touching scene in the brief drama of the republic, when Anson Jones, its last president, standing on the steps of the old capitol, lowered the old flag from the mast and reverently furling it, announced amidst breathless silence, "The republic of Texas is no more." Many a head was bowed, many a broad chest heaved, and many a manly cheek was wet with tears when that broad field of blue in the center of which, like a signal light, glowed the lone star, emblem of the sovereignty of Texas, was furled and laid away among the relics of the dead republic. But we were most of us natives of the United States, and when the stars and stripes, the flag of our fathers, was run up and catching the breeze unrolled its heaven born colors to the light, cheer after cheer rent the air. Methinks the star in the lower left hand corner should have been especially dedicated to Texas.

As was anticipated, the annexation of Texas again involved us in a war with Mexico, but how different from those that had preceded it! Instead of a few hundred poorly armed men, there was General Taylor, "Old Rough and Ready," who "never surrendered," and stern old General Winfield Scott, who won his first honors at Lundy's Lane thirty-five years before, and with them Grant and Lee and many others who developed into able commanders during the civil war, together with their thousands of soldiers equipped with all the latest appliances of war, and above this imposing array, not one lone, lonely star, but a glittering constellation of twenty-eight flashed defiance to all foes.

But Texas did not stand aloof while the United States fought her battles. The requisition made upon her for troops was promptly responded to, many being bitterly disappointed because the ranks were filled before they got in. Governor Henderson, assisted by Jack Hays, Ben McCulloch and Walter P. Lane, all of whom subsequently rose to distinction, took the field at the head of two regiments of cavalry and two of infantry, joining General Taylor, who had been ordered to Corpus Christi immediately after the passage of the annexation act, Mexico having previously warned the United States that such an act would be considered casus belli. Captain Ad Gillespie, killed in the storming of the fortifications on El Obispado, led the scaling party up the almost perpendicular steep and was the first man to mount the parapet surrounding the bishop's castle which crowned the summit, receiving his death wound in the act. Captain Samuel Walker was killed at Huamantla.

Active hostilities commenced with the battle of Palo Alto in May, 1846, and ended with the conquest of the Mexican capital in September, 1847. Thus was the old ambitious dream of the revolutionary army of '35 at last realized, though few, if any of them, were there to see it. But one regiment of Texas volunteers—Hays'—was in General Scott's division, and, I think, they were probably later additions to the fighting force of Texas. The Texas rangers were of invaluable service in the war, winning high encomiums from both Scott and Taylor, the latter designating them "the eyes of the army."

The halls of the Montezumas were occupied by the hated Texans, who, if not themselves dictating terms of peace to the crestfallen Santa Anna, were at least on hand to see it done and rejoice over his humiliation. And hard terms they were, those wrung from old Mexico for her temerity in flying into the face of our revered Uncle! The surrender, not only of all territory to which Texas laid claim, but also that now embraced in the states of California, Nevada, Utah, three-fourths of Arizona, nearly half of Colorado and New Mexico, with a triangular block in the southwest corner of Wyoming, the only compensation being a paltry $15,000,000, with the assumption of an additional $3,000,000 which was due citizens of Texas by those of Mexico, aggregating $18,000,000.

How contemptible and disproportionate the sum when compared with the $10,000,000 paid a few years later for the Gadsden purchase, that strip of Arizona and New Mexico lying south of the Gila river, three-fourths of which is desert; and the $10,000,000 paid Texas for that portion of New Mexico lying east of the Rio Grande, and to which the claim of Texas had never been recognized either by the United States or Mexico; no attempt having ever been made by the republic of Texas to extend jurisdiction over it, it remained under Mexican control, inhabited only by Mexicans and Indians. The only Texans who ever entered Santa Fe, the capital, went there in chains. The semi-official Santa Fe expedition was not authorized to do more than hold out inducements to the inhabitants to throw off the yoke of Mexico. Between the disputed territory and the outposts of the republic stretched six hundred miles of unexplored territory, inhabited only by savages. When General Sibley retired from the Rio Grande in disgust, after having tried in vain to oust Canby, he reported to the authorities at Richmond that "the whole territory was not worth the blood and treasure wasted on it."

General Scott having "conquered a peace," we were relieved from all further apprehensions of a Mexican invasion, but the Indians were still on the warpath, killing and driving off stock, and when a good opportunity offered, killing people. To check their depredations military posts were established at suitable points along the frontier and General Harney placed in command of the department, with headquarters at Austin.

Many of the old residents doubtless remember General Harney. He was then past middle age, with a fine, soldierly bearing. He had spent many years in the service and it was a cause of regret amounting almost to mortification that he had "not a single scar to show for it."

General Harney was an officer of the old school, a strict disciplinarian, admitting of no hesitancy about the carrying out of instructions. A story was told of him when he was on his way to Mexico; he engaged teams to transport the baggage, placing an independent Texan—Carter—in charge as wagonmaster. The streams were all up and Carter had a good deal of trouble, but whenever he demurred to the general's orders he was cut short with the admonition that all he had to do was to "obey orders." They camped one night near the Nueces river and Carter ascertained that it was impassable, but said nothing to the general on the subject. The next morning Harney gave the order to move on. Carter without a word started on with the train, but only proceeded as far as the river, where he halted till the general came blustering up to see what was the matter.

Perceiving the situation he turned to Carter.

"Didn't you know that the river was up?" he demanded.

"Yes, sir," meekly replied the wagonmaster.

"Why didn't you tell me?"

"You didn't ask me, sir. You said my business was to obey orders. You ordered me to hitch up and move on, and I did it."

"You did right, sir. Turn around and drive back to camp."

Carter used to tell the story, but always gave General Harney credit for being consistent, at any rate.

With the garrison at Austin were Major Fontleroy and Captain Beeal, both of whom had families. Beeal was a jovial son of Mars and a constant devotee of Bacchus, with whom he had many a bout, but generally came out best, the capacity of his stomach being inadequate to the quantity of intoxicants necessary to overcome his head. He was a great story-teller and always had a crowd of interested listeners.

Major Fontleroy, on the contrary, was rather retiring; though his appearance bespoke him every inch a soldier. In the course of a few years they all drifted away from Austin in the wake of the retreating savages and the places that once knew them knew them no more forever.

General Harney entered the army at eighteen, his first service being in the Seminole war; after which he participated in the Blackhawk war and then the Mexican war. From Texas he went to the Platte to subdue the Sioux, and from thence to Oregon, returning to the East in '61. While en route to Washington he was arrested by the Confederates at Harper's Ferry and taken to Richmond. Meeting General Lee, with whom he had fought in Mexico, Harney expressed regret at meeting him under such changed conditions. "General Harney," Lee replied, "I had no idea of taking any part in this matter. I wanted to stay at Arlington and raise potatoes for my family, but my friends forced me into it." Gen. Jo Johnston, another old comrade, expressed himself in the same way. General Harney was retired in '63 and in '65 brevetted major-general for long and faithful services. He died in 1889, being then in his ninetieth year. Major Fontleroy began his military career in the war of 1812, serving through the Mexican and Seminole wars, following the Indians on into Arizona and defeating the Apaches in 1855. When the late war broke out he entered the Confederate service. He died in '83, aged eighty-seven. Captain Beeal, like General Harney, won his first spurs in the Seminole war. After the close of the Mexican war, he sojourned for a time in Texas and then moved on westward; building all the forts from the Rio Grande to California. He was commissioned Colonel of Dragoons in '61 and retired in '62; dying a year later. Colonel Beeal had two sons in the Union army and one in the Confederate.

Among the first subjects that arose to vex the souls of those who had undertaken to guide the destinies of the new state was that of the public debt, which amounted to about $12,000,000, face value; but the legislature decided to pay the holders of securities only what they were worth at the time the holder became possessed of them, thus scaling the amount down to about

$7,000,000. Still there was no feasible plan for raising even that amount, the United States having absorbed all customs duties. In this emergency they fell back on the public domain, which it was proposed to sell to the United States. Said sale, however, never took place, as the boundary dispute soon arose and in the settlement of that the $10,000,000 spoken of above was paid over to Texas, the sum being more than sufficient to discharge the debts of the old republic as adjudicated by the legislature. These questions being satisfactorily adjusted, in 1853, the state entered on a new era.

In the meantime they had begun to "crowd" me in Webber's prairie and there being no further danger from Indians, I moved out on Brushy creek, where I could get elbow room, and went into the stock business.

The country was wild, and infested with predatory beasts, the most troublesome of which were the big gray wolves—lobos—the Mexicans called them. Many of them stood three feet high, measuring six or seven feet from tip to tip, with powerful jaws, which enabled them to drag down a grown cow single-handed if they could separate it from the band. Their endurance and speed were such that one could run down a deer.

Between my house and the timber belt of the Colorado, stretched a prairie about a mile across. One evening near sundown, myself being away from home, my wife, looking across the prairie, saw the milk cows coming on a run and behind them two big wolves. One cow, falling a little behind the band, was seized by the foremost of the wolves, but her calls for help caused the other cattle to turn and fight the fierce brutes back. The cows then started again for home, but the wounded one again fell behind and again was seized, but she managed to tear herself loose. By this time the chase had reached half across the prairie, and my wife, unable to stand and see one of her favorites torn to pieces by their ferocious pursuers, calling to the dogs, started to the rescue. The dogs, seeing the on-coming chase, dashed away and my wife after them, an unsafe thing, as the lobo had been known to make a stand and whip off dogs, and being intent on their victim, whose blood had already whetted their appetites, it would not have been surprising if they had refused to be vanquished. The dogs, encouraged by the presence and voice of their mistress, sped away on their mission of rescue, and, though wary of attacking the enemy, checked their advance, giving their torn and bleeding victim a chance to escape, till the wolves, catching sight of my wife, turned and made off to the timber. The cow was frightfully torn and died from the effects. After losing several cows and a number of calves, many of the latter being killed within a few hundred yards of the house, I began to treat the lobo family with strychnine, which noticeably decreased the loss of my cattle.

These wolves were a distinct species, having long, shaggy hair about the neck and shoulders, something like a lion's mane; they did not hunt in packs, like the northern wolf, but rather in pairs. Wild cattle when attacked by them would form a ring around their calves, and presenting a line of horns fight

them off; but gentle cattle were wont to break for home when frightened, as if understanding that they would be safe there, and woe to the unfortunate that fell behind. Milk cows lived on the range and were only separated from their calves during the intervals between milkings, the calves being kept up during the day while the cows went out to feed, and the cows kept in at night to give the calves the benefit of pasture; so that the little bovines were at the mercy of the prowling lobos, who, under cover of darkness, ventured quite near to the house; and sometimes before we had gone to bed we would be startled by a piteous bleating, followed by an answering bellow from the cows, which would break from the inclosure and rush to the rescue, together with dogs and men; but though the wolf was cheated of his prey, he had inflicted fatal injuries, not one of the victims ever recovering.

I tracked the marauders to the timber and set bits of fresh meat containing strychnine along the trails, sometimes finding them dead within a short distance. I kept it up vigorously until they were pretty well subdued.

There were many wild cattle along the river, descendants of the old Spanish cattle brought to the old mission San Gabriel away back in the eighteenth century. Some of these cattle were very handsome brutes, coal black and clean limbed, their white horns glistening as if polished. A couple of the bulls took up with my cattle and became quite domesticated, though they were as a rule very wild.

My nearest neighbor on Brushy was Jimmie Standefer, who lived three miles below me on the creek, his house being a kind of wayside inn for many travelers between Austin and points north and west. The old man came there with a large family and small means, and had a hard time for several years. He was very devout, but didn't allow that to interfere with business. One of his sons used to tell a story on the old man that will bear repetition. Jimmie had domesticated a number of hives of bees, the increase of which he was anxious to save. Bee-keeping then was not the science it is to-day; instead of separating the bees, they were allowed to take their own way and time for moving. This they did by swarming in the spring. Having noticed an unusual activity among his bees, Jimmie left some of his children to watch them while he went to breakfast. Before the rather long "grace" was finished his ear caught a suspicious buzzing, which caused him to hurry up the ceremony, but it had to be finished according to custom, though his impatience caused the introduction of a sentence not down in the ritual. Casting an anxious glance through the door as the concluding sentence fell from his lips, he called to the children: "Children, ain't them bees a swarmin'? Amen."

And while on the subject of bees, I will take the liberty of correcting a typographical error in a former article of mine. I had occasion to speak of "bee bait," which, perhaps being unintelligible to the compositor, he changed to "fish bait." As it made no material difference in the connection in which the word was used, I only recur to it for the purpose of enlightening those who are not versed in the primitive methods of obtaining honey. When we went out in serach of a "bee tree" we took along a vessel containing honey; this we placed in a situation to attract the attention of any bee that might be passing that way, usually at their watering places, and watching till they had filled their pouches and started for home, took note of the direction taken, and it being a well established fact that a laden bee flies in a "bee line," an expert had no difficulty in following them to their hive, which was usually in a hollow tree. This was called "coursing."

When left to settle their domestic affairs the young brood of bees, on arriving at maturity, are turned out by the heads of the hive to hustle for themselves. This creates quite a commotion. After being ejected the youngsters buzz around at a great rate and finally settle down on some convenient limb to hold a council, perhaps to dispatch agents to look up new quarters. At any rate, if not captured, they will, after remaining all clustered up in a ball for a short time, break up and take wing for their future home. To prevent their escape we used to throw water on them to prevent their flying and beat on tin pans and raise a general hullabaloo; and when we wanted to take honey from the hive, usually a section of a hollow tree with a board nailed on the top end, we pried off the board and smoked the bees out with burning rags, a process which did not tend to improve the flavor of the honey, but we were not fastidious in small matters, and fortunate indeed was the robber who escaped without stings.

But to return to my old friend and neighbor, Jimmie Standefer. Having a disagreement with one of his neighbors Jim Lewis, Lewis was relating his grievance to me. "Yes," said he, "I suppose he thinks he'll go to heaven with his long graces; but if his sort can go in at the gate, if I don't scale the wall d—n my soul."

After delving along there for years, himself and family working diligently, Standefer got forehanded enough to buy slaves, investing all his savings thus, only a short time before the war, which, of course, again left him stranded. He and his good wife have gone to their rest, several of their children being now in this state, California.

Lewis was a character. He came up to me one day on the race course at Georgetown. "Lend me $5," said he. I gave him the required amount in silver. He dropped it into his pocket and swaggered around loudly challenging a bet.

"Put up your property," said an accommodating sport.

"Property be d——d! If you bet with me you've got to fork up the dough." And Jim fetched his pocket a slap that set the half dollars jingling at a rate that bluffed the other fellow.

By and by he found some one with "dough," and by dint of much jingling, arranged a bet which he won; seeing which, parties who had advanced him loans gathered around for a divy.

Jim dramatically waved them away with the adjuration: "Depart from me ye workers of iniquity; I never knew ye."

Again, watching the fire in my forge, glowing at white heat under the influence of the bellows, he remarked that it was a hot place.

"O," said I, "that's nothing to what you will have when you get to hell, and you'll have to stand it forever." "That's all a lie. If hell's half as hot as that a dead man wouldn't last a minute," he retorted.

Lewis also came to California, where he took up the practice of medicine, and, settling on King's river, where the ague will shake a man out of his boots, dealt out calomel and quinine with remarkable success. He long since passed from earth. Whether or not he succeeded in scaling the walls of heaven deponent saith not.

In '52 Isaac Harris, an old San Jacinto veteran, caught the California fever and struck out across the plains, among the first to make the venture, bringing with him a large drove of cattle, as most of the early emigrants did. He came up to my place on Brushy and struck camp to wait for me to fit him out in wagons, etc. It was like going out of the world then to "go to Californy," but there was a great exodus that year, all of whom succeeded in running the gauntlet of Comanches in Texas, Apaches in Arizona, and lack of water; the large droves of cattle making a heavy draught on the scant water supply on their route. Yet gold, in its primitive sense, did not appear to be the object of their quest, most of them locating in Southern California where there were then no mines of importance. Their cattle, though, turned loose on the seemingly inexhaustible range of the sparsely settled country, brought them rich returns, securing for them the title of "cattle kings." With the influx of emigrants the pasture lands became farms and the glory of the "kings" departed. Their descendants are with us, but, like the old Mexican land barons, are practically wanderers on the face of the earth where once they reigned. The Spaniard despoiled the Indian, the American the Spaniard, and the "tenderfeet" the pioneer American. So it has been in Texas; so it is everywhere; so it must always be. It is the restlessness of the pioneer that impels him to seek fresh fields, seldom remaining to reap the reward of his toil and danger, or, if he does, he fails to take advantage of his opportunities, and old age often finds him without a place to lay his head.

CHAPTER 23

My landed estate on Brushy creek was not a valuable one from an agricultural standpoint, but there were some fine possibilities in the clay banks, which yielded a soft, fine-grained material, very pliable and adhesive, and would have yielded a handsome profit in the hands of any old-time potter. To me it was useless except for the enjoyment my children extracted from it in the manufacture not only of mud pies, but of bowls, and even crude attempts at toys, their wares when dry being quite durable.

There was also a fertile field for the archaeologist in the ledges of limestone, which in many places were many feet in thickness, holding in their grasp many interesting fossils, both organic and casts, veritable picture books of the prehistoric age.

The most conspicuous objects in these ledges were what at first glance would be pronounced petrified snakes, but as they were all coiled and headless, they would probably be classified under the head of Ammonites. The coils, many of which measured eighteen inches across, were very symmetrical and well defined, but rather more flattened than those of a snake. The absence of a head would naturally suggest that they were only casts, but for the presence of a vertebral structure, the joints of which were separable by blows, even the spinal cord being traceable, a feature which would seem to separate them from the Ammonites. But, on the other hand, I never saw a dead snake coiled. If they were really snakes, they must have curled up for the winter's nap and turned to stone while asleep; or perhaps St. Patrick passed that way. I presume there are still specimens embedded in those ledges, though many of them were removed during my occupancy of the place; and if any scientist cares to make a study of them he can no doubt determine their true character.

I don't remember the exact date, but think it was about 1848 that Fort Croggin was built on Hamilton's creek, where the town of Burnet now stands. Henry McCulloch had previously maintained a camp of rangers near there. Fort Croggin consisted of the usual log cabins, inclosed by a stout stockade, and was manned by one company of cavalry and one of infantry, the first commander being Captain Philip St. George Cook, who in 1843 arrested and disarmed a portion of the Snively expedition, for which act some of the parties so dealt with swore eternal vengeance on him.

Under these circumstances the position of post commander at Fort Croggin was not a comfortable one to Captain Cook, and he soon asked to be relieved. Lieutenant (afterward Captain) Blake succeeded to the command. Blake was in turn succeeded by Captain Lee, and Lee by Captain Sibley, later promoted to major, and to a general in the Confederate army. Christian Dorbandt, father of the present sheriff of Burnet county, was one of the men belonging to the post. Upon being discharged, he settled in the vicinity and is still there.

With this advance of the frontier the country between that and Austin settled up rapidly. As is usually the case, the fort attracted settlers, and thus the town of Burnet was born, though it was called Hamilton Valley for several years thereafter. Logan Vandever and William McGill, both San Jacinto veterans, were among the first arrivals, they having obtained a contract for furnishing supplies to the fort. Boland and McKee opened the first store. As was the case in every settlement, as soon as practicable a school was instituted, the promoters of the enterprise in Burnet securing the services of one W. H. Dixon, a graduate of Oxford university, as teacher. Under the efficient guidance of Professor Dixon the school attained high rank among the educational institutions of the western country and became an important factor in the growth of the town. There, in a little one-room log house, the young idea was taught to shoot straight toward Oxford, Greek, Latin and the higher mathematics sitting in the same room with the little tot with his pictured primer. As in most schools of that day, elocution was assigned a high place and embryo Websters and Adamses and Bentons harangued the school and its visitors at frequent intervals.

Finding a pastoral life unsuited to my taste, and the sparsely settled condition of the country in my vicinity rendering a blacksmith shop unremunerative, when the commander at Fort Croggin advertised for an armorer, I went up and worked a short time, long enough, however, to get an insight into the workings of the government machinery. There was a little upstart of a noncommissioned officer, who, having been made a sergeant, appropriated another fellow's wife and put on more airs than did the department commander. He set up a carriage and his wife had to have a servant and fine clothes. As his regular pay would not nearly pay his expenses he made up the deficit by cheating the government. He came into my shop one day with his scales, saying:

"I wish you would fix these scales for me so they will weigh a trifle light. The men all draw more rations than they can eat and it is just wasted. Now, if I could manage to save a little from each one they would never miss it, and where I issue several hundred a day it would amount to a good deal to me."

I told him that I was not employed to do that kind of business.

"O," said he, unable to understand my reason of refusal, "I'll pay you well for it."

In rather forcible language I rejected his offer, and he went away, a sadder if not wiser man.

Relating the incident to Logan Vandever, he laughed heartily at my verdancy.

"Why, that's nothing," said he. "When you've been here as long as I have, you will see that they all, from the commandant down, steal, each according to his opportunity. That man is only a poor little cuss. He has to steal by the ounce; others steal by the ton." A statement which I had an opportunity of verifying shortly after.

Some parties who had taken a contract for supplying corn for the horses drove up to the quartermaster's department late one afternoon and began to unload. The grain was put up in cotton bags supposed to contain two bushels. The "slack" of the bags, however, was so conspicuous that the commandant ordered them all weighed, calling on me as a civilian to witness the attempted fraud. Not one of those weighed fell short less than a peck, and some more. The quartermaster, with righteous indignation, ordered the guilty parties to reload the corn and take it away. Seemingly but little disturbed by the exposure of their dishonesty, the contractors drove across the creek and camped for the night. Early the next morning they drove back to the fort, where the corn was received without more ado, though the bags were just as slack as on the previous day. My observations since that time have not tended to disprove Vandever's assertion.

There was, however, one notable exception. Lieutenant Givens stands out in bold relief against this background of speculators and schemers. When the division headquarters were removed to San Antonio the quartermaster general arbitrarily usurped the functions of the local quartermasters, buying up supplies at San Antonio and hiring teams to distribute them among the posts, some of which were several hundred miles distant. The post at Burnet had been abandoned and the company to which Lieutenant Givens was attached moved out to some of the outside posts, where Givens was assigned the position of quartermaster, the responsibilities of which he accepted in good faith. Finding he could buy corn delivered to his post at a smaller cost to the government than that being sent out by the quartermaster general he proceeded to act on the information. This did not suit his highness, the quartermaster general, and seeing that corn in San Antonio was cheaper than corn nearer the post he sent on an accusation against Givens, charging him with fraud, also annulling Givens' contracts and placing him under arrest. The lieutenant was courtmartialed and dismissed from the service. He then sent on his report, showing the fraud that was being perpetrated, and having influential friends in congress his case was taken up in that body and resulted in his reinstatement and promotion.

After the Mormons were drowned out with their mill enterprise above Austin they went over on the Perdenales, about four miles from Fredericksburg, and built a mill, faring even worse than on the Colorado, the mill being entirely swept away and the burrs covered up in sand. Their village was also inundated. They had gotten a government contract and bought up corn and were in a fair way to retrieve their fortunes, but this new disaster blighted their prospects. Not to be discouraged, they went over on Hamilton's creek, eight miles below Burnet, where there was a fine site, and put in another mill. Their burrs being lost and having no money to buy new ones, they went out to the quarry and got out blocks of marble, of which they manufactured burrs, which answered for grinding corn, but they required frequent dressing.

Old Lyman Wight, the high priest, set about the task of recovering the lost stones. After wrestling alone with the spirits for some little time he arose one morning with joy in his heart, and summoning his people, announced to them that he had had a revelation, and bidding them take spades and crow-

bars and follow him, set out to locate the millstones. Straight ahead he bore as one in a dream, his divining rod in his hand; his awestruck disciples following in silence. Pausing at last in the middle of the sand bar deposited by the flood he stuck his rod down.

"Dig right here," he commanded. His followers, never doubting, set to work, and upon removing a few feet of sand, lo and behold, there were revealed the buried millstones. Wight said he saw them in a vision and his followers believed it.

Another miracle which the elder, in conjunction with the twelve disciples, performed, was related to me by one of the company. A boy fell from a tree and broke his leg. He was taken to the council chamber and the elder and his council were summoned. They laid their hands upon the broken limb and prayed; the boy then arose and walked. When the narrator had finished the above recital I looked him searchingly in the face and said:

"Did you feel of that leg and satisfy yourself that it was really broken?"

"No, I didn't; but 'the twelve' did and they said it was broken," he replied, with an air of wonder that any one should have the audacity to question a verdict rendered by such authority.

"I'm glad you didn't," said I, "for if you had told me that you yourself felt of that boy's leg and found it broken, I should never believe another word you speak."

The poor dupe looked as if thunderstruck. I was not so much surprised at him, but there were some really intelligent men among them, and it was a mystery to me how they could lend themselves to such a course, when there was so little to be gained by it.

In addition to the grinding mill the Mormons put in a sawmill and turning lathes, manufacturing chairs, tables, bedsteads, etc., with which they supplied the whole country. The most of their chairs were made of hackberry, the wood of which, being so white, required a good deal of washing to preserve its purity. One lady in Burnet, to obviate the necessity of such frequent cleaning, concluded to paint her chairs; that was before the days of chemical paint. We bought the pigment and reduced it with linseed oil. This lady, having no oil, and arguing that oil was oil and so was butter, during the summer, mixed her paint with butter and applied the combination to her chairs; the effect can be better imagined than described.

While some of the Mormons were engaged about the mill, others opened a farm, and some were employed in hauling off and disposing of their wares among which were very pretty willow baskets made by the women. Their houses were small and their furnishings meager. But, in spite of their industrious habits and frugal living, they became involved in debt and offered their mill for sale. Having all my life had a penchant for mills, I recognized this as "my long lost brother," and at once opened negotiations for it. The dream of my life was fulfilled and I was at last the proud possessor of a bona fide mill, and that in one of the most picturesque spots to be found. A mountain had been cleft from north to south, to permit the stream to pass through, and then from east to west, the southern portion having been entirely removed, so that the almost perpendicular walls between which flowed the creek, turned away at right angles at the mouth of the gorge, where the stream fell over a precipice twenty-eight feet or more in height into a deep pool below; thence rippling away between green banks, shaded by the various trees indigenous to the country. Just at the foot of the falls on the east stood the mill, a three-story frame building, the second story being on a level with the bank, with which it was connected by a gangway. A patriarchal pecan tree lifted its stately head beside the building, caressing it with its slender branches. On the upper side, connected with the falls by a flume, rose the huge overshot wheel, twenty-six feet in diameter, which furnished the power for the mill. The machinery was mostly of the rudest, clumsiest kind, manufactured by the Mormons of such material as was obtainable from natural sources. Great, clumsy, rattling wooden cog wheels and drum and fly-wheels filled up the lower stories, the upper one containing a small corn cracker mill and an old up-and-down sash saw, which, after all, had this advantage over the circular saw, that it could handle large timber. This was clearly demonstrated when a little later Swisher and Collins put in a circular saw over on Cypress creek, their saw being unable to cope with the largest and best timber, some of which was hauled to the Mormon mill a distance of fifteen miles.

And speaking of the circular saw, I shall always think myself the inventor of that useful device. I was born with a mechanical genius which I had ample opportunity of developing. My father, though not himself a smith, always kept a shop in his place, in which I early began to tinker; my first efforts being directed to the making of arrow points and putting pegs in tops, blades in knives and tongues in jewsharps. I had windmills on all the housetops and water mills—paddle wheels—in the creek wherever there was a little ripple. I presume everybody knows what a whirligig is. I had a varied assortment of them, some of which were made of scraps of tin. In these I conceived the idea of cutting teeth; then, while I operated the machine, my little brother fed it with cornstalks, turning out quantities of cornstalk lumber. To the shaft of one of my water wheels I at length attached a toothed whirligig, the power being sufficient to drive the miniature saw through a cornstalk. That was my idea of a sawmill; imagine, then, my surprise when on visiting for the first time a full grown mill I saw the old up-and-down sash saw, the operating of which I could not understand. That was years before Hoe patented the circular saw.

The sale of the Mormon mills created quite a ripple in the vicinity. After I had concluded the bargain I set out for my home on Brushy. As I jogged along on my Spanish pony a stranger overtook me.

"Can you tell me whether Colonel Smithwick's carriage has passed down?" said he.

"I have seen nothing of it," I replied, and he spurred on to overtake the imaginary turn-out.

There being no good milling timber in the vicinity we, my nephew, John Hubbard, having become a partner in the business, decided to throw out the saw and turn our attention to the manufacture of breadstuffs. In furtherance of this plan we decided to reorganize the machinery, throwing out all the old wooden cog work and substituting castings. And while we were about it we put in a new over-shot wheel, the shaft for which we procured on Cypress creek, selecting for the purpose a tree six feet through at the ground. This we dressed down to thirty-two inches square and eight feet in length. Into this shaft we inserted arms twelve feet long, upon which was built frame work supporting numerous buckets, each four feet in length, the completed wheel measuring twenty-eight feet in diameter. Besides the quantities of timber used in its construction, there was about a ton of iron. I have since seen a little turbine wheel one foot in diameter that I could lift with one hand running a six-foot circular saw. What a revolution!

We then put in a new set of burrs and added bolting works, the first flouring mill west of Georgetown. This gave a new direction to the farming interest, and soon the rattle of the threshing machine was heard in the land, and the reign of the corn-dodger was over in those parts. People came from all points to have their grain ground, and the capacity of the mill being very limited, sometimes when the mill was crowded they had to wait several days for their turn. Those who lived at a distance, many of them thirty or forty miles, struck camp and stayed it out. The Germans came from over at Fredericksburg. Like other German colonists, they had a hard scramble for the first few years, their crops failing, and for want of a knowledge of the use of firearms they were unable to utilize the game. Many of them gave away their children to keep them from starving. But when there was work to be done, the Germans could be relied upon to do it, and do it right, and were therefore an important factor in developing the country. They did not believe in wasting anything, as a story the miller told will show. McCartney, the miller, said that a German came into the mill one day, his clothes all patches and everything about him betokening extreme poverty. He looked around, and seeing flour and meal scattered around the room, where it had been spilled and trampled over and spit upon, asked if he might have it. Mac told him to take it. The thrifty Dutchman got a broom, and, sweeping it all up carefully, put it in a bag. Pursuing his researches further, he found a little heap of bran, and asked to be allowed to take that also. His sympathy being aroused, Mac gave him the bran also. Having thus collected all the sweepings, he then bought a peck of shorts and mixed with it, the whole making something like a bushel.

"Huh, bread fourteen days," he exclaimed, as he shouldered the bag. McCartney said he felt so moved with pity for the family, which he naturally supposed must be on the verge of starvation, that he made up his mind to give the poor fellow a bushel of meal, and with that purpose followed him into a little store on the premises. Just as he stepped into the door the Dutchman laid down a $20 gold piece in payment for a bill of goods, among which were several plugs of tobacco. But the Germans throve.

The Mormons broke up and scattered in every direction after selling out. Old Lyman Wight, with those who adhered to him, went over on the Medina river, where they again planted a colony, Wight dying there. Quite a number of them remained on the village farm and several worked for a time in the mill. I found them just the same as other people in matters of business. While some of them were honest and industrious, others were shiftless and unreliable; and this must ever prove a potent argument against community holdings—the thriftless got just as much as the thrifty. But though the industrious saint was thus forced to contribute to the support of his idle brother, he drew the line to exclude the worthless dog that is generally considered an indispensable adjunct to thriftlessness, the canine family being conspicuous by its absence about the domicile of the Mormon. Nor was there anything objectionable in the Mormons as neighbors. If there were any polygamous families, I did not know of them. To still further emphasize the perfect equality of all members of the society, all titles of respect were discarded, men and women being universally called by their first names. And these first names, by the way, were perhaps the most striking peculiarity about the Mormons. The proselytes were permitted to retain their Gentile names, but those born in the fold received their baptismal names from the Book of Mormon; and have no counterpart elsewhere. There were Abinadi, Maroni, Luami, Lamoni, Romali, Cornoman and many others equally original. The female children, however, were apparently not permitted to participate in this saintly nomenclature. It might be that women cut no figure in the Book of Mormon; at any rate, there was nothing distinctive in the names of the girls.

One of my first efforts upon taking possession of the mill was to get a school, and in this those of the Mormons remaining, ably seconded me. We secured the services of a wandering pedagogue, known from the lakes to the gulf, Abijah Hopkins by name. He was an able teacher, but was never known to teach more than six months in a place. He tramped back and forth from Wisconsin to Texas, teaching a term here and there on the journey. His hobby was mathematics, which he had for the most part mastered unaided. He said that the first class he ever instructed in algebra, he had to study the lessons at night he taught the day following. "The rule of three" was his main reliance in all difficult problems. "State it in the rule of three, and go at it in a businesslike manner." Though not at all cross with his pupils, he held them under perfect control, seldom having to resort to the rod, the urchins quailing at a glance. He had four daughters living in Travis county, some of whom may still be there.

Our schools in those days were crude affairs, but the children learned more in a day than they do in a week—yes, in a month—in our modern schools. They were private enterprises, which, in a measure, accounts for their efficiency. There was no red tape connected with them.

The Mormons had nearly all left there before I did; there being but five families in 1861, three of whom came to California with me.

On a high plateau some half a mile from the mill, on the opposite side of the creek, was the cemetery, where, notwithstanding the miraculous healing powers of the "twelve," a comparatively large number of the saints had ended their earthly pilgrimage. A neat wall of red sandstone inclosed this last resting place, each grave being marked with a headstone of the same. That silent spot perhaps holds all of the once populous community that remains in Burnet county.

CHAPTER 24

Hamilton's creek drains quite a scope of the country, and when swelled by heavy rains, the flood being congested within the narrow gorge above the mill, rises rapidly and comes down in a solid wall of water which pours over the falls like a miniature Niagara. The mill, however, is protected by the bluff. I have often seen the creek, which is ordinarily a trivial stream, become a torrent within a few minutes. On one occasion a party of sightseers had a narrow escape. Having wended their way up into the gorge, along the margin of the shallow stream, they were startled by a roar above them, and the guide being acquainted with the vagaries of the stream, ordered them to climb for their lives. Laying hold of the bushes in the face of the steep declivity, they scrambled up out of harm's way and watched the angry flood of waters rush past and leap the falls with a report like thunder, sending up clouds of spray. The visitors were treated to more of a show than they had contracted for, as if the creek had got up a special benefit for them. They had to climb to the top of the bluff and cross over the table land and scramble down on the southern side. High up in the face of the cliff on the further side from the mill was a cave-like opening in which a colony of bees had taken up their abode. It was a source of much aggravation to the boys that there was no way of appropriating the store of honey which was doubtless concealed within the cave, there being millions of bees to protect it. No plan was devised to oust them during my regime, and they are probably still in possession.

Back from the mill on either side of the creek stretched vast cedar brakes, the abode of wild animals innumerable, affording abundant sport for lovers of the chase. The Indians were gone and likewise the buffalo. The black bear being the next biggest game, I made a specialty of bear hunting, and to assist me in ferreting them out I trained a pack of dogs that made it decidedly uncomfortable for Bruin. Rare sport we had chasing them through the brakes, where it was impossible to ride, for they instinctively made for the most inaccessible places, but we were oblivious to obstructions when the dogs opened on the trail of a bear; they knew as well as we that it was a hunt for bear and were not to be tempted by other game. I also had a pony so well trained that I could leave him anywhere and trust him to remain there till he was wanted. We often had to rush in and dispatch a bear with knives when he was brought to bay, the dogs closing in on him so that it was impossible to shoot without endangering them. Occasionally we jumped upon a Mexican lion and sometimes ran into a drove of javalinas—Mexican hogs—the latter sometimes cutting the dogs before we could get them away. We gave the javalinas a wide berth, but we gave chase to the lions which took to trees, from which well aimed rifle balls dislodged them.

The Mormon mills came to be quite a noted place. Candidates began to find their way through the dense cedar brakes, which shut it in, and thither in the summer of '54 came Richardson, the advance agent of the Galveston News, the first of his calling to brave the terrors of the wilderness, and dearly he paid for his rashness. My house, like that of all old Texans, was open to the public and consequently became headquarters for Richardson while sojourning in that vicinity. It therefore devolving on me to do the honors of the neighborhood, I conducted him to the Marble Falls on the Colorado, some five or six miles distant, where never the sound of the woodman's ax had broken the primeval solitude. We rode over in the afternoon and devoted so much time to the inspection of the falls and to the discussion of the possibilities lying therein that it was nearing sunset when we started on our return. Our road being only a bridle path we took it in Indian file. Richardson, being mounted on a fine American horse, being the most conspicuous figure, took the lead, myself on my hunting pony, coming next and my dogs bringing up the rear. In this order we had proceeded about half way home when our attention was attracted by a number of deer feeding at a distance. Thinking to wind up the day's pleasure by bringing down a fine buck, I told Richardson to ride on and attract the attention of the deer away from me while I crept up within rifle range. I slipped off my pony, and throwing the bridle over the saddle, turned him loose to follow on with the dogs. The deer caught sight of the cavalcade, and seemingly assured of its harmless intentions, contented themselves with watching it, while I, unobserved by them, crept up in good range and was just drawing a bead on a fine head of horns, when the band simultaneously threw up their tails and scampered away. Turning to see what had frightened them, I saw my pony dashing away toward home, pursued by Richardson and the dogs. "Let him alone!" I yelled

at the top of my voice, but the dogs had by this time opened on the track and their clamor drowned my voice, and away they went, leaving me afoot. And worse still, I feared for the fate of my trusty pony if the dogs succeeded in overtaking him. The din of the chase died away, and full of wrath I shouldered my gun and started for home.

By and by I heard Richardson hallooing off to the left and knew that he was lost. The pony had made a bee line for home, taking a course that Richardson could not follow. I was so exasperated with him that I would not respond to his halloo, but kept straight on to the Mormon village, where I was relieved to find my pony safe and sound; he having been rescued from his pursuers by the inhabitants. I then began to feel some remorse for having failed to answer my guest's call for help. The night passed and still he did not put in an appearance, and I, having fully recovered from the annoyance caused by his mistaken effort to do me a kindness, was just getting ready to go out and hunt for him when he hove in sight, full of contrition for having failed to catch the pony for me. His gaze being riveted on the deer he did not see me dismount, and when the pony, after having stopped to graze a little, came trotting up behind him, he looked around, and not seeing me, naturally supposed the little mustang had run away from me; his first impulse, therefore, was to catch him, which he could easily have done by walking up to him, but instead he made a dash for him, frigtening the pony, hence this tale. Richardson, after wandering around several hours, stumbled upon a cow camp, where he tarried till morning, when he was sent on his way. He was a genial, companionable fellow, and I felt no shadow of resentment for the transitory inconvenience to which his good intentions had subjected me, and we parted the best of friends. But the story found its way to Austin, where it was considered too good to be lost. Ford, editor of an Austin journal, was anxious to write it up in style, but I laid an injunction on it. I never again had the pleasure of meeting Mr. Richardson.

Here, too, came Gail Borden, of condensed milk fame, whom I had known in old San Felipe de Austin away back in the '20s, when he was only a blacksmith. I had lost sight of him for years, when he drove up to my door at the Mormon mills, he in the meantime having been to Europe in the interest of condensed milk. He had also taken up the homeopathic remedies and prefixed a Dr. to his name. His business in Burnet county, however, had no connection with his inventions or his practice. He had land located on Sandy creek, and there had been some particles of gold found in the sand, which created considerable excitement, which Dr. Borden was curious to investigate. The gold mines didn't "pan out." There was an old silver mine in the vicinity, which had been worked by the Spaniards, but it had apparently "petered out."

Dr. Borden imparted to me the great secret of his school of medicine as he understood it. Said he: "It is no use to be a doctor unless you put on the airs of one. Nine times out of ten sickness is caused by overeating or eating un-wholesome food, but a patient gets angry if you tell him so; you must humor him. This I do by taking one grain of calomel and dividing it into infinitesi-mal parts, adding sufficient starch to each part to make one of these little pel-lets (exhibiting a little vial of tiny white pills), then glaze them over with sugar. In prescribing for a patient I caution him about his diet, warning him that the pills have calomel in them. Well, the result is that he abstains from hurtful articles of food, which is all he needs to do anyway. But I have strong medicine to use in cases of need." It struck me that there was a good deal of truth in his argument. After spending a few days with us Gail Borden, too, went his way and was lost to view. Another old time friend, one of the origi-nal three hundred, I found settled in Burnet county, Captain Jesse Burnham, with whom I had sojourned at his home near the site of the present city of LaGrange in the summer of 1827. He, too, had been "crowded" and conse-quently sold out and moved to Burnet, where he engaged in the sheep busi-ness, one of the first men in the country to try the experiment.

Burnet had by this time grown to be quite a village, although the military having performed its part had moved on. There were several stores, among them being one owned by Jack Haynie, a brother of Dr. Haynie of Austin. The first substantial building in the town was a two-story stone, built by Vandever & Taylor, the lower story being occupied by them as a store and the upper floor fitted up for the use of a flourishing lodge of Free Masons.

The Masonic hall was dedicated on the 24th of June, 1855, a grand bar-becue and ball being among the attractions of the occasion. The dinner was free to all and consisted of everything the country afforded, and in such abun-dance that after all who would had partaken freely there were quantities ap-propriated by the outside element. I saw one fellow who I knew had not con-tributed one cent to the dinner riding off on horseback with a quarter of roasted beef on his shoulder, upon which, with the assortment of cake, pies, etc., his thrifty helpmeet had collected from the table, the family no doubt feasted several days.

The houses of the early Texans were small, but their hearts were large enough to cover all deficiencies. No candidate for hospitality was ever turned away. After the danger from Indians was over we had all outdoors in which to entertain our friends. If there was a wedding everybody was invited and a long table set out in the yard, around which the guests stood while partaking of the cheer with which it was loaded. Then if the bridegroom had relatives they gave an "infair" on the day following the wedding, at which the outdoor dinner was repeated.

Among the early social events I recall an infair given by William McGill to his nephew, Louis Thomas, and bride, nee Miss Kates; also a dinner given by Logan Vandever at the closing exercises of the school, which was the pride of the town, besides several Masonic and Fourth of July dinners. These free-for-all dinners were discontinued after a few years; the hungry hordes that swarmed in from all parts of the country, not content with a hearty dinner, filled their pockets, reticules, baskets and handkerchiefs with the dessert provided by the ladies, till they went on a strike against the imposition, and thereafter only those having the password gained admittance.

Barbecues were a feature of all political gatherings, the most notable one in that part of the country being given at the Marble Falls on the Fourth of July, 1854, prior to which time only the sound of the water leaping down the successive steps or benches that form the falls, and the voices of occasional small parties that had visited the spot, had awakened the echoes of the surrounding hills.

Preparations on a scale proportionate to the place and the occasion were inaugurated several weeks in advance. Meetings were held, committees appointed with power to levy contributions indiscriminately, everybody cheerfully complying with the demands thereof and faithfully carrying out the parts assigned. The mills were called on for flour, and some of the Mormon ladies who were famous cooks manufactured it into bread. The Burnet merchants gave freely of their groceries. Old man Hirston, who lived on the creek which bears his name, a few miles below town, was put down for a wagon load of roasting ears; other farmers brought loads of watermelons and canteloupes, together with such vegetables as were on hand. Huntsmen brought in venison and wild turkeys, and beef and pork galore were advanced. Nor were more delicate viands wanting; there were pound cakes worthy of the name, warranted full weight, that deluding inflationist, baking powder, not having, as yet, found its way into that neck of the woods. There were wild grape pies and dewberry pies and wild plum pies; as yet there was no cultivated fruit to be had except dried fruit, which was very scarce and high.

Several families from Burnet, among them the Vandevers and McGills, ever foremost in such enterprises, went down beforehand and camped on the ground to superintend the final arrangements. There was a wide spreading arbor covered with brush, beneath which seats and a speaker's stand were arranged, the ground being carpeted with a thick layer of sawdust, which served for a dancing floor. People came from far and near, on foot, on horseback, in carriages and farm wagons. None stayed away for want of conveyance, and the seating power of the spacious arbor was taxed to its utmost.

The first number on the programme was a national salute fired from holes drilled in the rock. The band, consisting of a lone fiddle manipulated by Jabez Brown, then played "Yankee Doodle" and "Hail Columbia," the only national airs in his repertoire.

The literary exercises began with the reading of the Declaration of Independence by the young son of the writer, a lad of fourteen, one of Professor Dixon's pupils, whom the professor had carefully drilled for the occasion.

Dr. Moore, the orator of the day, then took the stand. He was as long winded as a silver senator. His stentorian voice rolled out from his perspiring visage, contesting supremacy with the falls, while his rotund figure shook with the energy of his gesticulation. The sun mounted the zenith, and stooping far over to the westward, peered curiously beneath the arbor to see what all the noise was about. Still the doctor's sonorous voice rang out the paean of liberty above the nodding heads of the weary audience, mingling with the roar of the water and reverberating among the distant hills. At last it was finished, and the famished multitude made a rush for the dinner which had long been waiting, the odor therefrom aggravating the impatience of the throng, to a large number of which the dinner was the principal feature of the occasion, they presumably having risen early and breakfasted on the anticipation of the feast. But there was enough and to spare for supper and breakfast for those who remained to participate in the sawdust dance which closed the performance. Long before night a space was cleared of seats and Jabez Brown took his place on the stand and sawed out reels, which he also called, until daylight the next morning, occasionally varying the programme by singing, in a strong, musical, though uncultivated voice, "The Maid of Monterey," and "The Destruction of Sennacherib."

It was the greatest event the country had ever enjoyed, and we did have a royal time, some of the participants remaining on the ground several days later, presumably to live it all over again in imagination.

Some months later Colonel Todd came out from Kentucky, purchased the land on the east side of the river, and laid out a town. He advertised a sale of lots on the ground, to which quite a crowd turned out. A number of lots were sold, some of them bringing as high as $200, but beyond one or two dwelling houses the city existed only in name when I left the country in 1861.

Camp meetings, too, became a recognized institution among the annual gatherings. The first one held in Burnet county, if I rightly remember, was by the Methodists at Sand Springs on the road midway between Burnet and the Mormon mills, in the fall of 1855, Parson Whipple, an old Texas pioneer, being the chief priest. The hungry, both spiritually and physically, were freely fed at these meetings, the preachers dispensing the stronger spiritual meat of fire and brimstone first and tapering off the feast with milk and honey, while outside at every camp long tables were spread, provided with comfort for the physical man, where all were welcomed, an invitation to that effect being extended from the pulpit in the name of the campers whose hospitality was grossly abused in consequence. As other denominations took up the work, a regular chain of camp meetings every fall, with the incidental dispensation of free grub, induced many not overthrifty people to become regular camp followers, and most of them being quite forehanded with children, they became a heavy tax on the good brethren. The meetings, however, were not then drawn out indefinitely, five days being the usual limit. There finally sprung up a sect in Backbone valley that discounted all others in spiritual

manifestations. Protestant Methodists they styled themselves, though just what the name implied I never learned. They had meetings every night, singing, shouting and going into trances, during which they spoke with tongues and played on imaginary harps, and, as a grand finale, springing to their feet and running as if pursued by the emissaries of Satan. Crowds of curious sightseers flocked to see the performance as though it were a circus.

On one occasion a stalwart, honest son of Ham, who, though a stanch Methodist, looked with profound contempt upon the performances of this latest addition to the good old family, was standing just outside the door while the meeting was going on. "If any of them try to run away, you must catch them, Jo," some one said to him. Jo waited till the spirit moved one of the entranced to rise running, making a straight line for the door, where Jo was supposed to be on guard, but instead of catching him, the disgusted and skeptical darkey stepped aside and let him go.

"Why didn't you catch him, Jo?" they asked.

"If God A'mighty make 'em run I ain't got no right to stop 'em," was the philosophical reply.

The men of the sect all felt themselves called to preach, and as the emoluments of office were not sufficient to support the whole neighborhood, they had to make up the deficit by hook and by crook. A whole batch of them were once summoned as jurors. One after another they arose and pleaded the statutes in their favor as ministers of the gospel. The judge finally arose and blandly inquired if there were any men in their neighborhood who were not ministers of the gospel. Shiftless at best, their hallucinations rendered them even more so; they had worked their credit for all it was worth and were almost on the verge of starvation. They had gotten into me for various amounts of breadstuffs and I decided to shut down on them, the more especially as crops were short that year and mill stuffs commanded cash.

One old fellow who had a large family had been particularly troublesome. Seeing him coming, I told the miller not to let him have anything more. With an empty bag in one hand and leading a thin, ill-fed looking little boy by the other, he assaulted my fortress with the usual request for a bushel of meal on credit, reciting the failure of his crop, which, by the way, he had neglected to plant, and the destitute condition of his family in consequence. Without daring to look at the child, I put on a severe look and replied: "I can sell every dust in the mill for cash, Mr. ———. It is therefore impossible to accommodate you." The poor creature turned away, and taking the little boy by the hand, said in tremulous tones: "Well, son, we might as well go." I involuntarily glanced at the child, whose appealing eyes were raised to my face; tears stood in the blue baby eyes, tears of hunger. "Here, John, give Mr. ——— a bushel of meal," I said to the miller. I never got a cent for the meal, but the joy that lit up that little wan, pinched face and sparkled through the tears in those little eyes amply repaid me. I knew that the father was improvident, but the child was not to blame for that. Verily, "the sins of the fathers," etc. That same man denounced me as an "infidel." "Well," said one of his neighbors, "he's better than you are anyway, for the Bible says, 'He that provideth not for his household is wuss'n an infidel.'"

Had it not been for the large number of cattle that were being pastured in the country, many of the poor people would have certainly suffered; but milk will sustain life, and milch cows were to be had for the asking. My old-time friend, Peter Carr, who had obtained large landed possessions in Burnet and moved his immense herd of cattle thither, was certainly a great benefactor in allowing the poor people to milk his cows.

CHAPTER 25

After a few year's residence at the Mormon mills, I procured a fine tract of land down on the Colorado, eight miles below the Marble falls, removing thither in the fall of '55. Here I opened up a fine farm of one hundred acres of bottom land, and built the first frame house I had ever owned, thinking myself settled for life. "Man proposes, but God disposes."

My location was rather isolated, being on the east side of the river, midway between the Doublehorn and Hickory creek settlements. Doublehorn, the name of a little creek which emptied into the Colorado from the west, was derived from the interlocked antlers of two bucks found near the source of the stream by early settlers. The bucks, presumably having met at the spring to drink, became engaged in a dispute, and in attempting to fight it out got their horns interlaced, and, being unable to extricate themselves, starved to death. At the bold spring which is at the head of the creek, in a beautiful grove of Spanish oak, was the home of Captain Jesse Burnham, his children, grandchildren and great-grandchildren living around in the vicinity. The other inhabitants were mostly Fowlers, one family of which, Levi Fowler's, were my nearest neighbors, the head of the family becoming my chosen companion in hunting bear.

The Doublehorn people were all in comfortable circumstances and had an excellent school, presided over by Professor W. H. Holland, a Yale graduate. The holdings of the different families were large; their houses thus being widely separated, the children had to go from two to three miles to school. The schoolhouse was four miles from my house, and across the river, but in order to give my children the benefit of Professor Holland's superior instruction, I mounted them on ponies and sent them on. The river in its normal stage was fordable, and when it wasn't they had to lose their time. Sometimes a sudden rise cut them off from home, when they had to be ferried over in a canoe, the horses swimming. Such were the difficulties we encountered in trying to educate our children in the sparsely settled frontier districts. The thirty-five pupils under Professor Holland's care ranged from four years up to twenty, their studies ranging over a correspondingly wide territory. I often think of that school when viewing the array of appliances deemed indispensable to the modern school. Among other things there was a large class instructed in the mysteries of astronomy, the only artificial agents to assist in which were maps, and hoops made of willow branches. Nature, however, came to the professor's aid, generously contributing an eclipse of the sun, I think, in '59, in which that luminary was fully two-thirds hidden, and a magnificent comet, the finest I ever saw.

My neighbors on the other side in the Hickory creek settlement were all in very reduced circumstances, though some of them had seen better days. They were scattered along the creek from its source to its mouth, each one having a little plot of tillable land. Some of them had a few cattle of their own, and others took stock to keep on shares, as the lower country became settled up. The families were mostly related either by blood or marriage, were all on an equal footing financially, all belonged to the same church, and, take them all together, seemed to be happy and contented.

There was one discordant element in the person of "Bunk" Turner, who was among the first to locate on the creek, having a few cattle, which multiplied and increased until with the influx from other sources the range became overstocked, a state of things which "Bunk" warmly resented. That seeming the only thing to do, he concluded to migrate.

"Where are you going, Mr. Turner?" I asked.

"I dunno," he replied, dropping into a poetical vein—

"Whar the grass grows and the water runs,
And the sound of the gospel never comes."

There were others that had to seek fresh pasture for the immense herds that roamed over the hills in that vicinity. Levi Fowler's sons in '58 located a stock ranch on Pecan bayou, then away beyond the limits of settlement, taking thence 7,000 head of cattle. Thus was the advice of Horace Greely being acted on, the westward movement beginning with the stockman.

Among the Hickory creek settlers was an eccentric genius who was noted in that peaceful community for his profanity till a camp meeting gathered him under its wing, when he repented of his evil ways and faithfully tried to break off his vicious habits, succeeding fairly well in his laudable efforts till Satan in the form of a light-footed ox came to tempt him. In stooping to hobble the beast, Jack incautiously presented a tempting target within range of "Bally's" dexter heel. Whack! Visions of childhood floated across his mind, but quickly recovering from the confusion occasioned by the sudden blow, Jack pulled off his hat, dashed it to the ground, and after a momentary struggle with conscience, addressed himself to the ill-tempered brute as follows:

"Well, Bally, I ain't swore none yet since I got religion, but ———— your soul." And with that he gathered a pole and proceeded to administer a more comprehensive rebuke. That was the story his brother-in-law told, adding his opinion that camp meetings would have to come often if they kept Jack straight. Contrary to experience, however, Jack not only kept straight but turned preacher.

Just below my farm there was a fall in the Colorado which again aroused my penchant for mill building, and having previously disposed of the Mormon mill, I set to work in the winter of '57–8 to build myself a mill from the foundation up. Calling to my aid the full working force of Hickory creek, and a contingent from Backbone valley, together with some stone masons, carpenters and mill-wright, we quarried stone, burned lime and coal and put in a stone wall three feet thick, forty feet long by thirty in width, twenty feet high, laying the foundation upon the solid rock which composed the bed of the river. On top of the stone wall we erected a heavy frame building two stories high, the whole surmounted by a hip roof. The frame was securely bolted down to stone work, the wisdom of such precaution being demonstrated later. The natural fall in the stream being only about three feet, we put in a coffer dam; to facilitate the construction of which we built a boat of several tons burden, which we later employed as a ferry boat for the convenience of customers beyond. The motive power was at first applied through the medium of an undershot or current wheel, which was replaced a year later by a small horizontal wheel known as the Littlepage wheel, the inventor himself manufacturing and putting it in. One wheel proving inadequate, I afterward put in a second. The mill was as well equipped as any in the country, and cotton raising not having then extended into the highlands, there was ample business to pay a handsome profit on the investment. And, by the way, I am of the opinion that farmers in the south will find it the part of wisdom to return to the raising of grain again, at least enough for home consumption.

The dam in the river made a pretty little lake above, which, with the boat above mentioned, became quite popular as a means of recreation, along with fishing parties, who came to avail themselves of the schools of fish that ran up into the tail race while the mill was running and were left high and dry when the water was shut off. A party of the elite once went to the Marble falls for a day's fishing. They had fishing to their heart's content, but the fish failed to respond, and as the dinner hour drew near, and like those fishers of old, "only a few little fishes" were on hand, an emergency for which no provision had been made, a negro was forthwith dispatched to my place to procure the requisite quantity. Making the situation known, the darkey was sent to the race with a bag, when the obliging miller shut down the mill, and in a few minutes the messenger was on his way back to the famished multitude with his sack of fine fish.

In the summer of '60 there came an unprecedented rise in the Colorado, the water climbing into the second story of the mill, doing no damage, how-

[241]

ever, except to float out a threshing machine which was not secured. A mile above the mill there is a cut-off which in a flood takes the current away, leaving the mill in an eddy. The threshing machine, therefore, floated off up stream some sixty yards, where we succeeded in lassoing it and anchoring it to a tree. The rise came very suddenly, the first indication being noticed about noon, the highest stage being reached in three hours, by which time the water was running over the fall without even a ripple to indicate its presence, notwithstanding the volume diverted by the cut. A half mile below the mill the two streams came together, the river bed there narrowing to a deep gorge. There the spectacle was appalling. The maddened waters, freighted with driftwood and trees torn from the banks, rushed into the gorge, hurling the drifting timber high in the air and dashing it against the rocky walls with the roar and crash of a mighty battle. I am told that another flood some years later, went that of '60 several better, rising even to the roof of my old mill, which I am gratified to know held its own and is still intact. Founded on a rock, bolted to the massive masonry, it will stand till the stone itself crumbles.

A man's fittest monument is that which he rears for himself. That old mill, which I believe still bears my name, is all the monument I desire. In justice there should perhaps be emblazoned on its wall an incident that occurred during its building.

My dwelling, which stood near the edge of a narrow strip of table land between the river and the hills, was headquarters for a number of the mill hands. One night, just after dark, my dogs ran to the edge of the hill barking furiously at something below. Stepping out to see what game they had flushed, I heard a stone fall among them, by which I knew it was some person, and suspected that he was skulking, as the road ran on the opposite side of the house. It was too dark to make observations and knowing the watchful nature of my canine guards, I didn't give myself further trouble. It was, perhaps, an hour later that a bright light like a campfire was noticed a mile or so above in the river bottom; coupling that with the incident earlier in the evening, we someway hit upon the theory that they must be runaway negroes, which were not desirable additions to the neighborhood.

We determined to investigate, but the light died down, and there being no other means of locating the supposed camp, we deferred the foray till morning. Bright and early a couple of the boys set out to reconnoiter. In an hour, before it was light, one of them returned, confirming our suspicions. A party of five of us then sallied forth, another having remained in the vicinity of the camp to watch the movements of the occupants, who were seen to be negro men. The runaways, too, were early astir, and by the time the storming column reached the camp were off. The dogs of course accompanied the chase, and among them was a noble fellow, half bloodhound, that could be depended on to track anything living. Tiger promptly took the trail and bounded away with the rest of the pack at his heels; we hurried on and di-

rectly heard the dogs baying and then a shot. In a few minutes the dogs came back, Tiger bleeding from a shot through the skin near the throat. This put a serious aspect on the affair; we had not counted on armed resistance. The sight of my wounded favorite aroused my wrath and what had before been a mere frolic now became a personal matter. Tiger, who was not seriously hurt, was also apparently eager for revenge, but to guard him against further injury I tied one of the ropes we had brought along to secure our contemplated prisoners with around his neck so as to keep him in hand. Finding him hard to manage I handed my trusty rifle to one of the boys, taking an old-fashioned horse pistol in exchange. The delay had given the fugitives a chance to reload and get away. The river being up prevented escape in that direction. A little way on we came upon a horse which they had stolen on Hickory creek; the animal had bogged down in crossing a little creek and, there being no time to waste, his captors abandoned him. The negroes then took to the higher ground. By some accident favorable to the fugitives our party became separated, three of them carrying rifles getting off on the trail with the dogs, leaving me, armed with the old pistol, and two others with only small pocket pistols. For some reason the negroes doubled on their track and came back in full view of our position. We intercepted them and demanded an unconditional surrender, the only reply being the presentation of a rifle in the hands of a powerful black fellow. Thinking that he meant business, I threw up my pistol and without waiting to take sight, blazed away. There was a deafening report and something "drapped," but it wasn't the darkey. I sprang to my feet, the blood streaming from a wound just above my right eye; my right hand was also badly torn and bleeding, and my weapon nowhere to be seen. I comprehended the situation at once. The old pistol had been so heavily charged that when I pulled the trigger it flew into fragments, the butt of it taking me just above the eye. My blood was now thoroughly up, and thinking that the negro had fired simultaneously with myself I snatched a pistol from one of my companions and called to them to charge while his gun was empty. I discharged my piece without apparent effect, the only remaining shot was then a small pocket pistol in the hands of Billy Kay.

"Charge on him, Billy," I commanded.

Billy charged and received a bullet in the groin.

The negro had reserved his fire. By this time the other boys came up, but the negroes had gotten the best of the fight and were off, with the dogs in hot pursuit. Tiger had gotten away when I fell; directly we heard another shot and the dogs returned, Tiger having received a shot through the body. Neither Kay nor the dog were disabled, but Kay's wound was a dangerous one and we made all haste to get him home and get a surgeon. The chase had therefore to be abandoned.

In sorry plight we returned home. In our haste to get off after the game in the morning, hoping to bag them in camp, we had not waited for breakfast, thinking to be back in an hour or two. A messenger was dispatched for Dr. Moore, our Fourth of July orator, sixteen miles away. The doctor came post haste, but could not locate the ball with which Kay was loaded. The neighborhood was aroused and the country scoured in vain. Several days later the fugitives were heard from over on Sandy, where they held up Jim Hamilton and made him give them directions for reaching Mexico. We subsequently learned that the negroes had escaped from the lower part of the state. They were never recaptured, though one or two other parties attempted it. I hope they reached Mexico in safety. That big fellow deserved to; he certainly was as brave a man as I ever met. Singlehanded—his companion being unarmed—he had whipped six white men, all armed, and as many fierce dogs. That was unquestionably the worst fight I ever got into. I think now, looking back over a life of ninety years, that that was about the meanest thing I ever did. Though having been all my life accustomed to such things I did not then take that view of it. The capture of fugitive slaves was a necessity of the institution.

Billy Kay was laid up about two months, the bullet finally causing suppuration, by which means it was located and removed. Tiger's wound eventually caused his death. My injuries soon healed, but I still bear the scar, which might well have been the brand of Cain. The only portion of the double-acting pistol that was ever found was the guard, which caught on a bush some yards away from the scene of battle.

It was curious to note the different views taken of that affair by the negroes—a man and a woman—in my possession. The woman, who was a mulatto, openly avowed her sympathy for the fugitives, while the man, a full-blooded negro, took the other side.

It was, I believe, in 1858 that the grasshopper plague visited our section. They came on the wing and in such numbers that the sun was literally darkened with them. Anyone who has ever looked toward the zenith during a snowstorm will remember that the snowflakes looked like myriads of black specks. That is just the appearance the grasshoppers presented when first discovered. Soon they began to drop and the ground was alive with them. It was late in the fall and they went into winter quarters, devouring every green thing in sight except the rag-weed, which is intensely bitter, utilizing the denuded bushes and weeds for roosting purposes. When the cold nights came on they were frozen on their perches, and in this state they fell easy victims to the hogs, which devoured millions of them, but there were still enough left to seed the ground for the next season's crop, which they did by boring holes into the earth with their tail-ends. They did not distribute themselves evenly, some farms being almost free of them. On one such place there were only a few dropped down, and the owner thereof, mustering his whole family when the hoppers began to light, gathered tin pans, beating them energetically until the main body of the pests passed over. After his neighbors had received

the full force of the invasion he was wont to attribute their affliction to shift-lessness. "If you had just got out and fought them, as I did, you might have saved your crop." Pretty soon, though, there came on another detachment. When they began to drop our hero got out with his tin pans and brooms and "beat" and "shooed" till he was exhausted, but the hoppers kept on dropping, and lost no time in getting to work, cleaning out everything in sight.

In 1859 the first Indian raid was made in the vicinity of Burnet. They were discovered near town, and a party immediately went in pursuit. Being over-taken, the Indians showed fight, one of them slightly wounding Adam John-son, later a general in the Confederate army, while he in turn wounded an Indian. Billy McGill, a lad of thirteen, had the honor (?) of killing the only Indian left on the ground, and on investigation it proved to be only a squaw. The savages got separated in the retreat, one party of them getting down into the cedar brakes below Burnet, where they made an attack on Joe Allen, the negro previously referred to. Joe had been spending Sunday with his wife at the Mormon mill, and started out very early Monday morning for home. In passing through the brake about daybreak he was fired upon by the Indians. He made haste to seek the protection of a house a short distance away, reach-ing it in safety, only to find it deserted. The enemy did not seem to be aware of the fact so they did not venture to follow. The alarm was given, and all over the country private companies were organized, guards being stationed at in-tervals, to watch for any signs of hostility. The Indian wounded by Johnson was found the next day and dispatched. That was the last Indian seen in the vicinity during my residence.

It would have been a distressing affair had old Joe Allen been killed, as he was the sole support of a poor widow with a large family, among them several grown-up sons. The injustice of the situation forced itself upon my recogni-tion at the time, and I often wondered how it fared with Joe and his wife Mandy when they were free. Two more honest, faithful people could not have been found in all the country. Joe was so entirely trustworthy that his mis-tress permitted him to hire himself to suit himself, himself collecting his wages, which were faithfully delivered to the mistress, while his own wife went barefooted and in rags, her hire and that of one of her children by a former husband supporting another white family. I had both Joe and Mandy in my employ, and never had the least cause to find fault with either one. At another time the widow's family had a narrow escape from losing their means of livelihood. Joe was wending his way to his work early in the morning, after having Sundayed with his wife, when he was bitten on the leg by a rattle-snake. He had a chunk of tobacco in his pocket, which he chewed up, hastily binding it on the wound with his handkerchief, and went on his way, not losing a day's work.

CHAPTER 26

In the summer of 1860 Colonel Dale came out from St. Louis, Mo., and bought land just below Burnet. He was connected with a manufacturing firm, which was projecting a scheme to build a woolen factory somewhere contiguous to the wool-producing section. The advantages to be gained by the utilization of the waterpower led Colonel Dale to the highlands of the Colorado. The Marble falls was the objective point in view, but the owner, Colonel Todd, held that site at a very high figure. My mill, having stood the test of the high water, next attracted the attention of Colonel Dale, and, after looking the situation all over, he made me an offer of $12,000 for it. Considering that sum a pretty fair return on my investment, and rather longing for more worlds, in the way of mill building, to conquer, anyway, I accepted the offer.

Colonel Dale then went back to St. Louis to report to his firm, proposing to return in the fall with the cash for the purchase, and the machinery for the plant.

In the meantime the presidential election came on, and the disturbed condition of the country arising therefrom knocked all enterprises out. We had had the locust plague, the eclipse of the sun, and the comet, all of which the superstitiously inclined averred foreboded war, and now the war was upon us. Scarce fifteen years had passed since we were rejoicing over being admitted to membership in the great American Union—fifteen years of comparative peace and unexampled prosperity. The country had settled up rapidly, capital was flowing in and new enterprises were being inaugurated. Schools, and good ones, were being organized all over the country, mail routes and postoffices established. The great overland stage route connecting the Atlantic and Pacific traversed hundreds of miles of Texas territory, with strong probability that a transcontinental railroad would in the near future supersede it. The iron horse had crossed the Brazos and was heading towards Austin. And now all the advantages accruing to us under Uncle Sam's beneficent rule were to be thrown to the winds. In vain our leading men—Houston, Culberson, Hamilton, Hancock, Throckmorton, Duval and many others—tried to reason with the excited populace. They were deaf to reason.

As the son of a revolutionary soldier, I could not raise my hand against the Union he had fought to establish. I had fought to make Texas a member of the Union, and I would not turn round and fight to undo my work. But when I talked of war my hearers scouted the idea. Many men offered to drink all the blood that would be shed.

"Oh, there won't be any war. The Northern men are all a set of d——d cowards; one Southerner can whip a dozen of them," said one.

"Well, Billy," I replied, "in former wars the Northern men have not shown themselves lacking in courage, and although I think I have as good a reputation as a fighter as most of you, when you parcel them out you needn't give me but one, and I don't care to have him a very stout one."

It was the prevailing impression that there would be no war; an impression to which the apathy of the outgoing administration gave color. Had there been an Andrew Jackson in the presidential chair, there would probably have been no war to speak of; his sentiments on the subject of secession being clearly defined in the case of South Carolina, twenty-nine years before. "By the Eternal, the Union must and shall be preserved." I was a Democrat of the Jackson school, my first vote having been cast for the hero of New Orleans, and when the term Democrat was made to mean secessionist I could go with the party no further. I was ever a man of strong convictions, and with me to think was to act. I was unalterably opposed to secession, both on principal and policy. I did not believe that the South would be benefitted thereby, nor did I believe that the North would tamely acquiesce in the disruption of the nation; and I felt a firm conviction that in case of an armed conflict the South must inevitably go down; a calamity from which I exerted all my little influence to save Texas, even taking the stump for the first time in my life, a course which placed me under the ban.

"Just wait till we get things fixed and we'll attend to your case," said one of the leaders, a man who never set foot in the country till all the danger from Mexicans and Indians had passed. I didn't wait. When the ordinance of secession passed, I immediately set about getting away. I sold my farm for $2,000. The mill for which I had been offered $12,000 I could not cash at any price. I was, however, bent on fleeing from the wrath to come, so I turned the property over to my nephew, John Hubbard, who, though also a Unionist, decided to stay and face the consequences; a decision that cost him his life. I didn't get a dollar for the mill, but took promissory notes, secured by mortgages, for $4,000. A fine young negro man that had a few months before the election been assessed at $1,500, I sold to Governor Houston for $800, and everything else in proportion.

Having decided on California as the land of refuge, and the trip thither to be made overland, the next thing was to provide means of transportation. As we had to run the gauntlet of two hostile tribes, we could not rely upon our horses or mules which were liable to be stampeded, so there remained only the slow, but sure ox or a train of burros. A number of my acquaintances joined the movement, and we rigged out a fleet of prairie schooners and gathered up a lot of wild, long-horned Texas steers, few of which had ever felt a rope except when they were branded. These we tied together in couples as the preliminary step.

"What are you going to California for? That state will secede before you get there," I was asked.

"Well, if it does," I replied, "I'll get me one of those big trees they tell about and dig me a dugout and go across to the Sandwich Islands."

I went down to Austin to lay in supplies for the trip. Speechmaking was the order of the day. Somebody, I don't remember who, was holding forth from the steps of the capitol. A big, rough looking fellow, a carpenter, I believe, stepped up among the crowd, and, after listening a few minutes, said to those in his vicinity:

"What the hell's it all about, anyway?"

"The nigger," someone answered.

"The nigger! H—l. I ain't got no nigger. Give me a nigger, some of you, and I'll fight for it as long as any of you. I ain't going to fight for somebody else's nigger." And yet that was just the kind that had to do a large part of the fighting.

I went to see General Houston and had a long talk. "General," said I, "if you will again unfurl the Lone Star from the capitol, I will bring you 100 men to help maintain it there."

"My friend," said he, "I have seen Texas pass through one long, bloody war. I do not wish to involve her in civil strife. I have done all I could to keep her from seceding, and now if she won't go with me I'll have to turn and go with her."

And so we parted ways. It was with a feeling of inexpressible sadness that I bade farewell to old Austin and the many friends who had been associated with me in our early struggles. Many of them were Unionists, some of whom like myself fled the country, while others, like General Houston, acquiesced in the will of the majority. Hamilton and Hancock were among the former.

Conspicuous among the latter was J. W. Throckmorton, whose memorable speech in the convention that passed the ordinance of secession deserves to live among the classics of the nation; he being one of the seven who voted in the negative. When it came to his turn to vote he arose to his feet. These, I think, are the words he used:

"Unawed by the reckless spirit of revolution around me, in the presence of God and my country and my own conscience, which I fear more than either, I vote No." As he sat down some one hissed. Springing to his feet, he exclaimed:

"Gentlemen, 'the rabble may hiss when the patriot trembles.'" How he reconciled his subsequent course with his conscience I do not know.

That Houston and Hamilton, both outspoken in their opposition to the secession movement, which was even then under discussion, were in 1859 elected by handsome majorities respectively Governor and member of Congress, is evidence of the loyalty of the people of Texas until carried away by excitement. Among other devices employed to influence the wavering, was a book entitled "The Armageddon," by one Baldwin, in which the author demonstrated to his own satisfaction that the impending conflict was that foretold in the prophecies of Daniel; in which the king of the North and the king of the South were to meet in battle, from which the king of the South was to come off victorious. Either Daniel, or Baldwin, was mistaken; but, the book had quite a run among the church people.

I was apprehensive that we had no time to lose, so we hastened our preparations, and on the 14th day of April, 1861, the very day that Fort Sumter was evacuated by the United States forces, though we were in total ignorance of the fact for many days thereafter, we started on our long, tedious, dangerous journey. For the second time I was being driven from the land of my adoption. There were about thirty-five souls in our train, of whom thirteen were men, all armed with revolvers.

At Fort Chadbourne we encountered the first visible effects of the impending war in the absence of the American flag from the fort where it had fanned the breeze so long. There were a few Texas rangers there, about one company, I think. There we struck the United States overland mail route to California, and in the dismantled and deserted stations thenceforward were constantly reminded of the disturbed relations between the two sections of the country. The road paralleled the Concho river many miles. Through all that fine fertile country there was not even a stock ranch. The Comanche was lord there. At the head of the Concho a protracted rain came on and, availing ourselves of the deserted station buildings, we awaited fair weather. During the sojourn we got our first Indian scare. A couple of the boys who were out herding the stock, ascended a high knoll to reconnoiter. Discovering a lone horseman approaching, they hastened to conceal themselves to observe his movements. They were seen by the object of their distrust, who in turn, taking them for Indians and having descried our camp, hurried on up to warn us of the danger. We hurriedly housed the non-combatant portion of our party and, being apprehensive of danger to the boys out herding, sent a party to their aid, which of course brought the matter to a solution. The lone horseman, Dr. Ferguson by name, proved to be the advance guard of a large train of emigrants from Dallas.

When the rain ceased we all started on together. With this accession to our strength there was little fear of an open attack from Indians; still we were in the Indian range and we older folks who had had experience in that line had much trouble in bringing our young folks to a realizing sense of their danger. Our girls would venture too far away from camp and our boys persisted in emptying their revolvers at everything and nothing, just for the fun of shooting. Many pounds of lead were thrown away in the vain attempt to kill a prairie dog, but if one was ever hit he tumbled into his burrow, to the mound surrounding the entrance to which he betook himself at the first alarm. Safe retreat thus secured they stood up on their hind quarters to take observations, emitting little yelps, dispatches presumably to the inhabitants within. "Bing! Bang! Bang!" The dirt flew and all that the quickest eye could catch was the twinkling of tiny feet as the unscathed rodent disappeared down the shaft of his tunnel. So persistent were the boys in their ambition to secure a prairie dog scalp that there were times when if the Indians had charged us there would not have been a loaded wagon in camp. When we struck camp we drew our wagons round in a circle, lapping the tongues upon the wheels of the wagons in front, securing them with chains; in this way forming a corral in which to keep our stock at night. We stopped long enough before night to give the stock a chance to feed, sending them out again as soon as it was light in the morning.

Guards were kept out all night, being relieved every two hours. One night one of the guards came to the wagon in which I was sleeping and rousing me told me that he had discovered a suspicious object out in the chaparal. With as little show of alarm as possible I arose and accompanied the guard to the further side of the enclosure, where he pointed out the object. It certainly did look in the dim starlight like a crouching figure and the guard was positive that it had but just come there. I told them to bring their guns to bear on it and if it did not answer when hailed to shoot. I hailed "Who goes there?" There was no reply. I repleated it, and still the figure neither stirred nor spoke. Telling the guard to be ready to fire, I was just in the act of hailing the third and last time when a woman in a wagon near by put out her head and called "Minerva," and the crouching figure answered "Ma'am." A cold shiver ran over me and I sat down as weak as an infant. The child had left her bed in obedience to a call of nature, and either did not know that the challenge was directed to her or did not realize her danger. That was another narrow escape I made from the brand of Cain.

Leaving the head of the Concho, we struck out across the staked plains. The Mustang ponds being the last living water until we reached the Pecos at the old Horsehead crossing, eighty or one hundred miles distant, we lay by there till evening before beginning the long, dry march. There was no station at the ponds, but as the next station out—Johnson's—had to haul their water from there, there had been a stone house built for protection in case of attack. In the summer of 1860, I think it was, Tom Johnson, a brother of General Adam Johnson, and another man having gone to the ponds for water, were surprised by the Comanches, and took refuge in the stone house. The Indians laid siege, keeping the boys prisoners three or four days, when the stage with its armed guard came along and broke the siege. Filling up our water barrels, with which we had provided ourselves before leaving Burnet, we started out late in the afternoon. Slowly the long train of white-covered wagons drew its sinuous length along, the steady tramp of the oxen and the monotonous grinding of the wheels on the gravelly road being the only sounds that broke the stillness of the night, save when the occasional pop of a whip told that some driver had stirred his lagging team. All night we kept up the pace, and morning found us in the center of the wide, treeless plain. Cattle and drivers alike were tired, so we halted for the day. There was plenty of green grass, fresh and dewy, on which the stock regaled themselves, but not a drop of water. Here we had the novel experience of digging for wood. The ground was full of mesquite grubs, though there was not a green shrub in sight. Unwittingly we made a dry camp within a few miles of water, our chart, a map sent out with the Texas Almanac, not correctly locating the Wild China ponds, which we would have passed early the second night but for the sagacity of our thirsty cattle. Scenting the water the team in the lead made a break for it, snapping the wagon-tongue. Another long forced march brought us to the Pecos river. Here the work of vandalism had already begun in the destruction of the ferry boat. There was a ford lower down, but the river was flush, and in order to keep our goods dry we had to lift the wagon beds and put blocks underneath, and then chain the beds down to prevent their floating.

Here again we filled out water barrels, another long, dry stretch intervening between the Pecos and Fort Stockton. Fort Stockton was held by a company of state troops. The stage route from San Antonio to El Paso here connected with the overland route so that communication with the balance of the world was restored. I do not remember how often the trips of the stage were made, but I remember how eagerly the stage was watched for, and how breathlessly we listened for the latest news of the war that was then only just beginning to take shape.

The station buildings had begun to feel the effects of abandonment. They were all adobe with earthen floor and roof, the latter requiring for its support heavy timbers. These, which with the heavy doors and jams had been procured with much labor and danger, many of them hauled hundreds of miles, were being torn out by emigrants for firewood.

In the Wild Rose pass we had another accession to our train, consisting of two families and several single men who were traveling under the escort of a Mexican government train. The head of one of these families was one James Brown, cousin to John Henry Brown, the historian. The pass through the Apache mountains was at that time a dangerous one, but we got through without trouble, though some trains that came later encountered the Indians. Fort Davis had a small garrison of Texans. From El Muerto springs across to Van Horn's well was another long, dry stretch, and another between the well and Eagle spring. We reached the latter place in the night, men and teams tired out, so the latter were just turned loose to seek water, which was in a dangerous canyon beyond the station. The next morning when the boys went out to look up the cattle they had all disappeared, but in looking around the boys found their trail where they had gone through the canyon, and following in their wake, were shoe tracks. This discovery reported in camp, we rallied our forces and started in pursuit. There were two men at the station. Their opinion was that it was the work of Mexican bandits, but bandits would scarcely have been on foot. We followed the trail several miles back into the mountains, at one place finding the carcass of one animal, from which a portion of the meat had been taken. A little further on in a secluded spot we found most of the herd. The poor creatures had not rested for twenty-four hours, and had not even reached the water when they were captured. We drove them slowly back, but so tired out were they that it was necessary to lay by another day before making the final march to the Rio Grande at Fort Quitman, which completed the first stage of our journey. Here we found the remainder of our cattle, they having taken the road and kept on it till they found water.

We drew a long breath of relief when we at last struck camp on the Rio Grande at Fort Quitman, though the flag under the folds of which we should have found protection, had been withdrawn. The fort was held by four men pending the arrival of Baylor. Having safely crossed the Comanche range we felt secure from bodily harm and so far as possible threw off the load of care and anxiety, resolved to take a good rest.

The river being low we were compelled to keep a close watch on our stock during their grazing time; but, obtaining permission to use the fort corral, we were relieved of the necessity of night guard.

We came near losing some of our stock, however, by the treachery of some of our own men, outsiders having induced two of our boys to join them, without divulging their plans in full, which were to run the stock over into Mexico. Through the men at the fort, to whom the leader of the conspiracy made overtures on the score of our being Union men, we learned of what was going on and took prompt measures to rid ourselves of such undesirable company. Finding the game up, the leaders skipped. The station men proposed following them and hanging them on general principles. Our two boys pleaded ignorance of any designs on our property, but the fact that they had secretly entered into negotiations with the other fellows to leave us, destroyed our confidence in them and we promptly dismissed them, and they went on and joined the other party.

In the meantime another large train of emigrants, hailing from McKinny, Texas, came up. Four families, Elliot, Kendal and Austin brothers, were taken into our train.

With few exceptions the Texans who came out to California that season (1861) were rampant secessionists, but they were better voters than fighters, they probably having every one voted for secession and then run away from the consequences. One of these braves was cursing Abe Lincoln.

"Well, what has Lincoln done?" I asked.

"Why, d—m him, he voted for the fugitive slave law," said he. And this was a fair sample of their intelligence.

From Fort Quitman up to Fort Filmore, where we crossed the river, feed and water being everywhere available, we traveled by easy stages, to give our stock a chance to recuperate for the long, hard, dry march across Arizona. There were many little Mexican pueblos along the way, the denizens of which came out with fruit and vegetables to sell or barter for coffee. At one place a wealthy ranchero came out and invited our young people to attend a fandango at his house in the evening. Several of the boys went out, and were made welcome by the host. They were cordially invited to participate in the dance, but as none of them could go through the dizzy maze of the waltz, and the Mexicans were equally as ignorant of the evolutions of set dancing, our boys were compelled to remain wall flowers. Some of them were induced to sample the mescal, the effects of which were painfully apparent. The Mexicans used to be very temperate drinkers, the act being more a social rite than to gratify a thirst. Their custom was to take a sip and pass the cup on, much as the communion cup is passed. When the Texas boys got hold of the cup they drained it. It was harvest time and in every village there was a threshing yard. The straw was arranged around a center pole, a band of horses driven in and started in a gallop around the stack, horsemen forming a ring around to keep them from breaking away, and also to keep them crowded toward the center till the whole stack was trampled down, when the straw was shaken and removed and the grain cleaned by a kind of dry washing process. The Mexican plow and cart were in general use, and when a swain wished to take his lady for a ride he seated her in his saddle and mounted behind her, to hold her on. There were white men at all the towns, and as a rule they were worse than the Mexicans. The day we reached El Paso, while we were stopped for dinner, our loose stock was left to graze in the vicinity of the camp. Elliot had three fine horses, on which he kept vigilant eyes, but while eating he observed one of them feed off around a little knoll, out of sight. He finished his dinner and went to drive it back, but it had completely disappeared, nor could any trace of it be found. Going on up to El Paso—Franklin, as the town on the American side was then called—Elliot made his loss known, when a white man offered him a Mexican pony for the chance of the American mare he had lost. A half loaf—even a quarter—beats no bread, so Elliot took the pony, and within a few hours the purchaser of the "chance" was riding the mare through the streets.

I asked an El Paso man how it was that such a large vote was polled in favor of the ratification of the secession ordinance in a county apparently so sparsely settled. "Oh, that was a light vote," rejoined he. "We could have polled twice that number if the river hadn't taken a rise." There was a well equipped flouring mill just above Franklin. The flour, however, was slightly gritty from the grain having been tramped out on the ground.

At San Elizario, White, one of the best men in the Dallas train, was accidentally shot, and having no family, two of his friends, Campbell and Kirkney, also single men, stopped with him. He lingered some weeks, but finally died. Campbell and Kirkney then joined some of the returning parties and probably went into the Confederate army.

On the evening of July 3rd we reached Fort Filmore and for the first time in many months saw Old Glory floating front the mast. That beautiful ensign never before looked so lovely to me, and I thought of Francis Scott Key when straining his eyes "through the dawn's early light," the "broad stripes and bright stars" floating over Fort McHenry, catching "the gleam of the morning's first beam," flashed them the signal that their friends still held the fort. But it harbored an officer beneath its folds, who a few days later made a disgraceful surrender of the place.

On July 4, 1861, we crossed the Rio Grande. At Mesilla the stars and stripes were flying, but the glorious old constellation had been cleft in twain. That was the only Confederate flag displayed along the route. At Mesilla we parted company with the Brown family, and also old man Hambrick, they deciding to stop there, and I never saw or heard of any of them again.

From Mesilla we struck out across the arid sands of Arizona, the long, dry stretches of sand being broken at intervals by rough, dangerous passes, through which we hurried with bated breath. The Apaches were literally in possession of the country, all the United States troops having been ordered to fall back to the Rio Grande. The Indians probably had not yet grasped the situation, otherwise our progress might have been interrupted. As it was, we saw no hostile parties on the trip, though we saw many evidences of their atrocious work. At the eastern outlet of Apache pass were nine graves where the overland mail coach had recently been ambushed, all of the occupants being killed. Apache pass is a narrow wash just wide enough to permit a wagon to pass between high overhanging walls of rock that seemed to look menacingly down upon the traveler, and had the Indians known enough to provide themselves with crowbars they could have dealt destruction to us in comparative safety themselves. The guards that always accompanied the stage were always on the lookout when approaching and in going through the pass. This the Indians had found out, so they built breastworks of stone at the farther end, and when the guards, having gone safely through the pass, relaxed their vigilance, the Indians made the attack. At another place were the charred remains of a government train that had been captured, the teamsters being lashed to the wagons, which were then fired. For this last outrage at least six of them paid the death penalty, the pursuing party catching them and stringing them up to the trees, where the mummified remains were still swaying in the wind. The coyotes had nibbled off their toes, but otherwise the forms were well preserved. There was an old regular with us who had been over at Filmore in the hospital. His company was stationed at Fort Breckenridge, and when the order was issued to abandon the place he wanted to join his company, and to that end asked to travel with us to the nearest point, which was forty miles north of Fort Breckenridge. He was with us when we came to the place where the Apaches were hanging some little way from the road. We stopped the team and every man, except the old soldier struck off to see the show. The old regular stayed with the train and deplored the thoughtlessness of the balance of us for leaving it defenseless in such a dangerous locality. At Dragoon springs, just on the western side of Dragoon pass, were the battered walls of an old stage station which had succumbed to the attack of a large force, the few men who were in it being killed. At still another place a family of emigrants had been attacked, and the father, mother, and several children killed, and a young lady taken prisoner. A boy of fourteen escaped by jumping from a high bluff. The name, I think, was Oatman.

It was so hot during the day that we had to keep up our night travels, during which every cactus was regarded with suspicion. Somewhere out in that desolate region we met A. Sidney Johnston and party hastening to join the Confederate army. Upon learning that we were from Texas he said with some asperity:

"I think you are doing very little for your country."

"Well," I retorted, "it seems to me you are doing equally as little for yours." Johnston had just resigned his position as commander of the Pacific Coast Division of the United States army.

We wanted to send letters back to friends in Texas by the party, but they did not care to have papers that would betray their destination in case they fell in with United States troops. They at least had the courage of their convictions, which was more than could be said of the current of emigration that was setting toward California. One large train of emigrants coming on behind us, learning of the approach of Baylor and becoming apprehensive that he might arrest their flight, crossed over into Mexico and did not recross the line until well on toward the Colorado.

General A. Sidney Johnston was killed in the battle of Shiloh.

Away back in Texas, at Fort Davis I think, I picked up a Mexican boy that wanted to go to California. He made himself useful and trustworthy, and when on the Rio Grande he met some friends who persuaded him to go with them, he came and told me of the change in his plans and offered to return the butcher knife I had given him. Up about Mesilla I picked up another Mexican. He also made himself useful, but not trustworthy, as I found to my cost. I had been riding and driving the loose stock, and being under the weather, when we went into camp on Rio Mimbres, about where Deming now is, I told the Mexican to get on my horse and go out and herd. That was the last I saw of the Mexican or my horse; my revolver was hanging on the saddle horn and my coat was tied on behind. It was a better outfit, no doubt, than the greaser had ever possessed in his life, and he could not resist the temptation. "Lead us not into temptation."

Just before we reached Tucson we espied moccasin tracks, and in reconnoitering discovered a lone Indian jogging across the country ahead of us. We immediately called a halt and held a consultation. Some were for pursuing the Indian and others for forming in battle array and awaiting developments;

but, as the Indian kept straight on without seeming to take notice of us, we concluded he was not hostile, and kept on our way. Pretty soon a train of squaws hove in sight, each one laden with a large basketful of mesquite beans, which the Indians used for food and also to make a beverage of. They were friendly, and our little people taking a fancy to the strings of beads with which they were adorned, traded off all the bread in camp.

We had heard much of Tucson as the seat of territorial government, and expected to see something of a place, but a dirtier, more disreputable den it would be hard to imagine. A little cluster of adobe huts, before one of which, suspended from a pole laid in the forks of two upright poles, hung three bells, typical of the Catholic church. There were a few American men there, but we saw no American women.

Lying over there a day, the boys out herding the stock, came upon a new made grave. The authorities were notified and they proceeded to investigate. A few feet below the surface the body of a man wrapped in a blanket was found. When the blanket was removed we recognized the features of one Hale, who had been traveling with the Brown family, but left them to follow the lead of another, thereby losing his life. There was evidence of foul play in a contusion on the back of the head that looked as if it might have been made with a junk bottle. Some of the front teeth were also knocked out. The authorities blustered and talked of sending out a posse to arrest the whole outfit, which had made haste to get away before our arrival, but a murder was an every day occurrence thereabouts and nothing to make a fuss about. We afterward overtook the train and a terribly scared lot they were when questioned about Hale. They said that a lot of them went into a watermelon patch to steal melons and were fired on, Hale being killed and one of the Bain boys being shot in the leg. The Bain boy did carry a bullet in his leg till one of our men cut it out, but the mark of the bludgeon on the back of Hale's head was not satisfactorily accounted for.

Our breadstuff having run low, we were obliged to replenish our stock at Tucson. The only thing in that line obtainable was an unbolted mixture in which sand and mesquite beans were present in considerable quantities, especially sand. The only way in which we could possibly eat it was to "bolt" it. We mixed up a batter of such consistency as to allow the cobblestones to settle to the bottom and then poured off the top, which was made into slapjacks, upon which we didn't dare to close our teeth. Our free, outdoor life gave us the digestion of ostriches, else the slapjack diet would have been fatal.

From Tucson the road followed down the valley of the supposed underground Santa Cruz river. The rainy season was on and waterholes were all full. From Casa Grande we struck straight across to the Gila at Sacaton in the Pima Indian reservation and were assured by the chief that we had passed the danger line and might therefore turn our stock loose with perfect safety; an assurance that brought relief to our souls after many months of incessant watchfulness. To the credit of those Indians be it said that not a thing was molested.

The Pima and Maricopa Indians farmed to some extent, bringing to our camp the cleanest, whitest wheat I ever saw. They also raised "frijoles," but didn't go back on the old reliable mesquite bean, which is really quite sweet and nutritious; cattle and horses eat them with avidity.

I do not know how the natives attired themselves in winter, but the summer costumes of the men consisted of a breech clout about ten inches wide and from two to four yards long, confined at the waist by a string. The only garment of the women—if garment it could be called, that had never felt scissors or needle—was a breadth of calico a couple of yards long, wrapped about the waist so as to extend to the knee.

The danger being passed, the bond of mutual protection that held the trains together was soon dissolved, and each one traveling to suit himself, we formed an unbroken line for many miles down the Gila. We had, however, to keep up our night journeys, it being August and the sun hot enough to roast Gila monsters. Excepting the space covering the mouth of the great bend we traveled in striking distance of the Gila clear on down to its confluence with the Colorado. Somewhere between the bend and Gila City we struck an old time resident of Bastrop county, who may still be remembered by some of the earliest settlers, James Dye. Though not a participant in the Texas revolution, he came to Bastrop shortly thereafter and was out trading with the Comanches during the time I was with them. Dye came to California in '39 or '40 and, after roaming over the state, drifted out to the Gila country where he took up a ranch, also keeping the overland mail station. The withdrawal of the stage line left him without any occupation to speak of, so he soon after returned to California, marrying and settling in San Diego county, where he died, leaving several children, who I believe are still there. About the middle of August we reached Fort Yuma, and with the most trying stretch of road on the whole route confronting us.

Yager was king of the civic portion of the place. He had the only ferryboat and had no conscience about charging for the use of it. It cost me ten dollars to get my outfit across the river.

Taking a good rest, we started from Yuma at sunset to make the last forced march across the great Colorado desert, ninety miles of sand with but one watering place for stock, the sun like a glowing furnace and a portion of the road below sea level. The wagon road took the nearest cut across, coming in south of the San Jacinto mountains, to the north of which runs the Southern Pacific railway. There is a stream laid down on the map called New river about midway of the desert, but the only water we found there was that deposited by the summer rains. But August being the rainy season on the desert, we found more water than we had expected, and there were tons of mesquite beans. We were unable to make more than fifteen miles a day, owing to the weakened condition of the cattle, and so were about five days crossing the desert.

Crawling along in the middle of the night, the monotonous grinding of the wheels in the coarse, loose sand was broken by a crash as an old wheel collapsed. As a large part of our original freight had been provisions, which were pretty well cleaned out, we transferred the contents of the disabled wagon, consisting mostly of human freight, to another wagon, and left the poor old hulk that had borne the most precious part of the cargo hundreds of weary miles stranded on the waste of sand. We had gone but five or six miles further when another wheel succumbled. As this wagon could not be spared, I sent two of the boys back to the wagon we had left to bring up a sound wheel from the wreck, and myself stopped with the wagon till their return, sending the balance of the party on to Indian wells. That was a long, lonely night, but not so dangerous as many vigils I have kept.

There were household goods, dead animals and broken wagons strewn all across the desert. At one place we found a complete set of blacksmith tools, including heavy anvil, which some poor fellow had been obliged to abandon on this last stage of the journey after having hauled them many hundreds of miles. I appropriated the set.

A sandstorm swept across our way, obliterating every trace of the road, but here again the bread we had cast upon the waters in taking in an old Californian at Tucson returned to us, said Californian safely piloting us through the trackless sea of sand by means of notes made on former trips. There were others not so fortunate, who got lost and narrowly escaped the horrible fate that has overtaken so many. Without further mishap we reached the land of the living, having spent four months on a trip that is now accomplished in three days, nights included.

At the western edge of the desert we met another party going on to join the Confederate army. Shortly afterward a third party led by Dan Showalter came on, but General Carlton with a column of California infantry was ahead of him and bagged the lot, putting them on parole. All of what is known as Southern California was then given over to stock raising, the inhabitants for the most part being of a class among which it was not desirable to bring up a family. So we kept on to Tulare county, remaining there till the advent of the railroad brought in another class of citizens, when we returned to Los Angeles, in the vicinity of which we have since remained.

On our way up to Visalia we fell in with an old time Austin boy whom the gold excitement had lured away years before, George S. Evans, son of Judge Evans who was connected with the land office during the days of the Lone Star Republic. George Evans at the time of which I write was a lieutenant-colonel of the Second California Cavalry, with a detachment of which he was on his way to Owen's river to quell an Indian outbreak. Later he was ordered to Visalia where we again renewed old acquaintance. He was soon promoted to full colonel and sent to Salt Lake to look after the rebellious Saints. He rose to brigadier-general before the close of the war. He was mustered out by the great ruler long years ago.

When after the close of the war, we established communication with friends in Texas, I learned of the fate of many of my Union friends, among them my nephew, John Hubbard, who was waylaid and shot down, his body being riddled with bullets. I felt that it would be unwise for me to return, as I should feel an uncontrollable desire to avenge his death. And yet up to the time I left Burnet county there had never been a case of murder in the county. But the dogs of war were literally turned loose, and the devil concealed in men, unchained.

Toward the man who, believing in the justice of his cause, had the courage to shoulder his gun and face his opponents on the field of battle, I harbor no resentment now, but for the cowards who, taking good care to keep out of harm's way, hunted down and murdered defenseless Union men—well, I have never been a believer in the orthodox hell, still, when I think of those wretches, I am forced to concede that it was an oversight in the plan of creation if hell was left out. Among the many good men who were sent to their long home by assassin's bullets in Burnet county during the war were the fathers of two young men who came away with us. "All that a man hath will he give for his life." I only saved mine by so doing.

I found a number of my old Mormon friends in California, and without an exception found them secessionists, not from any partiality for the Southern people, who were even more intolerant of Mormonism than the Northern people, nor yet because of any sympathy with the peculiar institutions of the South. They wanted to see the South succeed in its purpose to withdraw from the Union, thereby establishing a precedent which Brigham Young would have made haste to follow. Had there been no other reason for opposing secession, that dangerous precedent, which would have been a constant menace to the South as well as to the North, would have been sufficient ground.

It is extremely improbable that I shall ever see Texas again, as the first of January, 1899, ushered in my ninety-second year, but I will cherish the memory of the long ago spent on her soil, and wish her a prosperous future. I am proud to note the progress she has made, though I can scarcely realize the transformation that progress has wrought.

So few of my old time friends have kept pace with me, that in thinking them over, I, indeed,

> "Feel like one who treads alone
>   Some banquet hall deserted;
> Whose lights are fled, whose garlands dead,
>   And all but he departed."

Thanking my readers, if any there be, who have patiently followed me through the pages of this journal, I close the volume and bid you adieu.

Noah Smithwick

FINIS

THE TEXAS STAR

White star of peace! Mars' lurid light
No longer stains thy 'scutcheon* bright.
   On that clear field of blue,
Which seemeth but a fragment rent
From the blue vault above it bent,
   God's peace descends like dew.

No more the wolf's long quivering howl,
Or dismal hooting of the owl,
In woods where foes were wont to prowl,
   Thrills, like the knell of doom.
But, rising from each peaceful grove,
Soft notes of gentle woodland dove,
Cooing her sweet low song of love,
   Like benedictions come.

Exchanged the battle's bloody gage
For helpful staff of peaceful age:
   The roar and din of strife,
For bursts of childhood's mirth and glee,
As, from their throne upon his knee,
The patriot's great grandchildren see
   The gladsome dawn of life.

Thou wast his life's bright morning star.
Through the dark night, through want and war,
   He followed thee!
His long, long race is almost run.
Shining above life's setting sun,
His star of rest from work well done,
   O, may'st thou be!

Mrs. Nanna Smithwick Donaldson

*The field of the first Texas flag on which the Lone Star was displayed, was red. It was later changed to blue and has since so remained. Hence the above allusion.